A Constitution for the Common Good

Strengthening Scottish Democracy after the Independence Referendum

W. ELLIOT BULMER

Luath Press Limited

EDINBURGH

www.luath.co.uk

First published 2014
New Edition 2015

ISBN: 978-1-910021-74-3

The paper used in this book is recyclable. It is made from
low chlorine pulps produced in a low energy, low emissions manner
from renewable forests.

Printed and bound by
Bell & Bain Ltd., Glasgow

Typeset in 11 point Sabon
by 3btype.com

How splendid and honourable it is to mediate on government and public administration, on which our well-being, our health and our life depend.

FRANCESCO GUICCIARDINI,
Dialogue on the Government of Florence, 1527

For some men falsely persuading themselves that bad governments are advantageous to them, as most conducing to gratify their ambition, avarice, and luxury, set themselves with the utmost art and violence to procure their establishment: and by such men almost the whole world has been trampled underfoot, and subjected to tyranny, for want of understanding by what means and methods they were enslaved. For though mankind take great care and pains to instruct themselves in other arts and sciences, yet very few apply themselves to consider the nature of government, an enquiry so useful and necessary both to magistrate and people. Nay, in most countries the arts of state being altogether directed either to enslave the people, or to keep them under slavery; it is become almost everywhere a crime to reason about matters of government. But if men would bestow a small part of the time and application which they throw away upon curious but useless studies, or endless gaming, in perusing those excellent rules and examples of government which the ancients have left us, they would soon be enabled to discover all such abuses and corruptions as tend to the ruin of public societies. It is therefore very strange that they should think study and knowledge necessary in everything they go about, except in the noblest and most useful of all applications, the art of government.

ANDREW FLETCHER of Saltoun,
A Discourse of Government With Relation to Militias, 1698

Acknowledgements

Writing a book is a solitary endeavour, but producing a book – which involves turning the raw text into something publishable and readable – is always a joint effort. I particularly wish to thank: Dr Craig MacAngus and Dr Peter Lynch, both of the University of Stirling, for reviewing drafts and providing valuable feedback; John Drummond, of the Constitutional Commission, for his unstinting support; my parents, for their continued encouragement; Gavin MacDougall and the team at Luath Press, for their efforts in ensuring a swift turn-around from manuscript to finished book; my colleagues at International IDEA, especially Sumit Bisarya and Professor Tom Ginsburg; and lastly but most importantly my wife Eva who has fulfilled the duties of scribe, editor, reference-checker and caterer-in-chief with good cheer and patience.

Contents

Acknowledgements   6

Preface to the Second Edition   9

Introduction   13

CHAPTER ONE

Does the Constitution still matter?   21

i   *Independence, Democracy and the Constitution*   23

ii   *Independence, Sovereignty and Folkric*   27

iii   *The Constitutional Debate before the Independence Referendum*   29

iv   *Constitutionalism without Independence?*   36

   a   A Federal United Kingdom   39

   b   A New Treaty of Union   45

   c   Home Rule   47

CHAPTER TWO

How can Constitutions promote the common good?   52

i   *The Common Good as the Purpose of the State*   53

ii   *What is the Common Good?*   58

iii   *Common Good, Pluralism and Pre-commitment*   61

iv   *Political Liberty as a Common Good*   65

CHAPTER THREE

How prescriptive should the Constitution be?   67

i   *The Case for Procedural Constitutionalism*   67

ii   *The Limits of Prescriptive Constitutionalism*   80

iii   *The Relationship between Procedural and Prescriptive Elements*   84

CHAPTER FOUR

How could the Constitution strengthen democracy?   93

i   *Direct Democracy*   95

ii   *Representation and Inclusiveness*   104

iii   *Second Chamber: Senate or Tribunate?*   117

iv   *Local Democracy*   124

v   *Democratising Parties*   127

CHAPTER FIVE

How can the Constitution promote good governance
and accountability?   131

i Parliamentary Scrutiny and Fourth Branch Institutions   131
ii Recall and Popular Dissolution   139
iii Prime Ministerial Term Limits   143
*iv Guarding the Guardians: Supervision of the Military
and Security Services*   146

CHAPTER SIX
How can the Constitution reflect our values and identities?   152
i The Preamble and Para-Consitutional Covenants   152
ii Religion and State   159
iii Monarchy and National Identity   170

CHAPTER SEVEN
How can the Constitution help us to achieve social justice,
tackle poverty and reduce inequality?   177
i Social and Economic Rights   177
ii Judicial or Political Enforcement   181
iii Beyond Rights: Empowering the People   184

CHAPTER EIGHT
How can the Constitution promote public ethics?   187
i The need for Good Citizenship   188
ii Education for Citizenship   191
iii Principles of Public Life and Codes of Conduct   194
iv Public Honours   199

CHAPTER NINE
How can we build a new constitutional settlement?   201
i Does process matter?   201
ii Stages of the process   208
iii Possible next steps   213

APPENDICES   219
APPENDIX A   A Constitution for an Independent Scotland   221
APPENDIX B   'A New Treaty of Union'   270
APPENDIX C   A Home Rule and Full Fiscal Autonomy Settlement for
Scotland   277
APPENDIX D   A Constitution for a Federal United Kingdom   284

Endnotes   325

Preface to the Second Edition

THE FIRST EDITION of this book appeared in August 2014, shortly before the referendum on Scottish independence. This second edition appears after the May 2015 UK general election, in which the Scottish National Party achieved nearly a clean sweep of Scottish seats (56 out of 59, leaving Labour, the Liberal Democrats and the Tories with just one seat apiece). Much has changed over the intervening period. As the referendum result was to many a great disappointment, so the general election result was a sign of hope. It was a sign that all was not lost, that Scotland has emerged from the last few years stronger and more self-confident, and that the constitutional question is far from settled.

The general election result is a sign, above all, that Scotland can no longer be dealt with in the old colonial way, with a mild sop here and a messy fudge there. While the Tory establishment in London may wish to go back to the business of oligarchy as usual, the people of Scotland have sent a clear warning signal: 'We stayed in the Union on the promise of radical and fundamental change; deliver it, quickly, or we will leave'. Even the most arrogant, blinkered and conceited of British Prime Ministers cannot fail to hear that warning. Whether they have the sense to heed it, of course, is another matter.

It is clear, too, that the activism and engagement sparked by the independence referendum has not dissipated. Membership of the Scottish National Party tripled in the few weeks following the vote, whilst membership of the Scottish Green Party doubled. The networks, platforms, media channels and organisations created by the referendum campaign have continued to exist. People are 'not going back to their sofas', as Robin McAlpine, leader of the Common Weal campaign, put it.

Independence is off the agenda for now, but it might not remain so for long. If Westminster fails to change its ways, and if it proves itself incapable of accommodating a free and autonomous Scotland within a reformed Union, then one can imagine various scenarios in which the demand for a second referendum on independence – or on a package of constitutional measures very close to independence – may become irresistible. Scotland's First Minister, Nicola Sturgeon, has repeatedly stated that a vote for the SNP in the general election was not a vote for independence, and that there are no plans at present to hold a second independence referendum. This comes, however, with two very important caveats: firstly, that the SNP manifesto for the 2016 Scottish Parliament election is yet to be written, and that manifesto might well outline conditions under which another independence referendum would be held; and secondly, that a substantial change in circumstances – such as a vote on leaving the European Union – might force a second independence referendum rather sooner than many had anticipated.

Many of those who voted No in September 2014 did so only on a conditional basis, taking last minute interventions by former Prime Minister Gordon Brown as an indication that a No vote would guarantee much greater autonomy for Scotland within a radically reformed Union. A 'solemn vow' to this effect was publicly given by Brown and affirmed by the leaders of the Conservatives, Labour Party and Liberal Democrats. Thus the referendum can be interpreted not only as a rejection, for the time being, of full independence, but also as an endorsement of substantial constitutional change within the UK. Even if a second referendum on independence is not forthcoming, the deep constitutional problems facing Scotland and the rest of the UK are not going to go away. Scotland is still unequally yoked to an ill-constituted fading imperial state, in which dissatisfaction is still growing and tensions between different countries and classes are increasing. An acceptable and democratic solution to this problem must be found before unacceptable solutions, of a regressive and anti-democratic nature, are imposed upon us.

The SNP group in the Westminster Parliament, in conjunction with the Scottish Government, should push for the full implementation of the vow, taking advantage of the vow to claim the largest sphere of autonomy possible short of full independence. Now is the time to respond to the Scottish public's endorsement of fundamental change and to articulate a viable constitutional position that meets Scottish aspirations. There is an opportunity to capture the public imagination, to set the terms of debate, and to build a broad consensus around an intermediate position between independence and devolution that can unite both disappointed Yes voters and the broad swathes of No voters who still want real change. This intermediate position would not be merely a transfer of limited powers from one government and parliament to another, as envisaged by the lukewarm proposals of the Smith Commission, but a more radical reconfiguration of the state.

This second edition therefore contains a new section charting out three possible models of constitutional change that Scotland could pursue within the United Kingdom: a federal model, in which the UK would be reconstituted as an equal union of four nation states; a new Treaty of Union, which would provide for a bi-lateral relationship between Scotland and the rest of the UK, and a 'Home Rule' arrangement that would leave the central institutions of the UK relatively unchanged, but greatly diminish their influence and control over Scotland. Which track we take depends partly on the willingness of Westminster to give ground and partly on the extent to which the other parts of the UK wish to travel with us, but each of these solutions could in principle deliver the secure and substantial autonomy for Scotland promised in the vow. This means that Scotland could be fully internally self-governing and self-financing, and have a constitutionally secured position that is not subject to the will of Westminster, while remaining part of the UK for the purposes of foreign affairs and defence, and while sharing a limited range of powers in relation to passports, citizenship, the currency and similar matters.

The questions that were so energising and exciting before the referendum (What sort of country would we like to be? What sort of democracy do we need? How can we get there?) are too important to be forgotten and swallowed up in unedifying partisan tussles over a pinch of stamp duty here or a peck of income tax there. In taking this constitutional agenda forward, whether in an independent Scotland or in an autonomous Scotland within a reformed and 'loosely United' Kingdom, we (by which I mean all who care about the freedom and well-being of Scotland, whether for or against independence) must take care to ensure that democratic constitutional change does not take a back seat to technocratic tinkering. In particular, we must not allow ourselves, or our political representatives, to become so embroiled in petty wrangling about 'more powers' that we fail to engage in a deeper discussion about values and principles, or about improving democratic processes and safeguarding fundamental rights.

Introduction

IT IS NOW NEARLY four years since my first book, *A Model Constitution for Scotland* (2011),[1] was published. *A Model Constitution* stemmed from a belief that the Scottish constitutional debate needed to be refocused, away from the 'status question' of Scotland's relationship with the rest of the United Kingdom, and towards questions of good governance, democratic participation, citizens' rights and public values. I argued that independence alone would not deliver its promised benefits without a democratic constitutional foundation and that not 'mere independence', but the much nobler ideal of a 'free and civic way of life',[2] should be, and indeed long has been, the ultimate aim of the Scottish national movement.

This perspective is needed now, in the wake of the referendum, more than ever before. Since September 2014 there has been much talk of 'new powers', but almost no discussion of the constitutional structures within which those powers might sit, or of the constitutional principles that might guide and govern their proper use. The change that was worth seeking before the referendum was not simply a transfer of power from one Parliament to another; rather, it was the creation of a new and more democratic constitutional settlement for Scotland. In the post-referendum environment, when various forms of Home Rule or federalism are reappearing on the medium-term agenda, that desire for real constitutional change is as relevant and as challenging as ever.

I also sought to show that freedom cannot simply be defined in terms of economic freedom, or individual freedom to act without responsibility or restraint; such debased notions of freedom belong to tyrants, oligarchs and outlaws, not to citizens. Freedom in its civic, democratic sense necessarily includes active membership in a self-governing polity through which we the people deliberate upon and try to discern the common good. In other words, freedom is defined in terms of 'democratic voice', not just 'market choice'. Democratic citizenship is a communal, not an individualistic, preoccupation. It is always intimately and intrinsically connected to a concern for social justice, for the removal of gross inequalities in material condition and for the promotion of a good, flourishing life.

Aside from making these general, somewhat normative points, my intention in writing *A Model Constitution* was a modest one. *A Model Constitution* never claimed to be the final word on the subject of what form a Constitution for an independent Scotland should take. I simply wished to help inform public decisions by showing readers, most of whom have no experience of life under a written Constitution, and may never have even seen one,[a] what a workable, achievable and broadly acceptable Constitution for Scotland might look like. I sought neither to predict nor to prescribe any particular set of constitutional outcomes, but only to illustrate general principles by way of a 'worked example' in order to encourage more informed public debate and more committed public action. Judging by the comments I have received from readers and from my experience of attending public meetings in my capacity as Research Director of the Constitutional Commission, the book fulfilled these intentions with some success.

Over the last few years, I have had opportunities to discuss *A Model Constitution* with Scottish Cabinet ministers, members of the Scottish Parliament (from several parties), civil servants, academics in the fields of politics and public law, and members of leading civil society organisations. I have also presented the *Model Constitution* at many public meetings, and have learnt much from listening to citizens who, although they might have previously had no particular interest in constitutional affairs, have come to recognise that a Constitution is key to realising their desire to live in a better Scotland. More recently, through my work with the International Institute for Democracy and Electoral Assistance, I have been able to engage with people working on constitution-building processes in emerging democracies. These experiences have continued to refine my thinking about what sort of Constitution would be needed in Scotland, as

---

a   In this book, following the conventional usage of almost all democracies outside the United Kingdom, the word 'Constitution' refers always to a supreme law that, as a minimum: (i) defines the state; (ii) regulates its major political institutions and processes; (iii) protects civil liberties and fundamental human rights; (iv) is binding on all institutions of the state, including Parliament itself; and (iv) can be amended only by a special process, usually requiring a broader consensus than that required for the enactment of ordinary legislation. The UK, in this sense of the word, has no 'constitution' at all, and the idea of an 'unwritten, unentrenched, unenforceable constitution' is oxymoronic.

well as challenging some of my previous assumptions on the boundaries of constitutional possibility.

A Model Constitution concerned itself mainly with the institutional mechanics of a Constitution for Scotland. It discussed how to elect the First Minister, the powers of the Presiding Officer, the appointment of judges, the workings of the electoral system, the composition of the Electoral Commission, the process of enacting legislation, the rules concerning the dissolution of Parliament, different types of referendum, and other institutional matters concerning the form and structures of government. However, a number of difficult and controversial substantive issues (such as the relation of the state to religion, or the statement of values and principles in a preamble) were omitted, or covered only briefly. In some cases this omission was due to constraints of space and time, in others because I had not yet come to fully recognise their salience.

With increasing calls for a United Kingdom-wide constitutional settlement,[a] and Scotland's place within or relationship to the United Kingdom still very much in question after the independence referendum, now is an opportune time to reflect self-critically upon *A Model Constitution*, to update the reader on recent developments, and also to discuss questions of content, context and process that were not fully addressed in the earlier work.

This book takes a step back from institutional engineering to discuss the cultural, political and social considerations of constitutionalism. It marks a shift in emphasis from the letter of the Constitution to the spirit. Whereas *A Model Constitution* focused on the dry bones of 'rules and rights' in the Constitution, as they might feature in the work of politicians, civil servants or lawyers, this book also shows how the living flesh of the Constitution – reflecting our values, reinforcing our aspirations, and resonating in our hearts – can be relevant to the everyday lives of ordinary citizens.

---

a   The Political and Constitutional Reform Committee of the House of Commons has even gone so far as to publish a draft Constitution for the United Kingdom for discussion. This is a very centralising text, which would significantly reduce the powers of the Scottish Parliament, but it is at least a technically sound draft that reflects the basic principles of constitutional democracy. The text of the draft constitution is contained in the committee's Second Report, dated 3 July 2014: www.publications. parliament.uk/pa/cm201415/cmselect/cmpolcon/463/46302.htm

This book is written for four groups of people. Firstly, it is addressed to supporters of independence or substantially increased autonomy for Scotland who are unconvinced by, or uncommitted to, the principle of a written Constitution. It hopes to convince these people that the promise of 'more powers' would not deliver their expected social, political, economic and cultural gains without a commitment to democracy, human rights and good governance, underpinned by a strong Constitution. Secondly, it is addressed to those who wish to see progressive political change, notably in the areas of constitutional and institutional reform, but who see Britain through a Westminster-centric lens; I wish to show this group that, given the chronic structural failures of democracy the United Kingdom, a bit more devolution here and there is not going to do the job. Thirdly, I have in mind those who are already committed to independence or substantial autonomy and to a new constitutional settlement, and who wish to explore the ways and means of constitution-building in more detail. I hope that this group will benefit from the expanded treatment of the issues of substance and process that were not covered, or were only briefly discussed, in *A Model Constitution*. Finally, this book also hopes to make a modest theoretical contribution to public and academic discussion of constitutions, in terms of the relation of 'charter' to 'covenant', that will be of interest to people outside Scotland and the United Kingdom, whatever trajectory we take.

Going beyond the institutional focus of my earlier work, this book considers the wider aims, purposes, nature and scope of a Constitution, particularly as it relates to democracy, pluralism and the common good. The central problems of authoritarian backsliding, incumbent manipulation and corruption that any good Constitution must guard against, as well as the issues of identity, values and public ethics that any Constitution is required to address, will continue to face us whether we carry a Scottish or a British passport. The themes and ideas discussed in the book are therefore of direct and immediate relevance to Scottish citizens, and to people throughout the United Kingdom, as we go about the difficult process of forging a new constitutional order for ourselves, whether this happens to be in the context of an independent Scotland, in an autonomous Scotland trying to protect and improve itself through constitutional guarantees, or in a United Kingdom that finds the courage and ingenuity needed to reconstitute itself as a federation of free and equal nations.

Much of this book is devoted to the problem of how to reflect common values and promote the common good while preserving the diversity of a free and open society. It argues for a 'civic constitutionalism'. This differs from the liberal tradition in recognising that there is a 'common good' in society, and that a democratic state is required to play an active, positive role in the attainment of the common good. However, it does not accept the illiberal and utopian notion that there is any single, abstract, and universally evident expression of the common good to be discovered and imposed by a virtuous minority or by an arcane priesthood of ideological visionaries. Instead, the common good is recognised as existing in a contingent and ephemeral way; it is discovered as a result of pragmatic agreements arising from political participation, deliberation and negotiation. This applies: (i) generally, to the common good of society as a whole, which is the underlying aim of the common weal; and (ii) specifically, in relation to each policy decision.

If freedom from tyranny and oppression is essential to human flourishing, and if the common good is to be discovered and sustained through public deliberation, it follows that there must be freedom of conscience, association, discussion and political action, and that no one person, nor any particular group of people, should hold preponderant power in the state. The primary requirement of a good Constitution, then, is that it should protect fundamental human rights and democratic processes, and thus facilitate an open, pluralistic, deliberative politics under the rule of law. Yet this is not the only requirement. As well as being a legal charter, through which our rights are protected and under which our public institutions operate, a Constitution also embodies a national covenant. Without eroding or denying our many differences, it declares the promises that we make to one another as fellow citizens, declares the commonly agreed standards that we are determined to uphold in our public life, and so expresses our commitment not only to the rights and institutions, but also to the values and *mores* of the *res publica*.

The purpose of the Constitution, according to this understanding, is not to impose one single view of the common good on the whole of society (in contrast, for example, to the ideological constitutions of Soviet republics, or the theological constitutions of Islamic republics), but to reflect deep and enduring public agreements about the common good (its 'covenantal' function) while 'holding the ring' for public decision-making on how to resolve particular policy decisions (its 'charter' function). This requires a robust constitutional structure that: (i) protects against the manipulation of the rules by incumbents, guards against authoritarian tendencies, protects the rights of dissent and contestation through well-defended civil liberties, promotes good governance, defines the ethical standards of a healthy public life, and (ii) articulates the shared common values and the baselines of human flourishing which enhance the well-being of all citizens. This argument, together with its consequences for constitutional design, is a recurring theme of this book.

Chapter One explains why the constitutional question was so integral to the Scottish independence debate and why it remains integral to the debate about Scotland's future, whatever the extent of our relationship to the rest of the United Kingdom. 'More powers' or even 'full powers' for a Scottish Parliament would be of limited use or benefit if not backed by a clear commitment to democracy, good governance, human rights and public values. A newly added section discusses approaches to constitutionalism in a sovereign and self-governing but non-independent Scotland, either through a federal United Kingdom or by means of a new Treaty of Union or an autonomous 'Home Rule' Constitution for Scotland.

Chapter Two roots the constitutional project in a commitment to the common good. It makes the case for an open and pluralist democratic politics, in which various competing concepts of the common good can be expressed. This need not, however, necessarily result in a blind, purposeless 'constitution without values'. On the contrary, an open, pluralist and democratic view of the common good – as something to be discovered and determined through public deliberation – requires citizens to strive for a broad consensus not only on basic rights and ground rules, but also on the ethics, norms and values which will shape public life and enable the common good to be realised.

Chapter Three considers the extent, nature and purpose of the Constitution. Two contrasting elements of, or approaches to, a Constitution are presented: the procedural 'charter' and the directive or prescriptive 'covenant'. The term 'charter' refers to the set of rights and rules that structure political activity ('the rules of the state'), whereas the term 'covenant' refers to the ethical statements and values that shape politics ('the spirit of the country'). These distinctions cut across typical institutional categorisations, such as whether a state is unitary or federal, has one or two legislative chambers, uses a proportional or majoritarian electoral system, or has a prime ministerial or presidential executive. In exploring the distinction between these two constitutional approaches and understanding the connection between them, many theoretical and practical problems of constitutional design can be clarified. While both approaches are integral to the whole – a Constitution is both 'charter' and 'covenant', specific 'charter elements' and 'covenant elements' can be expressed and enforced in different ways, and to different extents, on a pragmatic basis, depending on the needs and aspirations of each society at a given time.

Chapters Four to Eight discuss the application of these general principles to the institutional and substantive provisions of a Constitution, whether for an independent Scotland, for an autonomous Scotland within the shell-state of the United Kingdom, or for a federal United Kingdom. This discussion includes questions of public participation and democratic quality (Chapter Four), accountability mechanisms (Chapter Five), issues of identity, religion and nationhood (Chapter Six), social and economic justice (Chapter Seven), and public ethics (Chapter Eight).

Finally, Chapter Nine considers the constitution building process. It charts a potential roadmap towards the establishment of a new constitutional order for Scotland, whether as part of a reformed United Kingdom or otherwise. Drawing on experiences from other parts of the world, it argues that the process of constitution making is as at least as important as the textual outcome, and that a well-structured, inclusive and consensual process is the best basis for a stable democratic future.

In summary, this book argues that if we wish to enjoy a flourishing life in a free and socially just Scotland (whether Scotland is an independent state or an autonomous state within a loosely federated United Kingdom) then we need a 'Constitution for everyone': a Constitution that is directed towards the common good of all its people, not towards the particular privileges of the rich, powerful and influential. Such a Constitution would facilitate all citizens to engage in an open and pluralist democratic process through which the common good – in all its plurality and variability, nuance and flexibility – can be identified and defended.

CHAPTER ONE

Does the Constitution still matter?

SCOTLAND IS CAUGHT between two conversations. One concerns Scotland's constitutional future, its institutions of government and its relationship to the rest of the United Kingdom. The other is a conversation about poverty, inequality and social justice, land reform and environmental protection, wages, working conditions and public services.

The London-based parties and their allied interests in Scotland have long tried to present these as separate, unrelated and perhaps even contradictory debates. Seeking autonomy or independence for Scotland was, according to the leaders of the Labour Party, a distraction from 'real issues'. This should come as no surprise. The Labour Party, despite occasional flirtations with devolution, has never felt comfortable with constitutional radicalism.[a] It has long had a 'Tory' streak within it, which has quite uncritically defended the traditional top-down institutions of the United Kingdom.[b]

However, the broad Yes alliance that arose during the independence referendum campaign started to connect the dots between these conversations. The SNP, the Yes Campaign, the Radical Independence Campaign, the Scottish Green Party, Labour for Independence, Nordic Horizons, National Collective, Women for Independence, the Reid Foundation and Common Weal[c] all recognised that policy and state structure were closely connected. These organisations appreciate that the constitutional structures

---

a   This may be a product of its roots in 'Fabian' centralism. The Fabians, like the Utilitarians before them, believed in using the power of the centralised, bureaucratic state to do 'good things' to and for people, but were extremely suspicious of allowing people to do good for themselves through democratic action.

b   It is said that Ramsey MacDonald, the first Labour Prime Minister, could not wait to get into court dress and rush along to Buckingham palace to kiss hands (see: Wilson, H. *A Prime Minister on Prime Ministers* (London: Weidenfeld & Nicolson, 1977)).

c   The Reid Foundation's 'Commonweal' project has arguably made the most morally engaging and intellectually coherent contribution to the revival of social democratic thought since the Beveridge Report of 1942, which laid the foundations of the modern welfare state.

of the state determine who has power, how they handle that power, to whom they are accountable, and, therefore, how the state will respond, in policy terms, to people's needs. 'Real issues' can only be addressed if we have real powers under the control of a real democracy.

Piecing these two conversations together, it appears that the unjust, short-sighted, elitist, London-centric policy outcomes of the UK are related to, and at least in part are a direct consequence of, its decrepit, ramshackle, unbalanced and oligarchic political structure. In an article in *The Herald* in 2013, I wrote:

> The electoral system for the House of Commons is unrepresentative, the composition of the House of Lords is indefensible, the powers of the Crown are excessive, secretive and unaccountable, rights are fragile, and privileges rife. There is a direct connection between allowing rulers to make up the rules as they go along and the failure of the UK state to serve the common good. The banking crisis, the expenses scandal, phone hacking, illegal surveillance, persistent unemployment and wage cuts, rising inequality, corporate lobbying, and the destruction of public infrastructure and services – all point to a state that has fallen into the hands of an unchecked oligarchy, bound by its own self-interest.[3]

Moreover, many have recognised that the process of making decisions – whose voices are included, and how they are listened to – can influence not only what decisions are taken (eg whether the local library is kept open as a public service or sold off to a developer for conversion into flats), but also the social and psychological effect of those decisions (eg whether the library really belongs to the local community, because 'we' built or saved it for ourselves and future generations, through institutions of local democracy that are participatory and close to the people, or whether it belongs to a distant, impersonal bureaucracy).[a]

It follows that the delivery of more socially just outcomes must begin with a revival and deepening of democracy. As Thomas Paine recognised, good Constitutions are known by their fruits:

---

a   This point is amply illustrated in relation to the control of land by island communities in Riddoch, L. *Blossom: What Scotland Needs to Flourish* (Edinburgh: Luath Press, 2014).

> When it shall be said in any country in the world, my poor are happy;
> neither ignorance nor distress is to be found among them; my jails are
> empty of prisoners, my streets of beggars; the aged are not in want,
> the taxes are not oppressive; the rational world is my friend, because
> I am a friend of its happiness. When these things can be said, then
> may the country boast of its constitution and its government.[4]

Those who expect the United Kingdom to start delivering progressive
policies, if only there were a new Prime Minister in 10 Downing Street,
are expecting a bad tree to bring forth good fruit: they are expecting an
oligarchic system to behave and to deliver like a good democracy should.
But that cannot and will not happen.[5] Oligarchy does as oligarchy is: it
brings forth rotten policies and rotten behaviour from its rotten nature.
To enjoy good fruit, in policy terms, we do not need a new government,
but a new state: not another rotten fruit from the same corrupt tree, but
a new tree. Whether that tree is a Scots pine or British oak is to some extent
a secondary issue, so long as it is a good tree and firmly rooted in a robust
constitutional order.

Of course, the benefits of a good Constitution are indirect and instrumental, just as the inedible root of a tree leads only indirectly to the fruit.
Even the best Constitution cannot pave a cycle lane or repair a bridge,
manage a clinic or administer a vaccine, educate a child or take care of an
elderly person. The Constitution, however, can uphold a democratic order
that enables us to make our own decisions and to develop policies that
serve the common good, while protecting human rights, promoting public
accountability, and guarding against corruption. The Constitution ensures
that those in charge of formulating policies, administering the state, enforcing
the law, and delivering services, are not a self-selecting, self-perpetuating,
self-serving 'parcel o' rogues', but the democratically responsible agents
of a free and self-governing people. It is with this in mind that the need
for, and purposes of, a Constitution must be understood.

i Independence, Democracy and the Constitution

Economic inequality has returned to levels not seen since before the
Second World War. One in five children live in poverty.[6] Many suffer from
a 'low-wage, long hours' economy, with all that means for stress, health,

diet and a relatively low quality of life. Austerity policies cut deep into the social fabric, causing a surge in dependence on food banks.[a] But for all that, life in Scotland could be much worse. We have running water and reliable electricity: no civil war, no ethnic riots, no masked men with AK47s extorting money at roadblocks. Some – perhaps even the majority – are lucky enough to have a decent job, a nice house and a pension fund that is worth a bit. As long as you are not old, young, poor, or disabled, you can enjoy a quality of life not too far from the European average.

Likewise, our democracy might be substandard compared to other Northern and Western European countries. Our constitutional arrangements might be absurd. The United Kingdom – under whichever party that happens to be in power at Westminster – might be ruled by institutions that are distant, exclusive, secretive, oligarchic, increasingly corrupt, often incompetent, belligerent, and contemptuous of Scotland's aspirations. The Scottish Parliament might hold its powers only at the grace and favour of another Parliament, which is barely representative, contains more nominated lords than elected representatives, and is in large part paid for by the private healthcare and fracking industries,[7] but at least there are no gulags, coups, purges or show trials. Government agents never (*'well, hardly ever!'*) raid newspaper offices to cover up their misdeeds.[8] As long as you are not a radical Muslim, an investigative journalist, or a peacenik environmentalist at a protest march, you will be safe enough.

The Yes campaign claimed that independence would transform Scotland, resulting in a more balanced and prosperous economy, better public services and a higher quality of life for ordinary people. However, simply leaving the United Kingdom would not, in and of itself, guarantee much improvement. An independent Scottish Government would have more control over its own resources and policies but, equally, such fragile blessings as we now enjoy could be lost if an independent Scotland, like many other newly-independent countries before it, were to descend into chaos, ethnic

---

a   The Scottish Government's (2013) report, *Overview on the Provision of Food Aid in Scotland*, identified a threefold increase in emergency food aid provision from 2012 to 2013 and noted that 'welfare reform, benefit delays, benefit sanctions and falling incomes have been the main factors driving the recent trend observed of increased demand for food aid'.

strife, instability or dictatorship, leaving the country bankrupt and isolated. It is easy to see why opponents of independence took the view that the potential rewards of independence were not worth the risks. They were being asked to give up that which they knew for something that seemed to offer little automatic benefit and some risk of serious systemic failure.

Once the symbolism and the emotive appeals to history, identity or nationhood are removed from both sides, the pragmatic case for independence rests on the argument that a Scottish state would better serve the people of Scotland than the United Kingdom has done. All the haivering about policies, currencies, embassies, oil, and whether Scotland would have a few million more or less in the treasury from day one of independence, was – and remains – ultimately irrelevant compared to the key question: whether the institutions of an independent Scotland would be better or worse than those of Scotland in the United Kingdom. If an independent Scotland were to represent the interests of the people of Scotland, protect their rights, and serve the common good through democratic processes, then the people would flourish and prosper, not only economically but also in terms of ethos, culture and character. If, on the other hand, Scotland were to squander resources on vanity projects; if a small, self-gratifying elite were to syphon off our wealth and stash it in secretive foreign banks; if the civil service were to become a reservoir of political patronage; if, in other words, an independent Scotland were to be badly governed, then we would be no better off, and possibly even worse off, than at present.

Too many newly independent countries have gone from bad to worse because they have failed to consolidate stable democratic institutions and to build an effective state that reflects all of society, responds to public needs and respects human rights. Even today, successes are rarer than failures. *The Economist's* Democracy Index of 2012 (not a flawless measure, but a reasonable one for these purposes) identified just 25 'full democracies' out of 167 states, or 15 per cent of the total number, containing 11.3 per cent of the world's population.[9] A further 54 countries, containing 37.2 per cent of the world's population, were classified as 'flawed democracies',[10] meaning that while competitive elections took place, sound democratic governance was hampered by failings such as human rights abuses, the exclusion of minorities, the weakness of the rule of law, endemic corruption or political violence.[a] Consolidating a democratic order is a particular challenge for newly independent states. Authoritarian populism, the capture of state institutions by corrupt oligarchs, intercommunal violence, and erosion of the rule of law, are just some of the risks to which new states are particularly vulnerable. The risks are even greater in oil-rich countries, where the prize of being about to control valuable resources is a strong incentive for foul play. If the essential contention of the Yes campaign was that the common interests of the people of Scotland would be better served by an independent state than by the United Kingdom, their desire to 'end London rule' had to be backed by a positive plan for the construction of an effective, stable and inclusive Scottish democracy.

This is why the adoption of a written Constitution, far from being peripheral to the independence campaign, was absolutely central to it. Only a clear commitment to a strong Constitution could ensure that a small, corrupt, unaccountable and lawless clique in London would not simply be replaced by a small, corrupt, unaccountable and lawless clique in Edinburgh. Only a strong Constitution could defend the institutions of Scotland against incumbent manipulation, authoritarian backsliding and corruption, and so force the Scottish state to serve the common good rather than the private interests of a few. A Constitution would provide ground rules, above ordinary party politics, for the resolution of political disputes. It would prescribe a framework for the functioning of public institutions, defend the integrity of electoral, administrative and judicial processes, and protect the rights of individuals and minorities. As such, only a Constitution could reassure the people that an independent Scotland would not belong to any one person or party, but instead would be the common possession of all its citizens: a *res publica*.

---

a   The United Kingdom sits near the bottom end of the 'full democracy' category: it is, by *The Economist's* measure, a democracy, but its quality of democracy trails a long way behind the front-runners. The top places on the democratic leader board are consistently held by the small, well-constituted states, such as Norway, Sweden, Denmark, Iceland, Ireland, Luxembourg and the Netherlands, which make up the 'arc of democracy' surrounding Scotland.

ii Independence, Sovereignty and Folkric

Independence is a worthy cause (and may still prove to be a necessary one, if the rest of the United Kingdom does not show a sincere intention to change its ways), but those who wish to see Scotland flourish should not make independence the primary goal. Our wellbeing will principally depend not upon the name or the boundaries of the state, but upon how well governed we are within that state. Even the word 'independence' is unhelpful, not only because it has become emotive and politically divisive, but also because it provides a misleading diagnosis of our problems and an incorrect prescription for how to cure them. Independence simply implies the absence of external constraint. To think that Scotland's problems will be solved by independence (or, for that matter, any degree of 'more powers') is to blame these problems solely or mainly on external factors. If Scotland is to flourish, we need not only to rid ourselves of control by Westminster (at least in its present oligarchic form), but also, more fundamentally, take democratic control and responsibility for our own country.

Instead of focusing on independence, we should seek '*folkric*', or democratic self-government.[a] *Folkric* is also an adaptation of the concept of *Swaraj*, which, according to Ananya Vajpeyi, was the principal motivating idea behind India's struggle for liberation:

> If there was one word that dominated Indian politics from the 1880s, when the Indian National Congress was first founded, until Independence in 1947, this word was *swaraj*. *Swaraj* literally means 'self-rule': the rule of the self, or the rule over the self. Both the subject and object of 'rule' (*raj*) is the 'self' (*swa*). A subjugated country is ruled by others; a free country rules itself.[11]

As Vajpeyi explains, *swaraj* has a reflexive quality:[12] the self (as sovereign) rules, and the self (as subject) is ruled. In the same way, *folkric* implies the rule over the people (as subject) by the people (as sovereign). This unity of sovereignty and subjecthood is the essence of democratic citizenship:

---

a For the coining of the word *folkric*, as a modern Scots translation of 'democracy', I am indebted to Krister Vasshus, Assistant Professor of Linguistics at the University of Bergen, Norway.

those who rule over others are masters while those who are ruled over by others are slaves, but those who rule over themselves are citizens.

Making *folkric* our aim reminds us that the change we seek is much more than – and does not solely depend upon – a symbolic change in borders, anthems, flags, or even a change in the geographical locus of power from London to Edinburgh. Independence could be a necessary step towards *folkric*, depending on the extent to which Westminster is able to either reform itself or to relinquish control over Scottish affairs, but the pursuit of *folkric*, unlike the pursuit of independence, is not primarily concerned with whether the Union Flag or the Saltire flies over Edinburgh Castle. If *folkric* is the aim, we cannot be satisfied until we have established a democratic constitutional state in which the rights, dignity and voice of citizens are respected. Crucially, however, we could (at least in principle) achieve that satisfaction either in an independent Scotland or in a Scotland that is substantially autonomous within a looser and more equitable Union.

Folkric, in contrast to independence, is not a desire for Scotland to be governed by Scots (which would be a nationalist position, in the narrowest sense of the word), but a desire to be ruled to the fullest extent practicable by the people of Scotland (a democratic position). To embrace *folkric* as the objective is to recognise the fact that, in almost all internal respects, Scotland has always been governed by Scots. Even before devolution, the day-to-day governance of Scotland has always been performed, in large part, through an autonomous network of judicial, legal, administrative, educational, ecclesiastical, municipal and charitable institutions, all of which operate solely in and for Scotland, and are staffed almost exclusively by Scots.[13] What there has not been, however, is much real democracy. The Scots who traditionally ran Scotland were not, in the main, chosen by or accountable to the people of Scotland; the state did not belong to the people, but to competing patron-client networks. In consequence, the MPs, civil servants, Edinburgh establishment and Labour party *nomenklatura* who actually ran Scotland learned to act as intermediaries and courtiers, but rarely as citizens.[a] They were often instinctively fearful of real democracy.[14]

---

a   A general overview of the way in which that 'courtier' relationship between patrons and clients corrodes the values and ethos of good citizenship can be found in Viroli, M. *The Liberty of Servants: Berlusconi's Italy* (Harvard University Press, 2011). 'For

In and of itself, independence says nothing about the continuation of power in these hands, nor about questions such as accountability, transparency, meritocracy and good governance. If we make *folkric* our aim, however, we would thereby commit ourselves to a democratic ideal that can go on illuminating our political life, acting as a standard by which to critique concentrations of power, erosions of rights and instances of nepotism. It centres our attention not just on 'home rule', but also on 'who should rule at home', and how.[a]

Striving for *folkric* is also a realistic objective in an interconnected world. Legally independent states like Norway and Iceland continue to work together and to share powers through international organisations that impose limits on their freedom of action. Unless there is a profound change in foreign policy, an independent Scotland would be part of the European Union, the Council of Europe, NATO, the Commonwealth and the British-Irish Council and, as such, would still have to respond to certain external obligations. These would limit 'independence', at least if we accept a rather simplistic definition of the word as 'free from external restraint', but would be compatible with *folkric*, provided these external obligations are supported by the people. In the same way, the sharing of certain powers on a UK-wide basis, if done in a democratic, consensual and equitable way, would fall short of independence, but would be fully compatible with a commitment to *folkric*.

iii *The Constitutional Debate before the Independence Referendum*

In making a case for independence, the Yes campaign frequently recognised the principle of democracy. They drew attention, for example, to the fact that Scotland in the United Kingdom is on the receiving end of policies – from the privatisation of the Royal Mail and the imposition of

---

a critique of cronyism and jack-in-office politics in Scotland and its contrast with Scotland's progressive self-image, see: G. Hassan, *Caledonian Dreaming: The Quest for a Different Scotland*, (Edinburgh Luath Press: 2014).

a   This phrase has been used to describe the motivating ideology of the American Revolution of 1776. See: Becker, C. L., *The History of Political Parties in the Province of New York*, 1760–1776 (Madison: University of Wisconsin, 1909), p. 22.

the Bedroom Tax to nuclear weapons and the Iraq war – that the majority of people in Scotland do not support. Independence was presented as a way of correcting this 'democratic deficit' and of ensuring that Scotland would always get the Government it votes for.

Meanwhile, the SNP's longstanding commitment to a written Constitution was reflected in the Scottish Government's increased attention to questions of constitutional transition and post-independence constitutional design. According to the November 2013 White Paper, Scotland would be governed during a transitional period immediately after independence by an 'Interim Constitution' (or 'Interim Constitutional Platform'), which would adopt the existing devolved institutions to the needs of independent statehood, protect human rights based on the European Convention, and provide a stable institutional basis for future constitutional development. This Interim Constitution, it was hoped, would lay the foundations for an inclusive and effective constitution-building process in a way that would transcend party divisions, heal the divisions opened up by the independence referendum, and reintegrate No voters into the polity. It would have to be sufficiently comprehensive and robust to enable it to perform the legal and political functions of a Constitution – in protecting rights, structuring democratic processes, and protecting against the abuse of power – during the life of the first post-independence Parliament. Then, in a second stage of the process, a constitutional convention would have been established by the Scottish Parliament to prepare a permanent Constitution.

In most countries that became independent from the United Kingdom between the 1950s and the 1980s, a pre-negotiated prospective Constitution was put to the people when voting for independence. Malta's independence referendum, for example, was not a referendum on the vague notion or principle of independence, but a referendum to adopt a new Constitution that happened to provide for Malta to govern itself independently. Policy documents from when the SNP was in opposition show a previous commitment to such a process; MacCormick's 2002 draft, discussed extensively in *A Model Constitution*, appears to have been written with the intention that it would be put to the people before independence, and would be the constitutional foundation on which independence would be based. The two-stage process adopted by the Scottish Government in 2013 and 2014 therefore marked a change from the SNP's previous policy.

There were good political reasons for this change of tack. The Scottish Government did not wish to dictate the terms of the future Constitution on the very sound grounds that a Constitution should be based on a broad consensus and should belong to all the people, not to the Government or any particular party. It would have been impossible to achieve such inclusion ahead of the referendum, since the parties, groups and movements opposed to independence would have no incentive to participate in the process. Also, the Scottish Government did not wish to alienate thrawn voters whose support for independence might hang on some small point of constitutional content, especially over controversial matters such as religion-state relations. Yet the Scottish Government could not shelve the issue of constitutional design until after independence. To do so would have created a constitutional vacuum and an unacceptable concentration of power in the hands of whoever might win the first post-independence elections. A two-stage process therefore seemed to provide at least some guarantee that Scottish democracy would be safe during the transitional period, while also enabling contentious issues to be delayed until after the referendum.

The decision to postpone permanent constitution making until after independence also opened up the possibility of greater public inclusion: not just an all-party deal, but an all-Scotland agreement. Favourable allusions to Icelandic-style 'crowdsourcing' were made. Although specific details of the constitution making process were never clarified, the 2013 White Paper promised that we would have a 'People's Constitution', and that it would not be imposed by Alex Salmond or the SNP. As never before in Scotland, ordinary citizens would have had the opportunity to engage in constituting their country. After all, the Constitution is an act of the whole people establishing a government, and its legitimacy rests on the widest possible public agreement.

The disadvantage of the proposed two-stage process, however, was that it seemed to present an undefined, vague promise to the people of Scotland. The vote was simply on the general principle of independence, with little substantive detail behind it of what independence would mean in constitutional terms. The success of devolution in 1997 owed much to the work of the Constitutional Convention, which had not only built a broad consensus in favour of devolution before the vote, but had also done much of the detailed work in designing and negotiating the devolution package. This meant that people were not voting for a vague promise. If another referendum on independence, or something very like independence, were to be held, consideration should be given to a pre-independence constitutional conference or convention which would draw up a draft constitutional text to be put to the people. The process of agreeing constitutional specifics, rather than arguing over ill-defined, emotive and divisive labels, could be very beneficial; it could not only reassure voters, and thereby help to secure a positive vote, but also result in a set of proposals that are clear, coherent and well thought through.

The increasing prominence given to matters of constitutional design and process in the months leading up to the referendum was a reflection of the Scottish Government's gradual realisation that their task was not simply to remove Scotland from the United Kingdom, but also to create viable and acceptable institutions for the new Scottish state. It showed a dawning awareness that constitutions, while not a panacea, do matter, and that having a written constitution to regulate the political institutions of the state is now the normal state of affairs for a democratic country. The Scottish Government and a broad range of civil society organisations recognised that a Constitution was not an 'optional extra' to be taken or left at will, but an essential basis for the legitimacy, stability, success and longevity of Scottish democracy. Although some commentators continued to defend parliamentary absolutism,[15] the centre of informed public debate has moved on. No matter how radical the idea of a written Constitution might still be in a UK context, in the context of an independent Scotland it has become an accepted and welcome necessity.

In the event of independence a written Constitution would have been demanded not only by the Scottish public, but also by international circumstances. The absence of a written constitution would be unthinkable in the context of a European country achieving independence in the 21st century. A range of international agreements, to which Scotland would remain bound on independence or, even if not, would almost certainly seek to embrace shortly afterwards, would provide a framework of internationally recognised constitutional standards to which states must adhere if they are legitimately to claim democratic status. These include the International Covenant on Civil and Political Rights, the International

Covenant on Economic, Social and Cultural Rights, the Convention on the Elimination of all Forms of Discrimination against Women, and regional instruments such as the European Convention of Human Rights and the European Convention on Local Self Government. Although these international agreements leave very wide latitude to states in how they choose to constitute themselves, they nevertheless provide clear minimum baselines that states must comply with in order to be legitimate.

With the question of principle generally settled in favour of a written constitution, discussion amongst the Yes campaign shifted to a more pragmatic and forward-looking discussion of what a future Scottish Constitution might look like, and what its purposes, design, nature, content and form might be. For the most part, there was agreement, at least within the Yes camp, on the basic institutional structures by which an independent Scotland should govern itself. The creation of the Scottish Parliament in the 1990s provided an opportunity for a wide consensus to be reached on the basic institutional design, and there was little desire to deviate from this. While remaining within the global family of Westminster derived institutions,[a] the Scottish Parliament embodied a number of reforms intended to correct the worst of the perceived failings of Westminster. These included the adoption of a system of proportional representation, fixed term elections (with the consequent removal of the Crown prerogative of dissolution at will), the formal election of the First Minister by parliamentary vote, a system of pre-legislative consultation, and measures designed to strengthen the role of committees in the legislative process. Although these institutions have been less transformative than first hoped – failing, for example, to overcome ingrained habits of adversarial politics[16] – they have nevertheless provided a form of government for Scotland that is both broadly accepted in terms of public support, and generally acceptable in terms of perform-

---

a   For a discussion of the 'Westminster model' in its manifold global variations, see: Bulmer, W. E. (2014) 'Constrained majoritarianism: Westminster constitutionalism in Malta', *Commonwealth and Comparative Politics*, 51/1, pp. 232–253; De Smith, S. A. (1961) 'Westminster's Export Models: The Legal Framework of Responsible Government', *Journal of Commonwealth Political Studies*, 1/1, pp. 2–16; Ward, A. J. (1987) 'Exporting the British Constitution: Responsible Government in New Zealand, Canada, Australia and Ireland', *Commonwealth and Comparative Politics*, 25/1, pp. 3–25; and Wolf-Phillips, L. (1970) 'Post-independence Constitutional Change in the Commonwealth', *Political Studies*, 18/1, pp. 18–42.

ance. There has so far been relatively little appetite, even from the radical left, to change the basic structure of existing parliamentary institutions.

Indeed it is quite rare, globally speaking, for the macro-level institutional design to be radically changed, even when states adopt entirely new constitutions. Parliamentary democracies rarely become presidential ones, and federal states rarely become unitary. Constitution makers are inevitably constrained by what a country has known in the past and, therefore, what those who use the political system, whether as politicians or as citizens, are already familiar with. This is not to say that important constitutional changes cannot take place, only that they do not take place in an institutional vacuum; changes usually occur within existing structures rather through the invention of entirely new ones. We can therefore reasonably expect that, if there had been a Yes vote in 2014, the resulting Scottish Constitution would have been based on a familiar combination of parliamentary democracy, proportional representation and a unitary structure. We can probably expect the same of any future Scottish Constitution building process, either if independence is achieved in the coming years, or in the context of an autonomous Scotland within a reformed United Kingdom. Fortunately, this combination, which is found in the successful, small democracies in the 'arc of democracy' that stretches across Northern Europe, is known to promote good governance[17] and democratic consolidation.[18]

Within these macro-level structures, there was nevertheless plenty of room for reforms, at the meso- or micro-levels, to improve the effectiveness, inclusiveness and openness of Scotland's institutions. As Negretto writes:

> At the macro level, foundational constitutional choices may seem to remain unaltered over time. Most countries in Latin America, for instance, have maintained the presidential blueprint adopted in the 19th century. But many institutions that have the capacity to transform the quality and performance of presidential regimes have changed in substantive ways over relatively short periods of time. Such is the case of electoral rules, presidential powers, decentralisation schemes, and the organisational forms and powers of the judiciary and oversight institutions. In other words, what looks like the same constitutional structure at the macro level may turn out to be a complete different set of institutions once we consider the accumulation of short-term changes at the level of secondary rules that affect the daily operation of a constitutional regime.[19]

A relatively small group of people – acting through such civic organisations as So Say Scotland, the Electoral Reform Society, the Reid Foundation, Common Weal, National Collective, Environment Link Scotland, and the Constitutional Commission – made important contributions to this debate on deepening, localizing and protecting democracy. Specific issues raised in the period before the referendum included the question of whether the ceremonial head of state should be hereditary or elected, whether constitutional review functions should be performed by the existing Court of Session or by a new Scottish Supreme Court, whether there should be an enhanced role for direct and participatory democracy alongside parliamentary mechanisms, and the role and status of local government in the Constitution. Other proposed reforms included an increase in the number of members of the Scottish Parliament (to staff the new committees and portfolios, such as foreign affairs and defense, that would be needed in an independent state), a quota or parity system to increase the parliamentary representation of women, minorities and marginalised groups, and the creation of a second chamber to assist in scrutinising legislation and overseeing the executive.

However, such institutional reforms did not greatly capture the public imagination before the referendum, and were hardly taken up by the political parties, with the partial exception of the Scottish Green Party. This, too, is understandable. The Unionist parties would not be drawn into a discussion of constitutional design, for to have done so would have made the idea of a Scottish state seem much more real, and therefore more attractive to voters. It would have been very difficult to defend British institutions while comparing them to the options open to an independent Scotland. Meanwhile, the SNP, as a majority party, was unwilling to commit itself to institutions that would take power out of its own hands; the veto mechanisms and counter-majoritarian provisions that were prominent in the party's 2002 draft silently disappeared from the 2014 interim text, and were absent from the party's public pronouncements on constitutional policy.[a]

---

a   Had independence happened, we might have seen some interesting reversals of position during the process of constitution building. For example, the Conservatives, despite having long opposed both proportional representation and written constitutions, might suddenly have become staunch defenders of both, as means of protecting themselves and their supporters from majoritarian rule by parties of the pro-independence left.

The Scottish Government and the Yes campaign focused instead on the declaratory, prescriptive and policy binding roles that a new Constitution could play in defining a new Scotland. They envisaged a Constitution that would confirm the active role of the state in the promotion of the wellbeing of the community, chiefly through the provision of public services and the protection of social rights. The 2013 White Paper noted that a post-independence Constitution could, for example, contain provisions on such matters as 'equality of opportunity and entitlement to live free of discrimination and prejudice'; 'entitlement to public services and to a standard of living that, as a minimum, secures dignity and self-respect and provides the opportunity for people to realise their full potential both as individuals and as members of wider society'; 'protection of the environment and the sustainable use of Scotland's natural resources to embed Scotland's commitment to sustainable development and tackling climate change'; 'a ban on nuclear weapons being based in Scotland'; 'controls on the use of military force'; 'rights in relation to healthcare, welfare and pensions'; 'children's rights' and 'rights concerning other social and economic matters, such as the right to education and a Youth Guarantee on employment, education or training the constitution.'[20] In terms that are discussed in subsequent chapters, such a Constitution would not only have been a charter of democratic rights and institutions but also a new covenant for the people of Scotland, symbolising a commitment to a more inclusive, communitarian and egalitarian society.[a]

iv   Constitutionalism without Independence?

The referendum question in 2014 was simply, 'Should Scotland be an independent country?' In answering this question in the negative, the sovereign people of Scotland decided (on this occasion, for now) not to

---

a   Many conservatively inclined lawyers were deeply critical of these proposed commitments to policies and principles, regarding them as somehow 'improper' to be included in a Constitution. As discussed further in Chapter Three, a prescriptive, policy-rich Constitution is potentially problematic, and is especially so when it attempts to constitutionalise the views of a particular ideological sect, rather than the broadly shared 'common grounds' of the community; this does not, however, render the inclusion of certain policies and principles in a Constitution illegitimate, in circumstances where they are deeply and widely shared.

exercise our sovereignty in the context of an independent state, but to do so as a substantially autonomous part of a United Kingdom. Until we, the people of Scotland, otherwise decide (and the decision is ours, and ours alone) we will continue to be citizens of the United Kingdom, and our relations with the rest of the world will be mediated through British institutions. We will continue to hold British passports, to be defended by the British armed forces, and to be represented abroad by British embassies. Scotland will not have its own seat in the United Nations. On these things the people of Scotland have (for now) clearly pronounced a decision.

In constitutional terms, however, everything else is still wide open. We may have voted to stay in the UK, but the rejection, for the time being, of independence, does not mean that we can simply go back to the old ways of thinking about the sovereignty of the Westminster Parliament. The principle of the Claim of Right – that the people of Scotland are sovereign and so can determine the form of government best suited to our needs – is stronger and more relevant than ever. The referendum was an endorsement and a confirmation, not a denial, of that principle.

Popular sovereignty does not demand the end of the United Kingdom. It demands only that, if the UK is to hold together, it must be based on a new constitutional settlement in which Scotland's place – and the rightful place of its people – is properly recognised. The people of Scotland still lay claim to this sovereign and constituent power, whether independent or not. In Scotland, 'we the people' may choose to govern ourselves as part of a United Kingdom, sharing powers with UK-wide institutions as we see fit, but only on such terms as we agree to, and only for so long as we wish.

It is worth reiterating that the Claim of Right is a national claim, not merely a nationalist one. It was advanced by an inclusive Constitutional Convention in which the Labour Party, the Liberal Democrats, the Scottish Trades Union Congress, Scotland's major churches, and other political and civic organisations, all played a prominent role. Its principles were not of their own invention, but were derived from a long tradition of distinctly Scottish constitutionalism with roots that can be traced back through the theo-political thought of the Scottish Reformation to the limited and contractual kingship of the Declaration of Arbroath. When the Claim of Right was placed before the Scottish Parliament for endorsement in January 2012, it was voted for by the Labour, Liberal Democrat and Green members, as well as by the SNP. The essence of the Claim of Right, in the recognition of popular sovereignty, was even incorporated into the Smith Report of 27 November 2014, indicating its acceptance by Unionist opinion and by the British state, as well as by nationalist politician.[21]

Whether in an independent Scotland or as part of a reconstituted and 'loosely-United' Kingdom, it is now widely recognised in Scotland that a written, supreme Constitution is both an essential expression of our sovereignty and a necessary safeguard of our liberty. Since the people are to be sovereign, there can be no change to the basic ground-rules – the rules by which our institutions are structured, powers are assigned, or the rights of the people protected – except by the consent of the people of Scotland. These restrictions and constraints apply not only to Westminster Governments, but also to our own Government and Parliament in Holyrood. These Scottish institutions, as much as their Westminster counterparts, are not sovereign by right, but mere agents of a sovereign nation. Thus a non-constitutional government – one that operates without clear and binding rules that have been endorsed by the people of Scotland – can no longer be seen as legitimate, whatever the boundaries, name and flag of the state might be.

This commitment to constitutionalism rules out any form of devolution as a lasting settlement. Devolution was designed to delegate powers from Westminster to Holyrood whilst retaining sovereignty in Westminster. 'Devolution Plus' and 'Devolution Max' focus solely on the degree of devolved powers, not on the location of sovereignty or the status of constitutional guarantees. Under the proposals of the Smith Commission, as under any devolved scheme, Scotland would continue to be dependent on Westminster's goodwill for the very existence of its democratic institutions. The Smith Commission's report refers to the Scottish Parliament being made 'permanent' by means of legislation, but it does not say anything about how that legislation is to be protected from or entrenched against hostile majorities in the UK Parliament.[22] This would be a violation of the Claim of Right, which asserts that only a decision of the people can legitimately define and limit the powers of the Scottish Parliament. Without popular sovereignty, the people of Scotland might enjoy certain privileges and powers by grace and favour, but we will not truly possess them by constitutional right. What has been given in devolution, by the benign indulgence of Westminster, might just as easily be taken away by their pique or jealousy. This is not an idle fear: the history of Northern Ireland – where devolution was brought to an abrupt end and direct rule re-imposed during the Troubles – shows that Westminster is willing to suspend or abolish devolved institutions, by unilateral action, when it sees a compelling motive to do so.

The strategic opportunity for the Scottish movement is to set out an intermediate position between independence and 'devolution max' that would respect the Claim of Right while remaining (for as long as a majority of the people of Scotland so wish, and on such terms as the people see fit) part of a United Kingdom. In principle, this could be achieved in three ways: by the creation of a federation of the home nations based on a written federal Constitution for the United Kingdom, by a new Treaty of Union, or by means of a Home Rule Act that would guarantee substantial autonomy for Scotland within the 'shell' of the United Kingdom.

a   A Federal United Kingdom

The word 'federalism' is increasingly used in Scottish and British political discourse, but often misunderstood or misapplied. In general usage, federalism is sometimes presented as a maximal form of devolution, such that federalism would result if Westminster were to devolve a certain set or range of powers. This is not the case. There is a difference of kind, not degree, between federalism and devolution. The defining characteristic of a federation is that there are 'two constitutionally established orders of government with some genuine autonomy from each other',[23] whereas the defining characteristic of devolution is that one order or level of government has inherent power (Westminster) and that devolved institutions are statutory creatures of, and ultimately dependent upon, that power.

In federal countries, the federal government cannot easily or unilaterally change the powers of the 'state-level' institutions, whose autonomous powers and rights are secured by a written Constitution.[a] Moving from

---

a   Simply by way of an illustrative example, any change to the distribution of powers

devolution to federalism would involve a restructuring of the United Kingdom, so that the powers and rights of the Scottish Parliament would be secured within a written constitutional framework that is beyond the easy reach of any parliamentary majority.

Genuine federalism, thanks to this constitutional specificity and rigidity, would in principle ensure a more secure, stable and balanced system of power sharing across the four home nations. To that extent it is an attractive proposition, even if the existing distribution of powers between Scotland and Westminster were to be retained. The process of negotiating, drafting and adopting a federal Constitution for the United Kingdom would also provide an opportunity to rectify other indefensible features of the United Kingdom, such as the absence of effective human rights protections, the disproportional electoral system for the House of Commons, the dangerous extent of Crown prerogatives, religious establishment, and the role and composition of the House of Lords.

Federations vary in the extent to which powers and fiscal resources are centralised. Some, such as Canada, are highly decentralised; others, like Austria and India, are more centralised, with the federal legislature having primacy across a broad range of policy areas and state-level units having relatively few autonomous powers. So replacing devolution with federalism would place the powers of the Scottish Parliament on a more stable and secure constitutional basis, but would not, in itself, enhance the scope of those powers. The draft Constitution produced in 2014 by the House of Commons Political and Constitutional Reform Committee is federal in nature, at least to the extent that the existence and powers of the Scottish, Welsh and Northern Irish institutions would be constitutionally recognised and protected. Furthermore, no change concerning these powers could be made to the constitution without a two-thirds majority vote in both Houses of Parliament and the consent of two out of three of these Parliaments or Assemblies.[24] However, this text (which is strongly

---

between the national Parliament and the States in India requires a two-thirds majority in both Houses of the national Parliament and the approval of a majority of the State legislatures. In Canada, most important amendments require the approval of the legislatures of at least seven out of ten Provinces, having between them a majority of the population (the latter provision is designed to ensure that Quebec and Ontario, the two largest provinces, have a mutual veto).

Unionist throughout) would actually reduce the powers of the Scottish Parliament. So we cannot say that federalism – whatever its other benefits might be – would necessarily give Scotland the powers that most Scots appear to want. Indeed, almost all existing federal systems give the federal level extensive competence over many aspects of domestic policy, including social security, taxation, and much of criminal law. These extensive powers would be unacceptable in a Scottish context, if the aim is to produce a compromise that would make the Union attractive to Yes voters.

If a workable and enduring federal solution is to be found for the United Kingdom, it should be a loose federation (or perhaps more precisely, a 'confederation')[a] in which limited powers over certain matters are shared between Scotland and the other nations of the United Kingdom on an equal, mutual, consensual basis. This arrangement ensures that: (i) sovereignty resides ultimately with the peoples of the states, who retain a right of secession;[b] (ii) the powers of the Union are more limited than is usual in most contemporary federations, being restricted to foreign affairs, defence, the monarchy, passports, immigration, the currency, and perhaps – for a transitional period – a few uncontroversial incidental matters where duplication would serve little purpose; (iii) the states contribute to the common treasury from their own funds, rather than being taxed directly; and (iv) the central institutions of the federation are kept relatively small and simple.

Federalism of this sort has considerable advantages. It would transform the United Kingdom into what many Scots have always claimed it to be in principle, but have long known it not to be in reality: an equal Union, entered into freely, for mutual benefit, on certain limited conditions, by sovereign entities. The concerns of Unionists, in matters such as

---

a   The technical distinction between federalism and confederalism is a fine one that has been much debated by scholars. The Germans differentiate between a '*Bundestaat*' (a federal 'union-state', with emphasis on the unity of the whole) and a '*Staatenbund*' (a confederal 'union of states', with emphasis on the distinct identity of each state). This expresses the essence of the distinction more neatly than is possible in English.

b   There are examples, even within these islands, of the recognition of the right of succession. The Belfast Agreement recognises the right of the people of Northern Ireland to leave the United Kingdom and to be reunified with the rest of Ireland. The Edinburgh Agreement similarly emphasised that Scottish membership of the United Kingdom is based on consent, and can be unilaterally withdrawn.

identity and security, and the aspirations of Nationalists, in matters such as economic and fiscal powers, would both be met on common ground of thinner, more equal and more democratic Union. It would guarantee the long-demanded wish of reformers for 'home rule all round' within a loose, consensual Union. It would be highly decentralised both in terms of the extent of powers exercised by each state and in terms of the recognition of the sovereignty of each state. As well as guaranteeing Scotland's autonomy, the Federal Constitution would also provide a means of protecting human rights, deepening democracy, and promoting political integrity across the United Kingdom. This would be attractive not only to many in Scotland, Wales and Northern Ireland, but also to sincere and long-frustrated democrats in England. Finally, it would ensure 'English votes for English laws', but in a balanced and coherent way that would not create complications for the rest of the United Kingdom.

Under such an arrangement, the United Kingdom could be divided into four states: England, Scotland, Wales and Northern Ireland. The present devolved Parliaments and Assemblies would become 'State Parliaments', and would have primary legislative authority over almost all policy areas. Instead of trying to transform Westminster into a federal Parliament, it might be wiser to replace it with a new Federal Assembly, and to relegate existing Westminster and Whitehall institutions to English matters only. Thus, the English members of the House of Commons and House of Lords would continue to sit as the Parliament of England, after the permanent withdrawal of the Scottish, Welsh and Northern Irish members. This means that questions such as reform of the House of Lords or changing the electoral system for the House of Commons can be dealt with as 'English problems', without either having to wait for English reformers to catch up with the rest of us (which they probably would, given time) or harming the quality of democracy in other nations of the United Kingdom while we wait.

I am a recent convert to the idea of an English Parliament as part of a federation of four nations. In the past, my main objection to such a scheme was that the relative size of England, in relation to the United Kingdom, would make federalism unworkable. The classic texts on federalism have always said that there should be a rough equality of size between the States, such that no one can outweigh or outvote the others.

The only prospect for federalism in the United Kingdom, in that case, would be if England were to be divided into regions, such that there would be not four, but perhaps a dozen or so, States in the United Kingdom. This would then lead, however, to other objections: how can Scotland be an equal *nation*, if it is treated on a par with mere *regions* of England? How can England have a sense of itself, if a thousand year old nation is divided into regions that have little historical, cultural or social relevance?

Now I see it differently. England's size could be an asset. If Scotland is to have a future in a federal Union, then England, as a country, could provide a counter-weight to the centralizing tendency of federal institutions. Rather than England's power being a problem, it could be the key to creating a balanced Union in which the federal institutions do not overshadow the States. In a four-nation federation a Prime Minister of the United Kingdom would have to share power with a First Minister of England – perhaps of a different party – who would have a broadly similar electoral mandate and an equivalent claim to legitimacy. The Parliament and Government of England would demand powers from the United Kingdom, jealously guard their autonomy, and ensure that the federal institutions do not overreach themselves. Mere 'regions' are incapable of that. In the political space between, say, a Federal Assembly for the United Kingdom located in York, Durham or Liverpool, and an English Parliament in Westminster, there would be room for Scotland, Wales and Northern Ireland to breathe.

The fact that English voters would, by virtue of their population, have the largest influence on federal policy need not be problematic, especially if the federal institutions have relatively little power over domestic policy in the member-states. The English electorate would predominantly shape the political composition of the federal government, but this would be acceptable, provided that the federal government be limited to foreign affairs, defence, and a few other matters that do not greatly impinge on day-to-day domestic politics, welfare, economics, health, education, or most of domestic spending.

English predominance could be limited in other ways, too, as part of an overall power-sharing arrangement. The usual way is to give each State equal representation in a federal Senate, while having representation by population in the lower house. This can work, especially if combined with a nuanced legislative process that allows the Senate to veto certain classes of legislation, while not necessarily frustrating clear decision-making in other areas. However, given the limited powers of the federal level, it might be worth considering other, simpler, alternatives such as the deliberate over-representation of Scotland, Wales and Northern Ireland in a unicameral Federal Assembly. One way of doing this would be to prescribe a formula for the distribution of seats that awards half of the total number of seats on the basis of an equal four-way split and the other half proportionally on the basis of population. On current figures, this would give English members a small majority, sufficient to pass ordinary legislation, but not a two-thirds majority necessary for certain key decisions – such as constitutional amendments – over which the representatives of the other three States would have a veto. Moreover, there is nothing in this proposal that would prevent the further devolution of the English Parliament, giving substantial powers to the English regions or counties should there be such a desire.[a]

Whatever the advantages may be, reaching political agreement on a federal solution for the entire UK will not be easy. The gaps between the constitutional conversations north and south of the border, and within Scotland between those seeking greater autonomy and those wishing to put the brakes on the process, are wide, and it is likely that anything acceptable to an SNP-led Scottish Government would be unacceptable to opposition parties in Scotland, and even less acceptable to Westminster.

Much of the difficulty in reaching a 'four nations' federal agreement arises from the fact that the English people (whose consent would be essential to the successful creation and operation of a federal system) have no collective say in their own national affairs. English interests are swallowed up, much like English identity, in a United Kingdom from which they cannot clearly distinguish or easily disentangle themselves. At present there is no English Parliament, only a UK Parliament in which the

---

a   In proposing a four-nation federation for the United Kingdom, I am not ignoring the North-South divide in England, the anomalous position of London, or the historical claims of certain parts of the country such as Cornwall and County Durham. I would be delighted to see English regions and counties having assemblies with substantial devolved powers, but I see this as a matter of English politics, to be determined by the Parliament and people of England, as part of England's movement towards democracy and maturity.

English have an overwhelming majority. Fundamental restructuring on this scale is politically difficult precisely because a federation – in creating a balance of power between the parliaments and governments of England on one side, and of the United Kingdom on the other – would split the England-UK axis and thereby weaken the power-base of the British elite. Besides, English legal conservatism is probably too strong to allow the United Kingdom's conventional system to be replaced by a modern, written, federal constitution of this type (even though the British Empire had a fairly successful record of creating federations in places like Canada and Australia, and the idea of federalism is therefore not entirely alien to the British constitutional tradition broadly conceived).

There are also potentially problematic fiscal implications for Wales and Northern Ireland, which would find it more difficult than Scotland to be fully self-financing, as well as the risk that a federal settlement could reignite tensions in Northern Ireland.

These are not necessarily insurmountable obstacles, and they need not prevent us from actively pursuing a loose federal solution, but we would have to be realistic about the prospects of success. Federalism does not depend on Scottish will alone, but on the will of the rest of the UK to reform itself. We would be wise to be ready with a back-up plan to protect Scotland in the event that the rest of the UK does not want to go down that road.

b   A New Treaty of Union

If a four-nation federation is politically unfeasible, a second line of approach is to pursue autonomy for Scotland by means of a bilateral renegotiation of the terms of the Union, to be expressed through a new Treaty of Union. This would replace the 'incorporating' or parliamentary Union of 1707 with a 'non-incorporating' or inter-governmental Union.

The terms of the Union would be broadly as follows: the United Kingdom would continue, from the outside, to be one state, with one army, one foreign policy, one head of state, one passport, and other such trappings of statehood. However, this would just be a 'shell'. From the inside, Scotland would be a distinct entity, with its own Constitution, full internal self-government, and full fiscal autonomy, meaning that Scotland would be responsible for raising and spending all of its own revenues.

There are various historical precedents showing how such a 'non-incorporating' Union might work. It could, for example, take inspiration from the Austro-Hungarian Empire under the 'historic compromise' of 1867. The Imperial Government, which had come close to ruin during the 1848 revolutions, and had maintained its power in the 1850s only by means of repression, decided to reconstitute the Empire on a more mutual and inclusive basis. It retained a single external identity in international law for the purposes of foreign affairs and defence. Internally, it was divided into two entities: (i) Austria (including the Czech, Slovak and Polish lands, and other parts of the empire outside of Hungary and Croatia) and (ii) Hungary (including Croatia, Transylvania, and parts of what is now Slovakia). Each of these two entities was fully autonomous over all matters of domestic law, policy and finance. Each had its own Parliament, its own responsible Government, its own constitutional arrangements and its own civil service. There was a personal union in the monarchy, such that the titles of Emperor of Austria and King of Hungary were combined. There were just three joint ministries: foreign affairs, war and finance. These ministers were responsible to the Emperor-King (unlike the Austrian and Hungarian Prime Ministers, who were responsible to their respective Parliaments). Besides the three common ministries, there was a Customs Union and common external trade tariff, negotiated between the two Governments, approved by the two Parliaments, and renewed every ten years. There was also a common coinage and a joint national bank, and co-operation on common projects, such as railways and postal services, all of which were negotiated between the two entities on an *ad hoc* basis and implemented through parallel legislation passed by both Parliaments.[25]

Patterning new institutions for the United Kingdom on those of the long-dead and little loved Austro-Hungarian Empire might seem improbable, but this idea should not be dismissed out of hand. It has many of the advantages of a loose federation, while being simpler in terms of its institutional form. There would be no need for England to adopt a written Constitution or for the status of Wales and Northern Ireland to change. There would be no need for a federal Parliament, just for coordinating institutions of an intergovernmental nature through which Scotland's interests in shared matters such as foreign affairs and defence can be expressed.

Of course, purists may argue that in the absence of separate states to act as parties to negotiations, a new Treaty of Union between Scotland and the rest of the UK would be impossible to negotiate. Scotland would first have to become independent, and then, perhaps a minute later, agree to new terms of Union. However, such purism overlooks political realities as well as historical precedents. The 1920 Anglo-Irish Agreement was pointedly not called a Treaty by the British, but it performed the functions of a treaty and achieved a similar aim of allowing a transition to extensive but limited autonomy.

c   Home Rule

A third option is for Scotland to be granted Home Rule by an Act of the UK Parliament. Home Rule differs from devolution not only in the extent of autonomy ceded but also in the enshrining of that autonomy in an overarching constitutional structure that would recognise the sovereignty of the people of Scotland and thereby free us from continuing constitutional dependence on the Westminster Parliament.

The principle of Home Rule is that while the Westminster Parliament, in the absence of a written Constitution, may not bind its successors, it can irrevocably limit the territorial extent of its sovereignty; if this were not so, the various Independence Acts which gave independence to former colonies could be repealed, and those countries thereby brought back under Westminster rule – an absurd proposition. So, if Parliament can relinquish its sovereignty over a territory entirely, by means of an Independence Act, it can also relinquish its sovereignty over a territory partially, by means of a Home Rule Act that, once it is enacted, deprives Westminster forever of the right to legislate for that territory in relation to the matters that are not reserved to Parliament.

A Home Rule Constitution for Scotland would be debated and negotiated amongst the political and civic actors in Scotland and then approved by the people of Scotland in a referendum as an act of sovereignty. For the purposes of legal authority and continuity, the Constitution would then by conferred upon Scotland by means of a Home Rule Act, to which it would be attached as a schedule. The Constitution would establish the institutions of government in Scotland, define the rights of the people in Scotland, and specifically and irrevocably renounce the sovereignty of Westminster over Scotland. The Home Act would set out some 'red lines' that Scotland would have to respect, namely: the reservation of the monarchy, foreign affairs, defence, immigration, passports and currency. Everything else would be Scotland's autonomous responsibility, including the right to raise and spend all of our own money.

Although the technicalities of our constitutional status would be different, Scotland under an autonomous Home Rule Constitution would, in practical terms, be in a position not unlike that of the Channel Islands and the Isle of Man, which also enjoy substantial autonomy while still being reliant on the United Kingdom Government for the purposes of foreign affairs and defence, and while still using the pound. The key difference is that Scotland would be a part of the United Kingdom, while the Channel Islands and the Isle of Man are Crown dependencies. Nevertheless, the Channel Islands and the Isle of Man show that the United Kingdom can be tolerant of substantial autonomy so long as its military and diplomatic interests are unchallenged. The same degree of autonomy enjoyed by the Channel Islands and the Isle of Man could be extended to Scotland, under suitable constitutional arrangements, without difficulty, and without loss of friendship or co-operation.

An even better example of Home Rule for Scotland's purposes is provided by the Cook Islands, a group of Islands in the South Pacific. The Cook Islands remain part of the Realm of New Zealand. The Queen, 'in right of New Zealand' is the Head of State, and is represented in the Cook Islands by a 'Representative' whose duties are mostly formal and ceremonial. Cook Islanders are New Zealand citizens. Since 1964, however, the Cook Islands have possessed a written Constitution that gives them full autonomy over almost all matters except for foreign affairs, defence and the issuing of passports, which remain the responsibility of New Zealand. New Zealand, like the United Kingdom, is one of the few countries in the world that lacks a written, supreme Constitution, but this has not prevented the establishment of a written Constitution for the Cook Islands. The Cook Islands therefore show that it is possible for Scotland to have a written, supreme Constitution of our own, even while being in a Union, for purposes of external relations and defence, with a country that does not have a proper Constitution.

Inspiration and precedents could also be drawn from the example of Gibraltar and other overseas territories. Under the Constitution of 2006, Gibraltar has its own Parliament and Government with full powers over all matters of policy except foreign affairs, defence and security, and with full control over all of its own taxing and spending. In Gibraltar, the UK Government is represented by an appointed Governor who is responsible for overseeing external and military matters. UK policies regarding Gibraltar are determined by consultation and mutual agreement. The preamble to the Constitution contains a declaration of sovereignty that asserts the right of the people of Gibraltar to self-determination. In other words, Gibraltar, a colony with a population of a few tens of thousands of people, has more autonomy, and a stronger democratic basis for that autonomy, than Scotland would have if the proposals of the Smith Commission or any other forms of 'enhanced devolution' hitherto put forward by the major parties, were implemented.

Unlike Gibraltar or the Channel Islands, which have no representation in the UK Parliament, and which pursue their interests vis-à-vis the British Government on an inter-governmental level, a Home Rule arrangement for Scotland could provide for the continued representation of Scotland in the House of Commons, in order that Scottish members might speak up for Scotland's interests and contribute to UK-wide policies in the limited range of shared competencies. However, it would be only fair and sensible for Scottish members to be excluded not only from voting on non-Scottish legislation, but also from votes of confidence and supply, from holding ministerial office, and from select and standing committees that do not deal with UK-wide matters. The votes of England, Wales and Northern Ireland would determine the composition of the UK Government, but this slight and imperceptible loss of shared ruled would be more than compensated for by greatly expanded self-rule.

The three proposals outlined in this section – federation, a new Treaty of Union, and Home Rule – offer workable intermediate positions between devolution and full independence. The peoples of these islands have stood together in war and peace, and most Scots evidently continue to value elements of their British identity. Unfortunately, the old arrangement through which Britishness was made manifest, the centralised 'Union-

State', did not work to our advantage. Too often, the distinctive voice and interests of Scotland were drowned out, and democracy stifled by the oligarchic and unresponsive institutions of the United Kingdom. If Scotland is freely and willingly to remain as part the United Kingdom, it must be as part of a very different one: a UK based on a constitutional foundation that recognises Scotland's sovereignty and right to self-determination, guarantees Scotland's autonomy over almost all aspects of domestic policy, and respects democracy and human rights.

These proposals for an intermediate position, if adopted in a spirit of sincerity, would enable Scotland and the rest of the UK to go forward together in a partnership of equals, sharing certain powers and responsibilities where this is in our mutual interests, while respecting the liberty, autonomy and distinct interests of each country. Such intermediate positions would be attractive to moderate Unionists because they would, obviously and visibly, maintain this connection. Scots would still be 'British'. We would still carry British passports. We could still join, and would be protected by, the British armed forces. We would still be represented abroad by British embassies and consulates. We would still use the pound. Likewise, moderate supporters of independence cannot fail to recognise that these proposals for intermediate positions offer real opportunities for democratic self-government. Federalism or autonomous Home Rule (the choice between them is essentially a pragmatic one, depending on the extent to which the rest of the UK is willing to transform itself) would give Scotland the ability to pursue very different models of economic and social policy, to address problems of poverty and inequality, and to fund those policies from our own resources. They would also remove any suspicion of Scotland being 'subsidised' by the rest of the United Kingdom, since Scotland would pay a contribution to London for our share of shared services and the UK Government would have no tax-raising powers in Scotland.

While these intermediate arrangements would still be inferior to independence in many respects, since they would still leave Scotland without our own voice in international affairs, and would still subject us to the military policy of a more belligerent neighbour, they might nevertheless provide blueprints for a generous and healing compromise, at least in the medium term. For some, this compromise could be an end in itself; for others, it could be seen as a further step towards full independence in the future. Finally, federalism, a new Treaty of Union or Home Rule could allow scope for the effective strengthening of democracy in Scotland along the lines proposed in this book and in *A Model Constitution*, while remaining within the United Kingdom. Some of the reforms outlined in the later chapters of this book would be possible only with full independence, but many are at least theoretically possible in a non-independent context.

CHAPTER TWO

How can constitutions promote the common good?

A MODEL CONSTITUTION argued for a 'civic' approach to democracy, according to which the protection of human rights would be complemented by a commitment to the realisation of the common good. In a civic democracy, our freedom is recognised as having an ethical purpose, which is intrinsically connected to the idea of the common good:

> We do not seek freedom so that we can please ourselves, but so that, as fellow-citizens of a free and just community, we may love and serve one another, and through such love and service, can grow into ourselves and become as good as we can humanly be. Freedom, thus understood, is a serious ethical vocation, which requires us to cultivate good character and civic virtues. It cannot and must not be mistaken for amoral license, its cheap counterfeit.[1]

Freedom, understood in this civic democratic sense, is not only essential for the protection of personal rights against the abuse of power, but also has a common purpose in enabling us to live well together, and to fulfil our civic duties as active members of a self-governing community:

> [A civic democracy] seeks not the hollow freedom of the market place, reduced to a choice between similar political products like that between two rival brands of cola. Neither does it offer the purely negative freedom to be left alone and shift for ourselves in an indifferent, uncaring world, as some extreme libertarians would have us believe. Rather, it strives for the freedom of the mature, morally responsible person, who is aware of their interdependence with their neighbours, their community, their country, and the world, and who seeks freedom to do what is right in concert with others.[2]

This chapter argues that such an ethically rooted approach to politics, with the common good (*folkweal*) as its focus and active democratic citizenship as its mainstay, is compatible with a diverse and pluralistic society.

Understanding the common good in contingent and pragmatic terms, it shows how a concern for the common good – rather than private advantage or special privileges of any person, faction or party – can best be expressed through a commitment to political liberty (*folkric*), which it is the first duty of the Constitution to preserve.

i The Common Good as the Purpose of the State

In 1780, John Adams, the principal drafter of the Constitution of the newly independent Commonwealth of Massachusetts (and subsequently the second President of the United States), declared the 'common good' to be the chief purpose of a legitimate government:

> Government is instituted for the common good; for the protection, safety, prosperity, and happiness of the people; and not for profit, honor, or private interest of any one man, family, or class of men.[3]

Adams was describing government in principle, not in practice. Most governments in history, he knew, had been set up for the benefit of a few: either a monocratic ruler and his court or a patrician oligarchy. However, in making this moral claim, Adams was digging into a deep tradition of Western political thought, according to which the chief aim and purpose of the state should be to serve the common good.

This tradition can be traced back at least as far as Aristotle (384 – 322 BCE) who made a basic distinction between 'good' (true) and 'bad' (corrupt) forms of government. The good forms of government are bound by law and aim towards the common good, whilst bad forms are capricious, arbitrary, and aim at the personal, private or sectional benefit of those who rule.[4] Aristotle's distinction between good and bad governments cuts across other classifications of states, such as whether the state is governed by one, the few, or the many. The good forms of government are monarchy (lawful rule by one for the common good), aristocracy (lawful rule by the best few for the common good)[a] and polity (lawful rule by many for the common good). The bad forms are tyranny (arbitrary rule by one for their

---

a The 'Aristocracy', in the Aristotelian classification, is not to be confused with the titled nobility or old duffers in ermine. The original sense of 'the most excellent' is perhaps better conveyed by the word 'meritocracy'.

own benefit), oligarchy (arbitrary rule by the rich few for their own benefit) and ochlocracy[a] (arbitrary rule by the mob, or masses, for their own benefit). This distinction also applies whether rulers are popularly elected or gain power through hereditary succession, appointment by peers, conquest, lot, or any other means. Elective tyrannies or oligarchies are no less tyrannical or oligarchical for being elective. They are not legitimised by the formality of the election if they fail to serve the common good.

A problem facing classical writers was that the good forms of government were highly unstable and prone to degenerating into bad forms. Monarchs became tyrants and aristocracies of genuine merit soon became oligarchies of wealth and privilege. Even democracy (polity) had a tendency to degenerate into mob rule – not the lawful rule of the whole community for the common good, but the arbitrary rule of the majority. To counteract this tendency, Aristotle, followed by other writers such as Polybius (200 – c.118 BCE) and Cicero (106 – 43 BC), argued for a 'mixed', 'balanced', or 'temperate' government. This would enable the advantages of each simple form of good government (monarchy, aristocracy, polity) to be enjoyed while mitigating, if not entirely avoiding, the corresponding disadvantages of each.[5] Thus the energy, unity and responsibility of the single leader could be coupled with the wise advice and counsel of the best citizens, and these together could be harnessed to the people who, in exercising their power of veto and contestation over public decisions, would keep the elites honest and accountable.[6]

This central concern for the common good, as the aim and distinguishing mark of a just and legitimate state, coupled with the 'mixed constitution' as the principal means of achieving it, was absorbed from Aristotle and Cicero, through Thomas Aquinas, into the Christian tradition. There it was grafted, without too much conceptual difficulty, onto the medieval system of government by estates (*ständestaat*) in which kings shared power with, and were limited by, assemblies of the 'estates of the realm': the nobility, clergy, burgesses, and, in some cases, non-noble

---

a   Technically, Aristotle used 'democracy' to describe the partisan, capricious rule of the lower orders, which is the bad form of rule by the many, and distinguished it from 'polity', or 'public government', which is the good form of rule by the many. However, this terminology is confusing, since the word democracy now has other meanings, so it makes sense to use the term for 'mob rule' (ochlocracy) to describe the corrupt form.

landowners.[7] John Calvin, in his *Institutes of the Christian Religion* (1536), acknowledged this connection between classical concepts of the mixed constitution and the institutional arrangements of the 'state-of-estates'. He referred to the best constitution as a balance of aristocratic and popular elements and likened members of the Estates of the Realm in his day to the ancient Spartan institution of Ephors: public officials established in order to protect the common good by restricting, limiting and guiding rulers.[8]

However, it was in the Italian city-states of the high and late Middle Ages that the search for a politics of the common good was most earnestly undertaken. The citizens of free cities like Florence, Venice, Genoa, Pisa, Lucca and Sienna, where 'there were no princes and no kings, but citizens living together under common laws and statutes'[9] grappled with problems remarkably similar to those of our own times. They had to work out how to maintain a free and civic way of life in the face of ambitious, aspiring tyrants and powerful merchant oligarchs; how to protect the *res publica* from corruption and to defend it against internal and external threats without undermining its liberty; and how to maintain a sense of civic spirit and public duty amongst an increasingly mobile, commercial and variegated citizenry.

Italian liberty was always volatile and often vulnerable. Many city republics fell into the hands of closed, corrupt patrician oligarchies, or into the hands of *signori* – singular rulers who treated the city as their personal fiefdom and its citizens as their servants. Yet, in addressing the practical problems of making freedom work, the citizens of Italian cities developed 'a distinctive body of political theory committed to sustaining the principle of liberty and to explaining the political and legal means to attain and preserve it'.[10] This body of republican theory, long neglected by British scholars of both left and right but now undergoing something of a resurgence, offers a good key both to understanding our present situation and to meeting our aspirations for a better future.

I wish to highlight two core principles that have come to us from this tradition. The first is that the quality of government matters, not as a theoretical abstraction, but as something that directly affects the quality of life enjoyed by ordinary people. This gives a special urgency and relevance to political, and especially constitutional, discussion – not as idle speculation, but as a subject of deep moral and practical concern to us all.

This passion for the quality of government was reflected in public art. In the Palazzo Publicco of Sienna, where the city's 'Council of Nine' met, Ambrogio Lorenzetti painted the *Allegory of Good and Bad Government* (1339). These frescoes represent 'the qualities that rulers ought and ought not to have' and 'the effects of the two kinds of government on the lives of ordinary people'.[11] In the *Allegory of Good Government*, 'the city is ordered and wealthy: we see artisans plying their trades, merchants buying and selling'.[12] The rural hinterland is filled with peasants who can 'till the earth and gather in the harvest' in peace and security.[13] The rulers are surrounded by the virtues of Courage, Justice, Magnanimity, Peace, Prudence and Temperance, while the citizens are united by a chord of harmony.[14] This happy condition can continue because the commune has 'stripped the wicked of all power'.[15] Conversely, in the *Allegory of Bad Government*, the ruler is surrounded by the vices of 'Avarice, Cruelty and Pride'; we see military occupation in the city, and a barren, devastated countryside.[16] The inscription reads: 'Because each seeks only his own good, in this city Justice is subjected to tyranny.'[17] As David Miller notes:

> The portrayal of evil government was not just an academic exercise: it was a reminder of what might happen if the rulers of the city failed in their duty to the people, of if the people failed in their duty to keep a watchful eye on their representatives.[18]

How does Scotland compare to Lorenzetti's images of good and bad government? Are the grey schemes and the barren town centres, the struggling villages and vacant shops, the food bank queues and the health statistics signs of a community in which the common good is at the centre of public life, or testimonies to self-interested powers beyond our control?

A second core principle to be derived from the civic republican tradition is that good government can be secured only through political liberty: the participation of the citizens in their own civic affairs through free discussion, inclusive representative institutions, and rotation in office. To preserve their liberty and ensure good government, the citizens of Italy's republics experimented with a range of constitutional forms. At the base of each city-state was usually an *arengo* (public assembly) or general council in which the citizenry was embodied. Executive and preparatory duties were delegated to officials, variously known as consuls, priors, gonfoloniers, doges, or signori, who would be selected by complex systems of lot, election and nomination to serve for short terms of office. They would be advised and assisted by intermediate councils, such as a senate, 'small council', or 'council of sages'. There were also special institutions through which the common people were represented, often with their own 'captain of the people' who acted as a popular check on the power of the (mainly patrician) consuls.[19] The guiding aphorism was '*ubi multa consilia, ibi salus*' ('Where there are many councils, there is safety').[20] As Viroli writes, this multitude of councils, allowing the citizens to partake in government – not as ruler and subject, but as peers, colleagues, and equal partners – was the best guarantee of good government:

> If public deliberations concerning the entire city are entrusted to councils representing the entire citizenry... it is more likely that sovereign decisions will affirm the common good, rather than the personal interests of rulers or a political faction or a social group, and will therefore protect the citizens from domination.'[21]

These two principles go to the heart of Scotland's independence debate. Aside from questions of identity, history and culture, the case for independence essentially rests on the belief that Scotland's common good will be better served by placing sovereign authority in the hands of the people of Scotland, rather than in Westminster and Whitehall. The underlying philosophy of the pro-independence cause is democratic and 'civic republican', in a way that resounds well with Viroli's argument, namely that 'the rule of the people is the best assurance of the public good', or, to put it into other terms: '*folkric is folkweal.*'

Regrettably, the centrality of the common good as the legitimating purpose of the state has been overlooked in modern Britain, and especially so in recent decades. Neo-liberalism (the near-hegemonic ideology of the last 30 years, now deeply embedded in the institutions, policies and assumptions of the UK state) has the denial of the common good at its root. Instead, it embraces Hobbesian 'rational egoism': a coldly amoral worldview of competitive individualism and self-gain, without commonality or solidarity, in which everything, even human relationships, must either be commodified and traded, or deemed to be of no value. The aphorisms of this ideology are 'Sink or swim'; 'You're on your own'; 'Get on your bike!'; 'Greed is good'; 'You've got to look out for number one'; 'Heaven helps those who help themselves'; and, perhaps most infamously, 'There is no such thing as society.'

One of the few encouraging developments of our political life since the financial crash of 2008 has been the return of the language of the common good to our political discourse. There is a growing realisation that there is such a thing as the common good after all, that a culture of selfishness makes us all poorer, that a simple metric of GDP growth does not reflect all that is truly important in life. More people are recognising that a well-functioning society needs public institutions that educate us, heal us when we are sick, and support us when we are down on our luck – and, crucially, that these institutions only work well if we all contribute our share.

This development has been particularly evident in Scotland, with various pro-independence voices trying to articulate policy proposals for an independent Scotland with the common good at its core. The 'Common Weal' movement has made a great contribution to this effort, challenging the neo-liberal 'London orthodoxy' across a range of policy areas.[a] Others, associated with movements such as 'Green Yes', Labour for Independence, the Radical Independence Campaign and Compass, have also used the language of the common good to criticise existing policies and institutions and to frame an outline for desired future developments.

ii   What is the Common Good?

Despite this resurgence of interest in a 'politics of the common good', it remains a slippery and often misunderstood concept. The 'good that we all share in common' stems from our common humanity and from the universal needs that we all have, and that must be met universally if we are each to enjoy a flourishing life. It is the good that we enjoy individually, but that is achieved only by collective provision that makes the same good available to each and all:

---

a   Common Weal's 'In Place of Anxiety' on reform of the benefits system, 'Silent Crisis' on the restoration of local democracy and 'Time for Life' on the idea of a shorter working week are worthy contributions to an important debate. These and other excellent publications are freely available at www.allofusfirst.org

The common good, then, consists primarily of having the social systems, institutions, and environments on which we all depend that work in a manner that benefits all people. Examples of particular common goods or parts of the common good include an accessible and affordable public health care system, and effective system of public safety and security, peace among the nations of the world, a just legal and political system, and unpolluted natural environment, and a flourishing economic system. Because such systems, institutions, and environments have such a powerful impact on the wellbeing of members of a society, it is no surprise that virtually every social problem in one way or another is linked to how well these systems and institutions are functioning.[22]

The specific conditions of human flourishing will vary with place, time and culture, but the generalities are remarkably universal, being rooted in the material, emotional and psychological needs of human nature. The vast majority of us would like to live in reasonable comfort and material security, with a safe roof over our head and good food on the table; to be free from fear, tyranny, abuse and oppression; to have useful and reward-ing work to do, balanced with adequate opportunities for rest and leisure; to be able to cultivate friendships and relationships; to have safe streets and public spaces, whose functionality is graced with a little beauty; to drink clean water and breathe fresh air; to raise a family in comfort and security; to have access to education and culture; to develop our skills and talents; to express our personality; to worship according to our conscience; and to be cared for when we are sick, injured, old, or otherwise in distress. These conditions allow humans to flourish, and the absence of any one of these will necessarily harm and diminish our lives.[23] I argued in an article published in the *Scotsman* in December 2011 that meeting these universal needs provides a common basis for political activity:

> The common weal includes the goods we all hold dear, whatever our politics or identity: it means peace, capable administration, honest justice, sustainable prosperity, livable communities, clean and safe streets, decent and humane working conditions, thriving towns, a social safety net that does not become a poverty trap, and high standards of education and healthcare. People rightly differ on how to balance, prioritise, achieve and pay for these goods – and politics

is the mechanism by which we resolve those differences – but there is near-universal consensus that these are the conditions necessary for our wellbeing, and that the state has some part in delivering, or at least promoting, them.[24]

A community in which a concern for the common good is placed at the centre of its politics, economics, law and administration will be one in which a sincere attempt is made to secure these conditions of human flourishing for everyone. Conversely, any deviation from the common good, through the perversion of public power for private or partisan ends, will inevitably undermine the capacity for flourishing amongst those citizens who are not part of the ruling cabal, or privileged class, as resources are diverted away from public needs and common purposes and into the private hands of the corrupt.

It is important to note that, although embracing the common good will require us to evaluate policies by how they affect the deepest concerns of the commonality, and not simply by the calculus of our own advantage, the common good is not simply – or even necessarily – synonymous with a leftwards turn in policy. It implies a broader ethical critique of self-seeking actions and vested interest politics, in which all conscientious and public-spirited citizens can make common cause. Left and right may differ in their view of the role of the market, the state and civil society in the achievement of the common good,[a] but everyone can unite in expressing repugnance against those who deny the common good by awarding lucrative public contracts on corrupt grounds, or putting expense accounts and ornamental duck ponds before honest public service.

The common good, secondly, is not the same as the 'good of the majority'. The majority may decide to persecute or exclude a minority, who are thereby denied a share in the common good. A majority vote may be the best way, pragmatically, to determine the course of action to be

---

a   For example, those on the left may want fee-paying private schools to be deprived of charitable status, while those on the right may favour a system that enables parents to pay for education with state-issued vouchers, but all – except the most doctrinaire extremists – can recognise, first, that an educated mind is conducive to the good life of the individual, and, secondly, that an educated citizenry is conducive to a good society, and that therefore the state has some role in ensuring that a decent education is available to all on fair terms.

followed in particular circumstances, but it is not applicable to all decisions. Sometimes, to defend the common good, religious, ethnic or linguistic minorities have to be given special protection, while the power of the majority has to be restrained to prevent oppression.

Neither is the common good the same as the 'good of all'. In particular, those who live by corrupt means – those who use power and influence for self-serving, rather than community-serving, ends – stand to lose, in a personal capacity, when the common good triumphs, even though they would share in the benefit, in their capacity as citizens, from such a triumph. Imagine that a city council were to pay off a former head of a city-funded agency who had given lucrative contracts to millionaire donors to the city's ruling party; in this purely hypothetical case, the individual concerned would have benefited, as might the party, but the common good would suffer. If the common good were to reign in that city, the personal interests of the wicked would be harmed, even as the city itself would flourish (if this were not so, and if the common good could be established without harm to the corrupt, then it would be easy to achieve, and the world would be a much better place).

iii   Common Good, Pluralism and Pre-Commitment

To establish the common good as the normative basis of the State and its Constitution is to unite the citizens as fellow members of the *res publica* and as equal participants in its free institutions and its civic way of life. It requires a general commitment to liberty, embodied in democratic govern-ance and the protection of human rights, to equality, in the sense that no one should have the power to 'lord it over' others, and to fraternity, expressed in willingness to pool risks and resources, and so bear one another's burdens.

These general commitments do not, however, require that all be alike, in terms of cultural homogeneity, unanimity of belief or uniformity of lifestyle. A Constitution for the common good would not eradicate the vital pluralism of our society, nor deny the free expression of particular identities, values and priorities, or sectional, local and personal interests. Instead, it would embrace our diversity and accommodate differences of origin, gender, religion, ethnicity, geography and language – and of tastes, proclivities, goals, priorities, passions, concerns and opinions. The defense of such pluralism, far from being incompatible with the common good, is integral to it. To use an old metaphor, the body is made up of many members – eyes and ears, hands and feet – which are different yet interdependent. Indeed, if the whole body were an eye, there would be nothing to hear with; for 'there are many members, but one body'.[25] Thus the common good of the body is served not by the uniformity but by the harmonious diversity of its members.

The reason for this defence of diversity is simple, but often overlooked, especially by those who are most sincere, committed and well-intentioned: namely, that while much common ground may well be found, some of the things that are true, right and obvious to us may be difficult and doubtful, or just plain wrong, to some of our fellow citizens. For example, for every person who insists that the Constitution should protect the 'right of a woman to control her own body', there is likely to be someone else – someone equally passionate, equally committed, and equally convinced of the inherent rightness of their cause – who insists on the 'right to unborn life'. These arguments are often highly polarised and difficult to resolve.

Fortunately, it is not necessarily the function of the Constitution to resolve them. The adoption of a (written, supreme, rigid) Constitution creates a distinction between the Constitution and ordinary laws. The Constitution is the act of the whole people in their original, constituent, plenary capacity, whereas ordinary laws are the acts of the majority of the people's representatives in their derived, constituted, limited, capacity.[a] The Constitution need not take sides between supporters and opponents of abortion, same-sex marriage, or other deeply divisive policy decisions.

---

a   The exercise of ordinary legislative power or the statement of an advisory opinion in a referendum is not an exercise of sovereign or constituent power: in these cases, the people are acting not as sovereign, but as a constituted body having certain decision-making rights under the Constitution. The difference is a fine one, but important: it means, for example, that if the people were to vote in favour of a law referred to them in an advisory referendum, the fact that it had been approved by the people would not prevent future challenge, through the courts, of the constitutionality of the law. The law approved by this specific act of the electors would still have to conform to the Constitution that reflects the sovereign people. Only when voting on constitutional amendments are the people truly acting in their sovereign capacity. (On this point I follow the terms of Jean-Jacques Rousseau, and, in particular, his distinction between the 'people' and the 'sovereign').

Instead of trying to settle every dispute in the text of the Constitution, it might be enough, and as much as we can realistically hope for, if the Constitution provides a framework of ground rules and basic rights through which disputes can be resolved democratically, by ordinary laws, in a discursive, pragmatic and contingent way.

All that is required, in that case, is a 'thin' pragmatic agreement on the structures of democratic government and on those rights and liberties that are necessary to sustain political liberty and an open, plural society. It is possible, by concentrating on these matters, to develop a Constitution that enjoys broad legitimacy, inclusion, permanence and universality – not because it is an ideal blueprint for society, but because it serves as a framework in which different visions, ideals and movements can coexist, and engage in democratic politics without any one person, party or faction being able to dominate.

A Constitution that reflects the common good will allow various 'members' of the state (persons, families, religious institutions, political parties, trade unions, charitable and voluntary bodies, professional associations, interest and campaigning groups and local communities) to remain true to themselves while also participating in the whole. Unity of action and purpose may be achieved, in relation both to the general structures and institutions of government embodied in the Constitution and to particular policy or legislative decisions, but such unity, in a free society, would not require uniformity. In the words of Hastings Lees-Smith, who was leader of the Labour Party in 1940, the unity of an open society is 'unity by discussion, persuasion, good will and good sense, instead of unity by the concentration camp, the rubber truncheon and the executioner's block'.[26]

In practical terms, this means that the Constitution must protect the basic rights of a free society – freedom of speech, religion, association and assembly, privacy rights, and equality before the law. There must be institutions, such as independent courts and an impartial civil service and police force, through which those rights can be maintained and defended. There is a need for inclusive representative institutions, through which the diversity of society can be expressed, and in which all can have an effective voice. There should be room under such a Constitution for the grouse-shooting carnivore and the vegetarian animal rights activist, for the

Catholic, Protestant, Atheist, Muslim and Jew, for the Thatcherite and Socialist. These people might vote for different sides of various issues. They might live much of their lives in different social milieu. They might argue vigorously and robustly. They would nevertheless be fellow members of the *res publica*: as co-owners and co-beneficiaries of the 'public thing', they would all be protected by a Constitution that guarantees their free participation in the management of common affairs and in the pragmatic realisation of the common good.

An important aspect of this approach, perhaps paradoxically, is to recognise the limits of constitutional prescription. If it is to stand as a framework of governance that is superior, in origin and authority, to any given parliamentary majority or policy decision, the Constitution cannot impose the agenda of any one party or ideological trend. This is not to say that the Constitution must be silent or 'neutral' on matters of value, only that the values embodied in it must be 'common values', both in the sense of 'those values commonly-held and widely-accepted among us' and in the sense of 'those values which pertain to our common good as citizens', rather than those things we value only a members of a special interest group (the inclusion of which may erode the Constitution's generality and universality). An overly prescriptive Constitution, which goes too far in specifying particular policy choices, may succeed for a short time in forcing the pace of change, yet, if such a Constitution divides rather than unites, it could fail, in the long term, to guarantee the stability of democratic institutions and processes.

A Constitution embedded in 'common values' must therefore help ensure that all citizens are able to enjoy, on broadly equal terms, the conditions of human flourishing outlined above, whilst preserving space for the expression of difference; it must help all citizens to live a good life of dignity, without trying to impose uniformity of beliefs, values or identity.

In other words, a Constitution must be both 'social' and 'pluralist', recognising the interest and responsibilities we have in common, whilst upholding the rights of groups and persons. Moreover, it must recognise that the common good is neither obvious nor eternal. Often there is no clear solution to political problems, no now-and-forever answer to what the common good might require in particular circumstances. Many problems are inherently *political*, rather than merely technical, precisely because they depend upon the resolution of differences in ethics, values and principles on which good people may sincerely differ. Thus, while a Constitution may pre-commit itself to the common good in a broad and general sense – the people covenanting together to be ruled not by the will, interests or capricious desires of any particular persons, but by common right and justice – the common good in particular circumstances, as applied to specific laws or policies, must be realised contingently and pragmatically, through institutions of political liberty.

iv Political Liberty as a Common Good

Political liberty is not the absence of authority, but participation in an authority that is inclusive, discursive, rule-bound and non-arbitrary. It is enjoyed when citizens have both an equitable share in collective decision-making and protection from the abuse of power.

The relationship of political liberty to the common good has three aspects. First, political liberty is itself an integral and essential component of the common good. One cannot flourish if one is subject to tyranny, oppression, dependency or arbitrary rule. A life overshadowed by the domineering power of others would be stunted and precarious. Without liberty, one may be fed and watered, clothed and housed, but one's condition will still be abject and servile, and one's moral and intellectual development will inevitably be distorted: cravenness, venality, envy, opportunism, irresponsibility, fear, paranoia and a dull resignation to fate are the consequences of a long exposure to being ruled by others. Conversely, the opportunity to exercise a responsible and equal voice in the co-determination of public affairs, secured through inclusive democratic institutions and fundamental human rights, empowers us to learn, think, meet, debate, vote and protest freely, and so enables us to perform our civic duties with honesty, integrity, courage and independence of mind. Liberty empowers us to judge fairly, to relieve the oppressed, and to plead the widow's cause, without having to bow, scrape, or cower.[27]

Second, political liberty is a necessary precondition for the on-going, pragmatic and contingent realisation of the common good. The more robust the rights of citizens, the more open, inclusive and equitable the political process, the more effectively officials are held to account, the more the common good will be protected from those who would distort the state for their own narrow and selfish ends, and the more likely it is that the common good will prevail over private interests in specific legislative or policy decisions.

A basic commitment to the common good, thirdly, is required for the full and sustained enjoyment of liberty. Without such a commitment at the heart of our public deliberations, liberty (to the extent that it can survive at all) will always be at the mercy of corrupt and selfish interests, and thus patchy, partial, diminished and fragile. If the common good is forgotten, elections cease to be an expression of public judgment over the best political direction for the country, and become a mere trial of strength between contending party leaders, each of which seeks to exercise power for private gain; public deliberations cease to be an honest search for the best solutions through reasoned and passionate argument, and become a hollow exercise in point-scoring and one-upmanship; public appointments cease to reward merit and public service, and become a source of patronage and clientelism, a reward for the sycophancy and dirty work of party hacks.

A Constitution for the common good (*folkweal*), with political liberty (*folkric*) as its root and foundation, must therefore do two things: (i) because political liberty is both an intrinsic component of the common good and an instrumental tool for the realisation of specific common goods in particular situations, the Constitution must establish and maintain, mainly through its structural and procedural provisions, the rights and rules of political liberty; (ii) because political liberty is dependent upon an underlying commitment to the common good, the Constitution must also reflect and embody that commitment, especially in those broad fundamentals on which the citizens are widely agreed. In performing the first of these functions, the Constitution serves as a procedural 'Charter': a set of guarantees. In performing the second, it serves a directive 'Covenant': a set of mutual promises. These two themes – the Constitution as procedural charter for political liberty and the Constitution as directive covenant mandating common ends – are further developed in the following chapter.

CHAPTER THREE

How prescriptive should the Constitution be?

IF SCOTLAND IS TO have a productive constitutional debate that leads to a good and stable Constitution – whether in an independent state, or as a sovereign and autonomous part of a 'loosely United' Kingdom – we need to clarify what a Constitution is, what it is for, and what a Constitution can and cannot achieve.

This chapter seeks to inform and clarify this discussion. Two contrasting views of the purpose of a Constitution are presented, labelled the 'procedural' approach and the 'prescriptive' approach.[1] The procedural approach sees the Constitution primarily as a 'charter of rights and good governance', which restricts itself to defending fundamental rights and institutions of democratic self-government, without prescribing any particular policy outcomes. The 'prescriptive' approach, in contrast, has more ambitious aims: it presents a Constitution as the 'national covenant' of a renewed society. For reference, the distinctions between these constitutional approaches are presented in Figure 1, on pages 93–94.

i   The Case for Procedural Constitutionalism

Much of the excitement in Scotland surrounding the prospect of adopting a Constitution ahead of the 2014 referendum centred upon the transformative opportunities that a Constitution might offer. The dry, defensive and procedural role of a Constitution, in protecting fundamental rights and sustaining democratic institutions, was mostly overlooked, and perhaps even taken for granted. This lack of attention paid to the institutional, procedural aspects of the Constitution was a mistake, which ought to be corrected as we move towards a future constitutional settlement. Before a Constitution can make things better, it must prevent things from getting worse. To understand this, it is necessary to begin by explaining why the lack of a written Constitution is so problematic, first in the context of the United Kingdom, and then in the context of an independent Scotland.

In the absence of a written Constitution to organise public powers, the United Kingdom falls back on the twin pillars of parliamentary sovereignty and constitutional conventions. Parliamentary sovereignty means that an Act of Parliament is the highest source of legal authority.[a] Constitutional conventions are unwritten, often unclear and always unenforceable rules regulating – or, more accurately, describing – the relationships between the major organs of government, such as the Queen, the Prime Minister and Cabinet, the House of Commons, the House of Lords and the civil service. The combination of a sovereign parliament with unenforceable conventional restraints means that a governing party or coalition with a loyal majority in the House of Commons can alter, reform, abolish or otherwise interfere with any public institutions at will.

A simple parliamentary majority, unbound by a written Constitution could, for instance, weaken supposedly autonomous and impartial institutions such as the Electoral Commission, restructure the courts, abolish or restructure the Scottish Parliament, or even change the composition of the Westminster Parliament itself, all without having to achieve either a broad cross-party consensus or to refer the question back to the people. Such a governing majority has, in essence, an arbitrary power – there is no law above it, to restrain or hinder it. In extreme cases, Parliament could enact laws making it very difficult for opposition parties to win elections, turning a system that has been described as an 'elective dictatorship' into a perpetual dominant-party state.[b]

---

a   At least, this is true domestically: European law, for as long as the UK remains in the European Union, and international human rights law so long as we are bound by the European Convention, introduce an additional level of complexity and nuance, although this does not detract from the overall argument that a Government in command of a majority at Westminster can make significant unilateral changes to our institutions and rights. (This is especially worrying in light of the UK Government's increasing pressure from its own right wing and from incipient UKIP challenges to its base, to throwing off both these external limits to sovereignty).

b   A good example of this is South Africa 1949–1983. South Africa had a flexible, non-entrenched Constitution based on a British model. Aside from the obvious issue of the exclusion of non-white persons from voting and office, party competition within the white minority was also restricted by various laws – anti-terror laws and public order laws, etc – that made political contestation very difficult outside of 'approved' limits.

In the British context, it might be argued, of course, that such outrageous abuses as the proscription of opposition parties have not occurred, and that the system is, in its practical operation, tolerably democratic by global standards. This is, however, to miss the essential point. A body invested with sole, absolute and unlimited power may choose to stay its hand, but it is no less domineering for it; the fact remains that a party with a parliamentary majority can change the rules whenever it chooses to do so, without having to account to anyone.

To argue that outrageous abuses have not occurred is also to read British history in a way that overlooks many dark episodes. Whenever the British ruling establishment has felt its power and privileges threatened, or when social and economic discontent has bubbled up to the surface of public life, the state has barely hesitated to use selective repression. It is not necessary to go back to the 1790s or 1820s, the events of 1919 in George Square when troops were deployed against the people or even the brutal running battles of the 1980s miners' strikes for examples of selective repression. For those who dare to look, there are many recent instances of the abuse of power by the agents of the British state and of measures taken to erode our civil liberties and deny access to justice – especially for the poor.

Aside from such *abuses*, a problem faced by countries without a proper written Constitution is that even the *uses* of power are unclear. In the British system, the relationship between the Queen, the Prime Minister, the Cabinet and the House of Commons rests mainly on unwritten conventions whose content is unclear, whose status is debatable and whose provisions can be modified by any Government with enough pride or power to insist on a new interpretation. This means that the gap between legal provisions and conventional practice is a dark and mysterious one. For example, one could argue that now, by convention, the House of Commons must debate and vote on the use of British military force abroad, in accordance with public expectations and the precedents set by Tony Blair in the build up to the Iraq war in 2003 and by David Cameron in the Syrian chemical weapons crisis of 2013. However, all attempts to regulate military powers on a statutory basis have so far failed; in law, the Crown – that is the Queen, advised in sworn secrecy by her Ministers – can act as it wishes. Likewise, Gordon Brown, when he was Prime Minister

(2007–2010), attempted to write down and thereby to solidify and to legitimise some of the key conventions of cabinet government in the so-called 'Cabinet Manual', prepared under the direction of chief civil servant Sir Gus O'Donnell. The Cabinet Manual, however, was simply a statement of usual practice. It was not formally enacted as a binding law, still less as a constitutional document, and it could therefore be changed, or ignored, with impunity. An unwritten, conventional Constitution fails to regulate and legitimate the use of power in ways that are clear and impartial. Terms of reference are unknown. The limits and structures of the major institutions of the state are mysterious, and the relationships between them are ill-defined. In such conditions, accountability is difficult to enforce, and even the rules of proper behaviour are vague.

Two recent examples demonstrate this problem. In 2011, Lord Patten was appointed as Chairman of the BBC Trust – without resigning from the House of Lords, the Conservative Party, the Chancellorship of Oxford University or the Advisory Board of British Petroleum.[2] Then, in 2014, *The Mirror* reported that Prime Minister David Cameron was accused of stacking other supposedly non-partisan public bodies, such as the Charity Commission and the Arts Council, with Conservative supporters.[3] This is, of course, exactly what Labour had done in Government. The UK has winner-takes-all politics in which the 'spoils system' has an increasingly prominent place. As functions are taken out of the professional, impartial civil service and given to non-departmental public bodies or private contractors, so the scope for patronage and corruption increases. Most of the time we are barely aware of it, but there are a lot of boards, panels, committees and commissions staffed with people who have demonstrated meritorious and selfless service to the public solely by making generous donations to the right party, or perhaps by long endurance as a reliable party standard-bearer who does not rock boats, wake sleeping dogs, or otherwise cause any discomfort to those who sit in big leather seats and enjoy large lunches at public expense.[a]

It is even difficult, when the standards of conduct are determined only

---

a   I say this with a certain amount of caution. As a former Naval Officer and as an International Civil Servant, I have on occasion had some very good lunches at public expense – although never in return for political donations!

by non-statutory rules and by unwritten conventions subject to arbitrary redefinition, it becomes difficult to say with any certainty whether this is improper. We might think it is corrupt and unacceptable, for example, when an MP claims twice an average working Scot's annual wage in expenses, but we cannot argue that such actions are unconstitutional when there is no constitution to violate. A system based only on practice, and not on principles, cannot correct itself when its practice becomes unprincipled. A written Constitution, on the other hand, could enshrine the principles of permanence, professionalism and impartiality in the public administration,[a] ensure that certain key institutions necessary for the protection of democracy and good government (such as the Electoral Commission, Ombudsman and Broadcasting Authority) are constituted on a non-partisan basis,[b] and authoritatively define the principles of good governance that are binding on all public servants.[c] In this way, the Constitution defends not only rights of citizens, but also the integrity of democratic institutions, public ethics, and expectations of honest stewardship.

These are the three great functions performed by a procedural Constitution. First, it provides relatively rigid, impartial and clear ground rules for the exercise of power by the several institutions of the state. This places procedural restrictions on the exercise and transfer of power that neither the Government nor the incumbent parliamentary majority may evade. This regulates the institutions of the state in such a way that those who currently exercise power are not able to easily or unilaterally change the procedures by which power is obtained, exercised, and lost.[4] Second, it protects fundamental rights from erosion or arbitrary suspension by those in power. Third, it prescribes principles of political and official

---

a   Article IV, Section 10, of the *Model Constitution* states, for example, 'The administrative officials, subordinate to the Council of Ministers, shall be organised as a permanent, professional and non-partisan civil service, which shall be based upon merit and shall be regulated by the Public Service Commission in accordance with the law'.
b   Articles VII and VIII of the *Model Constitution* prescribe processes of appointment and tenure that are designed to insulate these officials and commissions from party-politics and all other corrupt influences.
c   Article X, Section 5, of the *Model Constitution* gives constitutional authority to the principle that those in public office should 'perform their duties solely in the public interest' and gives a mandate to the Public Service Commission to establish a Code of Conduct for public officials.

conduct that are intended to restrain, reduce and mitigate, if not to entirely eliminate, the corruption of public life.

As such, a procedural Constitution not only contributes directly to the maintenance of a civilised society in which certain baselines of human decency, such as freedom from torture, slavery and arbitrary imprisonment, are placed beyond the easy reach of governing majorities. A procedural Constitution also – crucially – preserves a civic space, through freedom of speech, association and assembly, in which lively democratic contestation can take place. Without these protections, governments could restrict criticism, hinder opposition parties or movements, or otherwise attempt to unfairly maintain themselves in power.

Even those who are skeptical of over-constitutionalising policy directives, and who would rather emphasise the role of elected Parliaments over judges in public decision-making, now recognise the need for, and advantages of, such a Constitution. Without it, all our rights and our democratic politics would be at the mercy of those who have won the most recent election, without even any guarantee that there would be another election, or that the next election would be conducted according to free and fair rules.

In a recent article written for the Scottish Constitutional Futures Forum, Professor Stephen Tierney of the University of Edinburgh accepted the need for a procedural Constitution in the event of independence:

> In the event of independence some form of foundational written document will be needed to replace the Scotland Acts of 1998 and 2012; even if an unwritten constitution were considered desirable, it is simply impossible today to replicate the conditions under which the UK Parliament acquired its authority. The powers of the Scottish Parliament and Scottish Government will require to be defined, as will the court structure, its hierarchy and the limits of its jurisdiction. A proposal to make provision for local government (proposed by the White Paper) would also fit within this model of a limited, institution-framing constitution; all of which would serve as a democracy-facilitating rather than a democracy-constraining set of provisions. But is it necessary to go beyond such a minimal constitutional model which would still leave policy choices to the new parliament? A new constitution will be needed, but it does not require to contain detailed policy issues which should rightfully remain the preserve of the elected parliament.[5]

An important distinction can be made between what an old state can get away with and what a new state cannot. In a long-established state, the lack of a proper Constitution, no matter how indefensible in theory, may be accepted in practice due to the stabilising effects of historical inertia. A sense that the rules, while unwritten and unclear, do nevertheless exist, if only in the imaginations of those who operate them, may be a sufficient restraint against slight and accidental abuses of power (although not, it must always be emphasised, against calculated, determined or deliberate abuses).[a] In other words, the gown covering the nakedness of power might be torn and rotten, but it has acquired enough cobwebs to hold it loosely together. A new state, on the other hand, without a well-sewn Constitution, would be dangerously exposed to lascivious eyes of anyone who wanted to seduce her with his flattery and make off with her oil revenues.

Above all, by providing institutional stability through basic ground-rules that the incumbent government cannot easily or unilaterally change, a written Constitution guards against the personalisation of power. If we consider what frightened many people about the prospect of independence, it was, perhaps, the thought that an independent Scotland would not be *their Scotland*: it would be, they feared, Alex Salmond's Scotland, or the SNP's Scotland – a Scotland without room for them, and in which they could not imagine themselves. *The Telegraph* ran an article suggesting that a likeness of Alex Salmond would replace that of the Queen on Scottish coins in an independent Scotland.[6] Although published under the deniability of an April Fools' Day joke, it sought to present Mr Salmond as a megalomaniac, and independence as a threat to democracy. Anti-independence campaigners tried, perhaps with some success, to raise such fears in the Scottish electorate, seeking to portray Alex Salmond as a dictator-in-waiting, comparing him to other initially well-intentioned leaders of national independence movements who later became dictators. Firm constitutional guarantees can overcome these sorts of fears, ensuring that the Constitution remains above any one person, or any particular party.

---

a   This is what I call the 'good chaps theory of government', and it goes something like this: 'We, the people who matter, the people who rule, the people who use the rules, make the rules and break the rules only when we have a very good reason to, are all thoroughly "good chaps", so you oiks have nothing much to worry about. Now shut up, get back to work, and let us get on with it.'

A procedural Constitution therefore acts as a means of public reassurance and as a mechanism for building trust in the stability and impartiality of democratic institutions. Crucially, a written Constitution of an independent Scotland, broadly along the lines of the SNP's 2002 draft, or of that envisaged in *A Model Constitution*, would separate the state as such, and its permanent institutions, from the incumbent government or the ruling parliamentary majority. The Constitution would thus defend the state as a 'public thing' (*res publica*) that concerns all of us, includes all of us and belongs to all of us. It would thereby ensure that those who occupy high offices of state do so not as masters, to rule and dominate as they please, but as servants of the common weal: they would not possess and dispose of the state as if it were their own private patrimony, but instead would be bound to administer it as faithful stewards of the whole community. The power of the Parliament would not be absolute, sovereign or arbitrary, but would be limited by a higher law – a constitutional law – that emanates from the people; the representatives and officials of the people may govern, legislate, administer, scrutinise, deliberate and judge, but only the people as a whole, in their collective capacity, possess sovereignty. As a primer on constitutionalism produced by the International Institute for Democracy and Electoral Assistance put it:

> In choosing to adopt constitutional government, people are choosing to say no to despotism and to the precariousness of living under rulers who can act arbitrarily. They are choosing to acknowledge that certain rights, principles, values, institutions and processes are too important to depend on the arbitrary will of those in power – they should be entrenched in a way that makes them binding on the government itself. By this means, the people will live under a government of universal rules that are based on broad public consent, and they will have freedom from the arbitrary acts of the rulers.[7]

In protecting democratic institutions and fundamental rights, the chief hazards against which a procedural Constitution must guard include 'authoritarian backsliding', 'incumbent manipulation' and 'corruption'. Authoritarian backsliding can be defined as those measures that undermine civil and political liberty, unduly concentrate powers in the hands of one person or party, or shield governments from scrutiny, accountability or public displeasure. Incumbent manipulation refers to any tinkering with the basic institutional rules, such as electoral law, laws regulating campaign finance, or the timing of elections, so as to give incumbents an advantage over opposition parties and other candidates. Corruption includes any act that uses public power not for the 'peace, order and good government' of the community, but for private or partisan ends.

Corruption does not just refer to 'petty corruption' (the taking of bribes by police or officials, although such acts of petty corruption are to be condemned). It also refers to the gross and systemic corruption of any state that does not serve the common good, and instead becomes a brokerage for private interests. Since the purpose of any legitimate state is to serve the common good, and thereby to enable the people to 'live well together' in a free and flourishing mode of life, any state that deviates from this purpose, and becomes a source of enrichment for the wealthy few at the expense of the many, is by its nature corrupt. Hence an oligarchy, by its nature, and by definition, is a corrupt government.[8] We should not be surprised when we see acts of corruption – a large donation here, a lucrative contract there[a] – abounding in a state that systematically favours the privileged few over the many. It should not surprise us when we see an oligarchic state engaging in profitable but unjust and unwinnable wars, or spending millions on vanity projects while taking bread from the mouths of disabled people and their carers through austerity budgets – no more than we should be surprised by the wasp when it stings or the midge when it bites; they are acting according to their natures, and it would be absurd to expect anything else. Unless we defend ourselves, through the constitutional equivalent of wasp traps and anti-midge nets, we will continue, whichever party heads the oligarchic state, to be stung and bitten.

To protect the *res publica* from authoritarian backsliding, incumbent manipulation and corruption, even a procedural Constitution has a lot of work to do. It must identify, and close, the loopholes that would allow these evils to sneak undetected or unopposed into the apparatus of the state. It would be a mistake, therefore, to confuse a defensive Constitution with a

---

a   According to a report in *The Mirror*, a private healthcare company was said to have been awarded £1.36 billion worth of health service work after several of its investors gifted about £1.5 million to the Conservatives; the chairman of another private healthcare company was said to have been made a peer 'after boosting Tory coffers by £247,250.' (www.mirror.co.uk/news/uk-news/fury-tory-party-donors-handed-3123469)

weak or patchy Constitution. A very skeletal, minimal Constitution, which omitted such critical details as the structure of the electoral system or the integrity of electoral mechanisms, would fall short of the mark. The Constitution of France, for example, does not specify the electoral system, with the result that various governments have tried, over the years, to alter the electoral system, and in particular the distribution of seats, to the unfair advantage of the ruling party.[9] Likewise, the Constitution of Canada does not contain any provisions for an independent, non-partisan electoral commission; the responsible body, 'Elections Canada', rests only on a statutory, not a constitutional, footing, and, as a result, its powers, status and independence are now being eroded – some say dangerously so – by the incumbent legislative majority.[10] Perhaps most egregiously, the Constitution of the Irish Free State – otherwise a very sound Constitution[11] – was fatally wounded by the fact that it could be amended, for an interim period, by a majority in Parliament: the majority repeatedly used this loophole to extend the interim period, and thereby gave itself the authority to amend the text at will – turning it, in effect, from a proper Constitution to little more than an ordinary Act.[12]

Closing the loopholes may mean spelling things out in some detail. It would be incorrect, therefore, to assume that a procedural 'Constitution as Charter' is necessarily short and laconic, whilst a directive 'Constitution as Covenant' is long and detailed. The raw length of a Constitution, in terms of the number of articles, clauses and words, is a product of its scope (the number of subjects it covers) and its detail (the degree of specificity with which each subject).[13] This means that directive provisions may be quite short, if they are big on rhetoric but lacking in enforceable substance, while a procedural Constitution may be long, if it precisely defines the rights and institutions that it seeks to defend.[a]

It would also be incorrect to assume that a procedural Constitution is the same as a conservative one. On the contrary, it might take radical

---

a   A good Constitution does not have to be discouragingly long. The European average is around 15,000 words; the *Model Constitution* was at the shorter end of the usual range, at around 8,000. At public meetings, I have often held up – simply by way of example – a copy of the Constitution of Malta, or of the Netherlands. Many people, expecting to see something more in the order of a telephone book or dictionary, are pleasantly surprised to see such a slim, manageable, pocket-sized pamphlet.

steps in the direction of greater democratisation – the better to defend the 'public thing' against corruption and abuse, and the more effectively to ensure that those who govern do not dominate the state. Those who seek independence or substantial autonomy for Scotland, or who wish to reconstitute the United Kingdom as a confederation of equal parts, also generally wish to deepen our democracy: to make the voices, priorities and concerns of ordinary people more prominent in public decision-making, and those of the rich, powerful and privileged few less so. These are laudable aims – indeed, necessary aims, if 'democracy' in the 21st century is to have any life and substance beyond a mere competition for power and popularity between two slick, professionalised parties. Subsequent chapters of this book consider ways in which this might be achieved through the design of political institutions in a new Constitution.

A procedural approach to constitutionalism, then, is not necessarily characterised by a desire for a short, simple or minimal Constitution, but by a desire for a Constitution that provides a robust and broadly accepted framework of basic rights and institutions, within which lively, healthy and engaged democratic politics can take place. A procedural Constitution is characterised rather by its limited prescriptive scope: it does not seek to bypass democratic politics in order to pre-commit the state to a particular programmatic agenda or narrowly defined policy options; neither does it attempt to impose, through higher law, a utopian vision of how society ought to be. It does not presume that the common good is so universally well understood, or so monolithic or timeless, as all that. It seeks only to maintain and defend democratic institutions, through which a plurality of citizens, with different views and interests, can freely contribute – on broadly equal terms, by competition, collaboration and compromise – to the pragmatic and contingent realisation of the common good.

A procedural Constitution, moreover, is based on society as it is. It accounts for the divisions and divergent views in society, and allows society to resolve disagreements and overcome differences at its own pace, in its own time, through open, pluralist, democratic politics. It defines and orders the state, but it does not – crucially – redefine or reorder society. A procedural Constitution will typically define the electoral system in some detail. It will lay down the procedural rules by which the Prime Minister is chosen, indicate the circumstances in which Parliament may be dissolved, define the powers and functions of the Head of State, and say when referendums must or may be held. It will prescribe the process for appointing judges, and will explain how a corrupt judge may be removed from office. It will define the investigatory powers of parliamentary committees, provide for the election of a Presiding Officer, protect the autonomy of local government, establish independent institutions to maintain the impartiality of the civil service, and prescribe general rules to ensure the proper supervision and auditing of public funds. It will provide rules for its own amendment. All these provisions are compatible with (and even essential to) a procedural approach to constitutionalism. Likewise, a procedural constitution will invariably guarantee – as a minimum – the generic set of basic civil, legal and political rights.[a]

There is a critique of fundamental rights which dismisses them as 'liberal' (but anti-democratic) limits on the extent and reach of state power. Sometimes, this criticism of fundamental rights uses the language and concepts of the civic republican tradition in an essentially reactionary way, to defend the absolutism of parliamentary majorities and to resist the role of the courts in protecting civil liberties. My view is that this critique is: (i) unrealistic, because it attributes to elected Parliaments a deliberative and representative quality that they do not possess, while denying the deliberative benefits that come from interaction between legislatures and courts; (ii) historically inaccurate, because it ignores the honourable history of that tradition in embracing constitutionalism and higher-law restraints on the arbitrary power of rulers; and (iii) misleading, since it tries to present rights solely as an individualist anti-civic denial of 'the political', when in reality such rights can also be defended on communitarian democratic grounds as necessary to protect a free, open and civic space in which political activity can take place from those who happen to currently be in office. Rather than seeking to portray rights as pre-political restrictions on democratic power, it is better to understand rights (especially as formulated

---

a   David Law and Mila Versteeg argue that there is a 'generic' bill of rights, composed of the most common rights found in around 75 per cent of the world's constitutions. These represent the rights that have emerged, by experience and consensus, as essential to a democratic polity and an open society. (See: Law, David S. and Versteeg, Mila, The Declining Influence of the United States Constitution (2012). *New York University Law Review*, Vol. 87, No. 3, pp. 762–858).

in the European Convention) as broadly recognised, historically discerned, basic principles of a free society which, when touched upon by the legislator, require a higher standard of reasoning; the legislator must show that its actions are necessary and reasonable in a democratic society.[a]

What a purely procedural Constitution will not do, however, is try to define the nation (except possibly in narrowly legal terms, with respect to territory and the rules of citizenship). It will not attempt to recast society according to any particular ideological vision (except in the most generic and open-ended sense, of being an open, pluralist society with a democratic form of government). It will not prescribe any religious affiliation, pre-commit the state to any specific economic policy (neo-liberal, social demo-cratic, or otherwise), or attempt to change the views, habits or mores of society. Provisions such as those found in the Constitution of Bangladesh, which states in Article 9 that:

> The unity and solidarity of the Bengali nation, which, deriving its identity from its language and culture, attained sovereign and indepen-dent Bangladesh through a united and determined struggle in the war of independence, shall be the basis of Bengali nationalism

will be notably absent.

A technically sound, broadly agreed and well-enforced procedural Constitution, which establishes and maintains political freedom, while restraining authoritarian backsliding, incumbent manipulation, and corruption, is therefore the supreme common good. It ensures that those who govern do so only as public servants not private rulers, that they must give a public account of their actions, that their decisions are subject to debate and to public challenge, and that the public is able to censure, remove and replace them. It also ensures that they can rule neither by arbitrary command nor capricious order, but must respect the due process of law and must uphold the equal rights of all citizens before the courts and administration. In this way, the Constitution ensures that we are governed in a free and civic way – by our equals. Those who hold public office might have specific functions, responsibilities, powers and burdens

---

a   Even Sonu Bedi, a critic of fundamental rights, assumes there must be protection for freedom of speech and assembly as part of a democratic order. See: S. Bedi, '*Rejecting Rights*' (Cambridge: Cambridge University Press, 2009).

for which they have been chosen and set apart, but they remain our equals in status: they are citizens governing fellow citizens in a consensual way, not lords and masters dominating the rest by fear or power.

ii The Limits of Prescriptive Constitutionalism

Most contemporary Constitutions are more than dry rulebooks of democratic procedures and generic declarations of fundamental rights. Often produced in the aftermath of a revolutionary upheaval or following a struggle for national independence, many recent Constitutions have sought to redefine society and its values according to a new vision. They have attempted to say something about who 'We the people' are, where 'we' have come from and how 'we' intend (according to the authors of the Constitution) to progress together into a brighter future. In other words, such Constitutions are 'nation-building' as well as 'state-regulating' instruments. They seek social transformation as well as institutional reform.

The appeal of such a Constitution is greatest at times of transition, when the pillars of the old order are shaken, and there is an opportunity for national soul-searching, for reconciliation and for deliberate public acts of reorientation. The mistakes and injustices of the past can be admitted and repented, and sincere resolutions for a more democratic, inclusive and humane future can be made. A nation which has, in the past, been divided against itself may, through the process of transition, seek a new unity, binding itself together through a Constitution that envisages a better society for all its citizens. There are many examples of Constitution-making processes which have had this transformative intent. Those of India (1950) and South Africa (1996) are perhaps the most well-known. Responding in one case to the legacies of British rule and caste discrimination, in the other to the indignities of apartheid, and in both cases to deep economic inequality, the founders of the Indian and South African Constitutions sought not only to establish democratic institutions of self-government, but also to embed those institutions in a new, radically inclusive and economically progressive constitutional order that would endeavour to bring freedom and dignity to all citizens regardless of race, caste or class.

Such prescriptive Constitutions have an ideal of the 'good society' to which they point, and which is either made explicit in the text of the Constitution (typically in the preamble or in introductory clauses defining the aims, purposes and nature of the state) or implicit in the Constitution's substantive provisions. Usually, this ideal tilts, to some extent or other, to the left: the transformation sought is from an unequal and repressive society to a more egalitarian and liberated one.[a] However, a leftwards tilt is not a necessary or defining characteristic of prescriptive constitutionalism. The Irish Constitution of 1937, for example, was infused with Catholic Social Teaching and militant Irish republicanism; its provisions, particularly in regard to property, religion, education and the role of the family and of women in society, were socially conservative.[14] Likewise the 2011 Constitution of Hungary is laden with conservative nationalism.[15] Despite the conservative or even reactionary inclination of these Constitutions, they are both undoubtedly of the 'prescriptive' type, because they seek to impose a particular ideological vision on their societies that is intended to be both declaratory of the state's identity and directive of the state's future development. These Constitutions do not merely set up a framework of rights and institutions for democratic self-government, but also seek to pre-set the direction that such government must take.

Prescriptive constitutionalism is widely criticised as undemocratic, since it commits the state to particular policy positions and therefore limits, so it is argued, the scope of democratic politics. However, while prescriptive constitutionalism may be undemocratic if it tries to impose controversial positions contrary to common consent, it is not necessarily so. Indeed, so long as the Constitution is the product of decisions made by the people as a whole, and is capable of being amended by the people, a constitutional rule committing the state to a particular course of action can be regarded as a clear and direct act of democratic delegation. To limit Parliament in this way is not to restrict democracy, but to enforce it, by preventing thin, fragile majorities from going against a wider democratic consensus, or by preventing politicians from going against the express will of the people as embodied in the people's supreme law, which is the Constitution.

---

a   The Constitutions of Soviet-bloc countries could perhaps be described as 'pseudo-prescriptive': they served as ideological markers of the state's identity, declaratory emblems of its achievements and signposts of its intended path towards the 'building of communism', but did very little to defend democracy or human rights.

Apologists for the British system of parliamentary absolutism, who maintain that the legal supremacy of a Constitution – prescriptive or otherwise – is undemocratic since it excludes certain fundamental questions from public consideration and debate, are mistaken. As we have seen in the independence referendum, placing questions of fundamental constitutional importance before the sovereign people, rather than allowing these issues to be settled by a parliamentary decision, does not exclude them from politics, but rather raises them in the public consciousness, and so broadens and extends the scope of political debate.[a] Rather than shifting power away from elected Parliaments and into the hands of unelected judges, as opponents of constitutional rule would portray it, it would be more realistic to see constitutional supremacy as shifting power away from the Government and into a wider public community, with the judiciary performing an ancillary role as guardians of the people's Constitution. This is not to deny the political role of judges – rather, it is to acknowledge it, as we should also be bold enough to acknowledge the political role, in the 'small-p' sense, of all other public institutions, from the civil service and the police to the monarchy and the military. If a Supreme Court annuls a law passed by Parliament as unconstitutional, or if it orders the Government to fulfil a constitutional mandate, it is not limiting the sovereignty of the people, but rather defending and giving effect to that sovereignty; it is keeping the elected Parliament and Government, who are but agents of the people, to their duty, and so protecting the sovereignty of the people against the wayward decision of legislators. In these terms, prescriptive constitutionalism can be profoundly democratic, if the goals set and values proclaimed in the Constitution at a moment of national foundation or refoundation are genuine expressions of the sovereign constituent power of the people, and if the people can change them, if the need or desire arises, by constitutional amendment.

The difficulty with prescriptive constitutionalism is not, then, that it necessarily limits democracy, but that it can undermine the generality, neutrality, and stability, of the Constitution as a fundamental law. If a

---

a   For an excellent and extensive treatment of democratic deliberation in referendums, see Tierney, S. *Constitutional Referendums: A Theory of Republican Deliberation* (Oxford: Oxford University Press, 2014).

Constitution is to perform its core function of providing a framework for democracy through the protection of democratic procedures and fundamental rights, it must rest on a broad social consensus that transcends party politics. A Constitution that embodies the ideology, national vision or policy priorities of one party or section of society, and which fails to integrate the rest of society into the political system, must either bend to the shifting will of the majority – and so become a blunt instrument of domination in the hands of that majority – or break. A Constitution that declares grand visions and makes sweeping promises would be more of a manifesto than a fundamental law; it might contain a wish list of policies and priorities that reflect the ideology of one party, but which do not reflect a genuine public consensus. Such a Constitution is unlikely to achieve a position of relative neutrality and of transcendent legitimacy above party politics, and so unlikely to outlive its makers. In other words, a Constitution that attempts to be too prescriptive will lose its defensive capability.

History is replete with examples of overly ambitious Constitutions whose authors, in a desire to transform society in accordance with their own vision, have alienated other sections of the public and thereby undermined the institutions they sought to create. The Spanish Constitutions of 1931 and 1978 are illustrative. The short-lived Constitution of 1931 not only attempted to establish democracy, but also to establish that democracy on a progressive, anti-clerical and radical-republican basis. The result, perhaps predictably, was a violent reaction from the right wing, which resulted in civil war and dictatorship. The 1978 Constitution was based on a more pragmatic compromise. The all-party drafting committee was careful never to be more radical in the substantive provisions of the text than the consensus of society (including reactionary, military and clerical elements) would bear. By the retention of the monarchy, a more conciliatory attitude towards the Roman Catholic Church, and a deliberate fudging of issues concerning national identity and centre-periphery relations, they succeeded in establishing a viable and acceptable democratic order without alienating conservative elements.[16]

This is not to say that a Constitution cannot have prescriptive provisions, only that any such provisions must (if the Constitution is to be viable, acceptable and lasting) reflect a widely shared public consensus, and not the imposition of the narrow agenda of particular sections of society over the rest. Neither is it to say that the Constitution must be 'value neutral', because every Constitution contains some commitment to values, even if these are expressed only in rather thin and generic terms, such as the commitment to 'human dignity' in Article 1 of the German Basic Law (1949/1990), or even if these values are simply implicit in the Constitution's prosaic provisions.[a] It does mean, however, that no workable Constitution can provide a shortcut to utopia, nor a way of conveniently entrenching every progressive policy on one's idealistic wish list.

iii The Relationship between Procedural and Prescriptive Elements

It is possible to identify some Constitutions, such as those of Canada (1867/1982) and the Netherlands (1814/1983),[b] which are mainly procedural charters. Others, such as those of Ecuador (2008) and South Africa (1996), have a more prescriptive and covenantal feel.

However, there are no 'pure' examples of either type. All extant democratic Constitutions are a mixture of both procedural 'charter' and prescriptive 'covenant', with the charter-provisions and covenant-provisions being mutually complementing. The 'Constitution as Charter' expresses the *how*: the institutions, the processes and the rules. The 'Constitution as Covenant' expresses the *what*: the aim, the vision and the common purpose. It is not a matter of charter *or* covenant, but of charter *and* covenant, charter *for* covenant, and covenant *through* charter. The covenant includes the injunction that we uphold the charter (we agree to be bound by the Constitution and to be governed by the rules and institutions it creates), while the charter enables us to maintain our

---

a The Canadian Constitution, for example, says almost nothing in declaratory or prescriptive terms about what sort of country Canada is to be, or about the ideologies that the Constitution is supposed to encourage in public life. Nevertheless, Canadian jurists have identified (through and under, if not in, the text) certain defining and guiding principles – federalism, democracy, constitutionalism and the rule of law, and the protection of minorities – that have become part of Canada's perception of itself. (See: Mullan, D. J., 'Underlying Constitutional Principles: The Legacy of Justice Rand', *Manitoba Law Journal*, 34/1, 2010.)

b The first date in parenthesis refers to the year on which the Constitution was adopted, the second date to the late major or fundamental revision.

covenant (it creates the rules and institutions by and through which the common good is reached).

To reiterate, therefore, the foregoing sections should not be interpreted as rejecting prescriptive constitutionalism. They should be read only as advising against imposing a divisive, one-sided, ideologically driven prescription by a narrow majority (or, worse, by a convinced and zealous minority who wish to rebuild society in their own image). Where there is a 'thick' consensus on aspects of identity, direction or programme, this may be reflected in more covenantal or prescriptive provisions; where there is not, a procedural charter, relying only on a 'thinner' consensus to govern ourselves peacefully, honestly and democratically must be, and can be, sufficient. A workable Constitution will almost certainly be a prescriptive, transformation covenant where it *can* be, to the extent that the consensus of society will bear, and defensive procedural charter where it *must* be.

At the root of the distinction between these two approaches is a difference in the extent and depth of our common life. The 'Constitution as Covenant' implies a more intimate and interconnected civic bond than that implied by the comparatively thin and generic agreements on which the 'Constitution as Charter' rests. The 'Constitution as Covenant' is the rule by which we live – almost in the sense of a monastic rule, that reflects a commitment to a certain way of life. The 'Constitution as Charter' provides the rules by which people may lead their own lives and pursue their own conceptions of the good life while still existing harmoniously in a society that, despite difference, has certain common concerns that can only be addressed pragmatically through collective action. This is the same distinction that Aristotle makes between the *politia*, which is a communion of citizens united in accordance with certain agreed principles of justice, and a mere 'treaty of alliance', where people agree not to harm one another without sharing a common commitment to the same vision of a 'good life'.[16] It is similar, also, to the medieval distinction between a *universitas*, which is a community gathered according to a shared vision, purpose and way of life, such as a monastic community, and a *societas*, which is a community gathered together on pragmatic grounds of cohabitation and co-operation, but without a common vision, purpose or way of life to unite its consociates. Members of a *societas* make practical agreements for the management of certain things they have in common, members of a *universitas* live their lives in pursuit of a common goal. It is possible, therefore, to envision that a Constitution for an independent or fully autonomous Scotland, resting upon a deep sense of national comm-unality, would contain more covenantal provisions than a Constitution for a confederal United Kingdom, which would rest mainly upon a pragmatic agreement amongst the four home nations.

Although Scotland does not have much direct experience of govern-ment under a written Constitution, we have a long tradition of covenantal government:[a] government according to mutual promises, by which people are bound together into a community according to certain express aims, purposes and conditions. The Declaration of Arbroath of 1320 took the form of such a covenant, according to which the 'whole community of the realm' bound themselves to support the king on the condition that he would maintain their freedom and not betray the national cause.[18] The National Covenant of 1638 and the Solemn League and Covenant of 1643, although primarily religious in character, also had important political and constitutional aspects, underlining the conditional, contractual and limited nature of the monarchy in Scotland.

This tradition of covenanting re-emerged during the long campaign for devolution. The Scottish Covenant Association, which sought to establish a home rule Parliament for Scotland in the 1940s and 1950s, adopted both the language of 'covenants' – the making of mutual promises – as well as the technique, pioneered 300 years before, of seeking legitimation through the gathering of signatures. In its specific demands, which were explicitly devolutionist and rejected independence, the Covenant seems tame and deferential by the standards of today, but its language nevertheless remains interesting. The Covenant takes the form of a promise made by 'We, the people of Scotland who subscribe to this Engagement', who 'solemnly enter into this Covenant whereby we pledge ourselves [...] to do everything in our power to secure for Scotland a Parliament with adequate legislative authority in Scottish affairs.'[19]

---

a   It would be amiss not to acknowledge the dark side of the 'covenanting' legacy in Scottish political thought: its association with sectarianism. Yet this is not intrinsic to the idea of a covenant. If we seek the common good, the covenant establishing the new Scottish state must be one that embraces and includes the whole people, as fellow citizens, regardless of religious, linguistic or ethnic background.

Similarly, the Claim of Right, issued by the Scottish Constitutional Convention in 1989, also used the language of covenanting and promising; the signatories *pledged* to put the interests of the Scottish people first.[20]

The idea of a 'national covenant' has continued resonance in the debate on a future Scottish Constitution. There is a desire (evident, at least, from personal experience, from public meetings and from following the discussion in Scottish civic society in person and online) for a document that would define the principles and set the tone of political life. It is intriguing, for example, that Angus Reid's *A Call for a Constitution*, written on the walls of public buildings, from shops to schools to bus shelters, refers to 'a form of words to model a nation's *behaviour*'. This concern with behaviour (not structures, institutions, or even rights) reflects, in Reid's words, a desire for a 'contract between a people and a government built from the core question: "What kind of country do you wish to live in?"'[21] The need for effective ground rules – setting out the procedures of government – is usually acknowledged, but is often portrayed as a matter of detail that is subordinate to the more fundamental questions of principles, values and ethics.

In introducing principles, values and ethics, we appear to return to the problems of pluralism and pre-commitment previously discussed: namely, that in a pluralistic society we all have different views on what sort of country we would like to live in. It might appear, therefore, that any common vision, if it is to be more than the imposed vision of one party or section of the population, must necessarily be thin and generic – of the sort that is capable of sustaining a 'Constitution as Charter'. The idea of a 'Constitution as Covenant' seems incapable, at least on the surface, of accommodating itself to pluralism.

However, this need not be so. First, there may well be principles, values and ethics, beyond merely procedural commitments to democracy, which are widely held in society. For example, there may be near universal agreement on the principle that no one should be denied educational opportunity or necessary medical care on ground of inability to pay. There may be differences of opinion on how best to realise these aims in terms of specific policy, but this need not preclude a constitutional recognition of the principle that realising these goods is part of our covenantal undertaking to one another as fellow citizens.

Second, to be in a covenanted relationship does not require unanimity of opinion. In this sense, a covenanted community differs from a creedal one. Membership of the latter is predicated on sharing the ideological beliefs around which that community is organised. Those who do not subscribe to those beliefs are not full members. We have seen examples of creedal political communities in states that have proclaimed their allegiance at a constitutional level to a single ruling party or ideology. Marxist-Leninist states, in which to be an anti-communist was to find oneself a non-citizen, are the most notorious examples of this type. A covenant, meanwhile, speaks not so much of what one *believes* but of how one undertakes to *act*. Its essence lies in the articulation of mutual promises, which may be based on shared values, principles and objectives, but which are broader and less exclusive than a creed. Covenantal communities recognise that we do not have to believe alike or be alike in order to work together. Trade unions, guilds, cooperatives and even some self-help groups might be regarded as 'covenantal communities'. They contain within them people of different ideologies, opinions, or creeds, who might disagree about fundamental aspects of belief, but who promise to work together for mutual purposes.

Third, since the covenant regulates our behavior, it need not always be expressed in terms of substantive outcomes, rights or policy commitments. The ethical behavior of public servants, a commitment to transparency and equity in campaign finance, and an undertaking to maintain the neutrality and integrity of bodies such as the Judiciary and the Electoral Commission, can all be a part of our covenant, which unites all of us in a pledge to political ethics that goes beyond ideological difference or particular interest.

There may therefore be scope, even in a diverse, pluralist society, with multiple political opinions and ideological creeds, to go beyond a merely procedural constitutional charter, and to embrace elements of a civic covenant, at least with respect to those principles, values and ethics on which a sufficiently broad and deep public consensus exists. Indeed, in a divided society, a statement of values and principles may provide a basis for co-operation, despite ideological differences. In Tunisia, after the revolution of 2011, communities recognised that there was no one unifying vision of Tunisian identity. Urban-rural, young-old and religious-secular cleavages divided society. Yet all were able to recognise that clean streets, public safety, and functioning infrastructure were in the common interest of society, regardless of their differences of identity or ideology. They also recognised the need for mutual accommodation, tolerance and respect, if they were to achieve these common goals. In many cities, statements of values and principles were accordingly drawn up by city authorities and civil society organisations. These statements served as local 'covenants'; despite divisions, and without ignoring those divisions, these statements attempted to express those values and principles that were held in common.[a]

If the Constitution is to be viable, acceptable and enduring, its prescriptive provisions must be limited to those things that are held '*quod semper, quod ubique, quod ad omnibus*'. That is to say, it should not reflect the intense but passing political issues of the moment, particular interests, or the imposed agenda of particular sections of society over the rest, but only general provisions that reflect a broad, deep, lasting consensus.

The question of what is sufficiently broad, deep and lasting is not easy to answer in categorical terms. The people themselves, at moments of constitutional founding and of constitutional revision, have to make and remake these judgments. Constitutional amendment rules are designed to provide the means by which a sufficient consensus, worthy of being reflected in a nation's Constitution, can be distinguished from the simple and transient majorities sufficient to enact ordinary laws. These may include a requirement for a three-fifths or two-thirds majority in Parliament (as in Slovakia and Portugal), appeal to the people in a referendum (as in Ireland, Denmark and Australia), two decisions separated by an intervening general election (as in Iceland and Sweden), or some combination of these rules.[b] The fluctuating winds of political passion, the will of the bare majority, or the programme of one party, are unlikely to be to pass such hurdles, whereas those things that enjoy broad agreement and represent the settled will of the people will be adopted. In this way, just as

---

a   I am indebted to Dr Neila Akrimi, of CLIG International, for these observations on the Tunisian experience.

b   For a more complete survey of constitutional amendment formulas and their consequences see: Boeckenfoerde, M. (2014) 'Constitutional Amendment Procedures', *International IDEA Constitution Building Primer series*: http://www.constitutionnet. org/vl/item/constitutional-amendment-procedures

the people contingently, pragmatically and deliberatively determine their own common good in relation to policy decisions through the 'chartered' institutions of the state, so also they determine, contingently and pragmatically, their own common good in relation to the covenantal provisions of their Constitution – albeit with a higher threshold of deliberation.

Typically, if the Covenant of the *res publica* is explicit, it will be contained in a Preamble or Declaration, which is often non-justiciable and removed from the prosaic portions of the Constitution. If the Covenant is implicit, it may be buried in various constitutional or quasi-constitutional documents. For example, the Canadian 'Covenant', it could be argued, is to maintain 'peace, order and good government' through a parliamentary democracy 'similar in principle to that of the United Kingdom'. It is also possible to have a Constitution with only a very thin and implicit Covenant, which may be necessary in situations where consensual agreement on ultimate aims and purposes is difficult to find, but where agreement can be reached on basic democratic procedures.

Fig. 1 Two Constitutional Archetypes

	Constitution as Charter	Constitution as Covenant
Understanding of the Constitution	'Procedural': Constitution as a neutral framework of institutions and rights constituting a democratic system. Legal and political aspects of the constitution emphasised.	'Prescriptive': Constitution as the organisational and ethical foundation of a democratic society. Social and political aspects of the constitution emphasised.
Rights provisions	Limited and Concrete: often limited to generic fundamental human rights; may include additional rights if these reflect a pragmatic consensus. Rights are usually directly enforceable and do not require progressive realisation.	Extensive and Aspirational: will typically include a range of social and cultural rights, directed towards the progressive realisation of a shared (or claimed) vision of the good society.
Other substantive provisions (settling policy-questions in the Constitution)	Absent or minimal: preference for policy questions to be resolved by ordinary (sub-constitutional) political processes; any substantive content in the constitution is likely to reflect the pragmatic resolution of historical disputes in a pluralistic society.	Extensive: many policy issues will be settled in the Constitution, reflecting the ideological orientation, values and policies endorsed by the constitution-makers; sub-constitutional political processes have only limited scope to re-shape the state's policy direction.
Relationship of 'right' to 'good'	Rights dominant: in the absence of agreement about ultimate ends and purposes, rights take precedence over any substantive goods.	Goods dominant: rights are present, but stem from, and are subordinate to, the declared principles of a good society.

	Constitution as Charter	Constitution as Covenant
Understanding of social relationships	'Gesellschaft' (Society): pluralist, open society; united by mutual convenience, pragmatic agreements, and physical cohabitation in the same space.	'Gemeinschaft' (Community): socially and culturally homogenous society; united by shared values and ethos.
Understanding of democracy	Pragmatic: democracy as a means of solving common problems by fair and peaceful means; 'democratic system' compatible with many modes of life.	Ideological: democracy as a way of life; 'democratic society' incompatible with alternative visions of society or modes of life.
Key political values implied by Constitution	Liberal: negotiation, tolerance and compromise; contractual citizenship.	Republican: civic virtue and dedication to the public good; active citizenship.
Degree of social and political pre-commitment on which the Constitution rests (or claims to rest)	Thin: 'agree to disagree'; agree to resolve disputes by peaceful and democratic procedures; no (or limited) agreement about substantive ends or purposes.	Thick: reflects (or claims) deep and broad agreement about identity, values and common purposes of community.
Style of constitution-drafting	Rational-Legalistic: Constitution written in neutral, technical and dispassionate terms.	Rhetorical-Political: Constitution may be written in ideologically-loaded and rhetorical terms.
Mode of Constitutional Amendment	Consensual: Requires broad re-negotiation and co-decision by multiple actors.	Populist: Typically by majority decision in a referendum.
Examples close to archetype	Canada (1867/1982), Netherlands (1848/1983)	Bolivia (2009), Ireland (1937)

CHAPTER FOUR

How could the Constitution strengthen democracy?

A Model Constitution took a 'moderate reformist' approach to constitutional design. As an educational tool and as a basis for further discussion, it was intended only to provide an example of what a viable and acceptable Constitution for an independent Scotland might look like, within the general patterns and norms of modern democratic parliamentary constitutionalism. As such, it presented a text that would build on the achievements of the Scotland Act, correct the worst flaws of the British system, and compare favourably – in terms of content, ethos and technical quality – with the Constitutions of other modern European and Commonwealth democracies. Above all, it sketched out a realistic, pragmatic text – one that reflects Scotland's political and social conditions and one that could conceivably emerge from a messy, imperfect, real-life constitution-building process.

This decision meant that anything deemed too daring was omitted. *A Model Constitution* used only the institutional technologies of accepted current constitutional practice, as found in most other Western democracies. It was radical only in the context of the constitutional backwardness of the United Kingdom; in comparative terms, it was based on models that are tried, tested, and not in the least bit innovative.

Utopian scheming was specifically rejected. There is a place for utopianism (indeed, as a society we are in need of more vision and imagination, and it would never be my intention to limit the possible to the present boundaries of the actual) but I took – and still take – the view that a Constitution for a newly independent Scotland should, before all else, provide guarantees for the effective and secure workings of parliamentary democracy, as known and practised in most democratic nations. Anything more than that – although we can and should aim for much more than that – is a bonus.

With regard to matters such as the structure of government or the organisation of the major institutions of the state, this chapter seeks neither to repeat nor to contradict the arguments made in *A Model Constitution*. It does, however, seek to explore several additional proposals for the strengthening of democracy, and, in particular, for the reinforcement of the 'popular' element of the Constitution against oligarchic and elitist forms of rule. It expands on certain institutional aspects that were not covered, or not covered in sufficient detail, in *A Model Constitution*, such as the use of referendums, increasing the inclusivity and representativeness of Parliament, the question of whether we need a second chamber and the regulation of political parties and primary elections.

The originality of this chapter lies in its discussion of non-elite representation. It considers the possibility of augmenting existing forms of representative government, which are structured through party-politics and tend to replicate a professional political class, with alternative forms of representation favouring ordinary citizens. Some of the ideas presented in this chapter diverge radically from existing institutional orthodoxies, and drawing deeply from the well of classical and medieval civic republican constitutional traditions of thought and practice.[a]

Crucially, these ideas – which are offered not as specific proposals, but simply as speculative examples of what might be achieved if the political will were present – apply to the 'charter aspects' of the Constitution. Radical democratic renewal is not presented, primarily, as an extension of the list of socio-economic rights (although, as discussed in Chapter Seven, there may be room for those too), but as an extension of political liberty. The institutions discussed in this chapter are intended to augment the democratic part of the Constitution, rebalancing of powers away from rich and powerful elites and into the hands of ordinary citizens; with stronger mechanisms of democratic contestation, the citizenry would be better able to articulate the common good, and to resist the tendency of

---

a   I am particularly indebted for these insights to J. P. McCormick's idea of 'Machiavellian Democracy' (see: McCormick, J.P. *Machiavellian Democracy* (Cambridge: Cambridge University Press, 2013). Also see: Smith, G., *Democratic Innovations: Designing Institutions for Citizen Participation* (Cambridge: Cambridge University Press, 2009).

rulers to engage in authoritarian backsliding, incumbent manipulation and corruption.[a]

It should be noted that many of the reforms proposed in this chapter would not necessarily require an independent state. They could also, to a greater or lesser extent, be incorporated into the constitutional structures of an autonomous Scotland within a reformed United Kingdom, if such an opportunity were to present itself in the future.

i Direct Democracy

One victor in the independence debate is the referendum itself. Once a rare and distrusted novelty, often held to be incompatible with parliamentary democracy,[73] the referendum is now an accepted part of our political life. It is acknowledged that the direct voice of the people speaks with greater authority than that of their representatives.

At least in principle, the referendum is an anti-oligarchical and anti-elitist device. By giving every citizen a direct vote on a salient issue, referendums embody the principles of political equality and inclusiveness in a way that is hard for representative institutions to match. In most democracies, parliamentarians are drawn largely from those who are separated, by their wealth, status, education and life experiences from the average citizen.[1] Even if the sociological composition of parliaments were to be democratised, through measures intended to increase the representation of non-elite groups, the representative process is still, at best, highly imperfect. Members of Parliament are elected typically for a term of several years, and on the basis of a party manifesto which includes a range of policy issues. Factors other than policy preferences, such as character, competence, record in office and local connections can also determine election results. Add to this the fact that parliamentarians, once in office, can easily be 'captured' by the influence of special interests and lose touch with the views of their voters, and it is easy to see why the parliamentary

---

a   'Democratic contestation' is a term used to encompass the right and power of the people to challenge, oppose, review and veto public decisions. On the concept, and the role of contestation in securing political liberty and a politics of the common good, see: Pettit, P. *Republicanism: A Theory of Freedom and Government* (Oxford: Oxford University Press, 1997).

majority may differ markedly from the popular majority on a particular issue. The referendum potentially offers a way of closing this gap between the preferences of the people and those of their representatives. The referendum is also useful in other ways: it provides a way of overcoming internal differences on divisive questions, of gaining support for a controversial course of action and of legitimating difficult decisions.[a]

However, since the SNP has come to power, the party's constitutional rhetoric and the Scottish Government's policy proposals have paid no attention to direct democracy beyond the independence vote. Neither the draft Interim Constitution nor the White Paper made explicit provision for direct democracy. The minority-veto referendum, which was such a prominent and original feature of the SNP's 2002 text, was silently dropped from the SNP's proposals, as was the need for a referendum on further constitutional changes.

It is therefore unclear what role referendums are to play in the SNP's vision of the future. Are referendums to be used only in an opportunistic way, so that having once voted for independence – if and when that happens – we are then required to cede power to a sovereign Parliament again, with the expectation that we can trust governing majorities, for a four- or five-year lease of power, without effective control or restraint? Or are we to have a Constitution that includes the people, that keeps sovereign constituent power in their hands and that lets the people have a decisive and direct vote on matters of great public controversy? Only the latter would be consistent with the SNP's own proclaimed principles.

A distinction can be made between states in which the referendum is an everyday part of democratic procedure, and those in which it is a more occasional feature of the political system. In Switzerland, national, cantonal and local referendums are a frequent occurrence,[b] with 12 national referendums being held in 2012, 11 in 2013, and 12 in 2014.[2] In contrast,

---

a   In 1940, the Liberal government of Canada under William Mackenzie King was elected on a promise not to introduce conscription, but by 1942 the call up of citizens to arms was judged by the government to be necessary for the successful prosecution of the war. A referendum was held to gauge public support for conscription, which the government won.

b   For a good general introduction to the Swiss political system, see: Steinberg, J., *Why Switzerland?* (2nd edition) (Cambridge: Cambridge University Press, 1996).

Luxembourg has only held four referendums, and Sweden only six, in the last 100 years. Between these extremes lie countries such as Italy, which has held around 20 referendums since the restoration of democracy in 1946, and Ireland, which has held almost 40 since independence in 1922.[3] In those countries where referendums are relatively rare, the matters most often put to the people include: (i) questions of statehood, or the reorganisation of boundaries; (ii) constitutional amendments; (iii) relationships with supranational organisations (eg Spain's referendum on NATO membership in 1986, and Denmark's referendum on joining the Euro in 2000); and (iv) issues that are socially divisive and may cut across party lines (eg Portugal's referendum on abortion in 2007 and Malta's referendum on divorce in 2011).

The people of Scotland have been asked to vote in five referendums, of which: one (in 1975) concerned membership of the European Economic Community, two devolution (1979 and 1997), one a change to the UK Parliament's electoral system (2011) and one the question of statehood (2014). Scotland, within the UK, has therefore made only occasional use of referendums. The question, from the point of view of constitutional design, is whether we would wish to make provision for more frequent use of referendums in a new Constitution. Should there be circumstances in which a referendum is mandatory? Should someone other than the Government – be it the parliamentary minority, or even the people themselves, have the right to demand a referendum? If so, should the results be binding, or merely consultative?

A Model Constitution suggested that provision be made for four types of referendum: (i) a mandatory, binding referendum on constitutional amendments; (ii) an optional, but binding, referendum, called by the Government, in cases where the parliamentary minority has exercised its right of suspensive veto; (iii) optional and consultative referendums called at the discretion of the parliamentary majority; and (iv) optional, consultative referendums called by local councils, on matters within their competence. It also envisaged a weak form of non-binding petitionary initiative, whereby 5 per cent of the electorate would be able to present a bill to Parliament for debate. These proposals, although not exhaustive, are a good starting point for discussion.

If sovereignty is the power to make supreme law, and if the

Constitution is supreme law, then the power to make or amend the supreme law (that is, the Constitution) must be retained in the hands of the people as a whole.[a] We might be governed, primarily, through representative institutions, but those institutions, while they act on behalf of the people in the matters delegated to them in accordance with the Constitution, should not be able to change the Constitution by their own will, without referring back to the people for authorisation. To uphold 'the sovereign right of the Scottish people to determine the form of government best suited to their needs', as proclaimed in the Claim of Right in 1989 and reaffirmed by an overwhelming majority in the Scottish Parliament in January 2012,[4] the Constitution must always remain in the people's hands, and there should be no major change in the ground rules without a referendum.

In the UK such an appeal to popular sovereignty is not enforceable. Although various grounds on which a referendum might be held may now be conventionally recognised,[b] the decision of whether to hold a referendum and the determination to be bound by the result remain solely at the discretion of the parliamentary majority.[c] In many countries, by contrast, the principle that constitutional changes must be approved by the people is written into the Constitution itself. In Ireland, Denmark and Australia, all constitutional changes, no matter how minor or technical, require popular approval. The Constitution of Spain can be amended by a super-

---

a   The *sovereignty* of the people as constituent power should not be confused with the *power* of the people. Sovereignty of the people requires that the people have the sole right to adopt and amend the fundamental laws – it operates at a constitutional level. The power of the people refers to the extent of popular control in ongoing political decision-making – such power operates under, and in accordance, with the Constitution.

b   The House of Lords Constitution Committee listed these as abolition of the monarchy, leaving the EU, independence of any nation from the UK, abolishing either House of Parliament, changing the Commons' electoral system, adopting a written Constitution, and changing the currency. A substantial change to devolved powers might also fall into this category. (See: Teirney, S. *Constitutional Referendums: The Theory and Practice of Republican Deliberation* (Oxford: Oxford University Press. 2014), pp. 108; 300–301.)

c   The Political Parties, Elections and Referendums Act 2001 is the main piece of UK legislation setting out general rules for the holding of referendums, but in the absence of constitutional provisions, there is little to prevent the parliamentary majority for altering these rules on an ad hoc basis for its own advantage.

majority in Parliament, but certain fundamental changes require a referendum.[5] Likewise in Latvia, a two-thirds majority of the members of Parliament can amend parts of the Constitution, while other parts, which are most fundamental to the nature of the state, can be changed only by referendum.[6] In Sweden a referendum must be held on constitutional amendments if one third, and in Luxembourg if one quarter, of the members of Parliament so insist.[a] Under these rules, the right of the people to have their say would not depend on the whims of the governing majority.

On the grounds of popular sovereignty, the SNP's 2002 draft Constitution, like the Scottish Provisional Constituent Assembly (SPCA) text[b] before it, would have required a referendum to approve all constitutional amendments, no matter how minor, technical, or uncontroversial these might be. The 2011 *Model Constitution* followed the same pattern, and for the same reason. There might, however, be a case for being less 'absolutist' than this, and for allowing minor and uncontroversial amendments to be made without the time, expense and inconvenience of a referendum. Such multi-tier amendment processes, reflecting different levels of entrenchment, are a feature of several post-colonial Commonwealth Constitutions. In Jamaica, as a typical example, there are three levels of entrenchment: certain minor provisions can be amended by an absolute majority in both Houses, other provisions only by a two-thirds majority in both Houses, and the most fundamental parts only by a two-thirds majority in both Houses followed by a referendum.

In Scotland, it would be quite possible, for example, for the Constitution to divide its provisions into two categories: (i) those that are essential baselines of a free, democratic order, and need to be specially entrenched, such as those concerning fundamental human rights, the electoral system, terms of office, the basic form of parliamentary government, judicial independence, and so forth; and (ii) other provisions, such

---

a   Luxembourg makes further provision for defending popular sovereignty by means of a rule that enables 25,000 electors, or about five per cent of the total population, to demand a referendum on constitutional amendments. (See: Constitution of Luxembourg, as amended, Art. 114).

b   The Scottish Provisional Constituent Assembly was an off-shoot of the Scottish Covenant Movement which published a draft Constitution for an independent Scotland in 1964. See: Moffat, R. *Scotland's Constitution* (Glasgow: Moffat Press, 1993)

as those providing for the details of public administration, finance, the organisation of state bodies, that are still of constitutional significance, but less fundamental in nature. Amendments to provisions in the first category would always require a referendum; amendments to provisions in the second category would only require a referendum if so demanded by, say, one-quarter of the members of Parliament. This would give opposition members, in most cases, or even a bloc of third-party or minor-party members, an effective veto.

This would be a concession to those who are concerned that requiring a referendum for all amendments makes Constitution too inflexible and unwieldy, while still upholding the essence of popular sovereignty. The important things, whether these rules be incorporated or not, are that: (i) no important or fundamental change to the Constitution should be made without the consent of the sovereign people, and (ii) that the right of the sovereign people to exercise this control should be embedded in the Constitution itself, and not granted by the 'grace and favour' of the Government or of the parliamentary majority.[a]

The second form of referendum contained in the *Model Constitution* is the minority veto referendum,[b] which was borrowed from the SNP's 2002 text with only minor changes:

> Under this mechanism, two-fifths of the members of Parliament (i.e. 40 per cent of the total membership) may demand that any bill (other than a money bill or a bill that is certified as urgent by the unanimous decision of the Parliamentary Bureau), be suspended for at least 12 months. After this period of suspension has elapsed, the bill may be put to the vote again in Parliament, with or without amendment, and may be passed by absolute majority vote. During the period of suspension, however, the Government may decide to override the

---

a   In this regard, the interim Constitution proposed by the Scottish Government and opened for consultation on 16 June 2014 is grossly deficient: the Constitution, and the revised Scotland Act that would form the basis of the institutional structure, would be capable of amendment by a simple majority of the Scottish Parliament – a state of affairs that would, despite fulsome promises of a commitment to popular sovereignty, simply transfer the effective exercise of sovereignty to Parliament.

b   For a fuller analysis of the minority veto referendum in comparative perspective, see: Bulmer, W. E. 'The Minority Veto Referendum as an Alternative to Bicameralism', *Politics*, (31/3, 2011).

suspensive veto by putting the bill to the people in a referendum. If the bill is approved by a majority of those voting in the referendum, it is at once presented for royal assent; if not, it is deemed to have been rejected'[7]

The purpose of this provision is not necessarily to elicit a popular vote on an issue – although that might be the occasional outcome – but rather, to strengthen the Opposition against the Government. Even the best Governments, if backed by a solid and well-disciplined parliamentary majority, are likely to make mistakes. They legislate in haste. They lose touch with the people. They break election promises. At present, opposition parties can complain about such behaviour, but they have no authority to counter-act it, and therefore no responsibility. A minority veto referendum system would give opposition parties real power, and with it, responsibility. They would have the power to inflict a frustrating delay on the Government's legislative agenda, or else force the Government to face the people in a referendum, and the responsibility to use this power only when they believe it truly in the national interest to do so. The balance of power in the chamber would shift, from the dominance of the majority to a more moderated form of government, with the people introduced as final arbiter.

The other forms of referendum provided in the *Model Constitution* are optional, non-binding, referendums, which provide a way for the Government (or, in the case of local referendums, the Council) to solicit an authoritative statement of public opinion with regard to a specific question placed before the people. These are the types of referendum with which we are familiar. They are called only at the discretion of the Government, and, given the choice, most Governments will call a referendum only if they believe they have a realistic chance of getting the outcome they want. Such referendums are a useful means of resolving issues that cut across party lines, or of legitimating difficult or important decisions, and it is proper that the Constitution should make explicit provision for them; by doing so, the Constitution recognises the rightful use of referendums and, by attaching certain rules and conditions, prevents their misuse.

The provisions of the *Model Constitution* are not the only way, and perhaps not even the best way, of incorporating referendums into the

Constitution. Italy, for example, provides for *abrogative referendums*: this permits any five of the country's regional councils, or a petition signed by 500,000 people, to trigger a referendum on the repeal of laws.[8] Latvia's Constitution allows the people a strong right of *initiative* – allowing the public, by petition, to propose new laws and bring them to a public vote, by-passing Parliament altogether.[9] In New South Wales, Australia, legislative disputes between the two Houses of Parliament can be resolved by means of a referendum.[10] Denmark's minority veto referendum system enables one-third of MPs to actually demand a referendum (and not merely, as in the *Model Constitution*, to suspend a bill, pending override by a referendum if the Government sees fit).[11] The Constitution of Slovenia allows one third of the members of the lower House, a majority of the upper House, or a petition of 40,000 electors, to call a binding referendum on any matter that may be regulated by law.[12]

If referendum rules loosely based on these examples were incorporated into a Scottish Constitution, the referendum would not be a 'use and discard' tool for achieving statehood. Rather it would be a periodic (if still occasional)[a] feature of our political life, which would restrain incumbent majorities, protect the people's sovereignty with regard to constitutional amendments, and facilitate the authoritative resolution of the most difficult and important political controversies by transferring them from Parliament to the people.

Whatever the precise form of referendum rules adopted, it would be beneficial for the Constitution to make some procedural provision to prevent the abuse of referendums. In particular, the Constitution should consider the formulation of the referendum question, the compatibility of

---

a   My aim is not to replace representative democracy with direct democracy, but only to use direct democracy to correct some of the faults of representative democracy. It would be unhelpful to end up in a situation like that in California, where it is not unusual for people to vote in more than ten referendums a year, and the hands of legislators are so tied by that policy coherence and responsibility are diminished. None of the referendum rules outlined in the *Model Constitution* would come close to that situation, since both consultative and minority-veto referendums would require the legislative initiative to be taken by Members of Parliament. If we were to adopt abrogative referendums, as in Italy, the people by petition would be able to demand a referendum only on the *repeal* (not enactment) of laws, and so the legislative impulse would still lie with the elected assembly.

the submitted proposal with the Constitution and the conduct of referendum campaigns. If these matters are handled in a relatively neutral and universal way in the Constitution (i.e. in such a way that the incumbent government cannot manipulate the rules to its own advantage) then the legitimacy of the referendum as a genuinely democratic decision-making mechanism can be preserved.[a] So, for example, the Constitution could require that any proposed referendum question be referred to the Electoral Commission for approval of the clarity and objectivity of its wording before being voted upon. Likewise, the Supreme Court might be mandated to perform an abstract review of legislative referendums to ensure their compatibility with the Constitution.

It is also usual to prohibit referendums on certain types of question. For example, any question concerning budgetary issues could be excluded on the grounds that the budget needs to be under the direct responsibility of Parliament in order to ensure fiscal discipline.

Fig. 2 Examples: Citizen and Minority-Triggered Referendum Rules

---

Constitution of Italy, Article 75

1 When requested by 500,000 voters or by five regional councils, a popular referendum decides on total or partial repeal of a law or other acts with legal force.

2 No such referenda are allowed for tax or budget laws, amnesties, pardons, or ratification of international treaties.

3 Citizens entitled to vote for the Chamber of Deputies may also participate in a referendum.

4 The referendum succeeds if a majority of those eligible have participated and if the proposal has received a majority of the valid votes.

5 The law establishes procedures for referendums.

Constitution of Latvia, Articles 72–75

72 The President of State shall have the right to suspend the promulgation of a law for a period of two months. He/she shall suspend the promulgation at the

---

a In this regard, the *Model Constitution* was arguably deficient, since it included no provisions requiring that: (i) that the substance of a consultative referendum must be certified to ensure compliance with the Constitution; and (ii) the wording of the question must be approved by the Electoral Commission, who would have a duty to ensure that it is clear and unbiased. The examples included at the end of this book correct these omissions.

request of not less than one-third of the members of the Parliament. This right shall be exercised by the President of State or by one-third of the members of Parliament within seven days after the adoption of the law by Parliament. The law thus suspended, shall be submitted to a referendum, if not less than one-tenth of the electors so request. Should such a request not be formulated within a period of two months as mentioned above, the law shall be promulgated upon the expiration of that period. The referendum shall not be taken, however, if Parliament puts this law to a vote once more and if then not less than three-fourths of all the members are in favour of its adoption.

73 The following matters shall not be submitted to a referendum: the budget, laws concerning loans, taxes, custom's duties, railway tariffs, military service, the declaration and commencement of war, the settlement of peace, the declaration of a state of emergency and its termination, mobilisation, demobilisation, foreign agreements.

74 A law adopted by Parliament and suspended in the procedure set forth in Article 72, may be annulled by a referendum, if the number of participating electors is at least one-half of those who participated in the previous parliamentary elections and if the majority has voted for the annulment of the law.

75 Should the Parliament determine the urgency of a law with a majority of not less than two-thirds, the President of State may not demand a second review of the law; it may not be submitted to a referendum and shall be promulgated within three days after the President has received the adopted law.

Constitution of Slovenia, Article 90

1 The National Assembly may call a referendum on any issue which is the subject of regulation by law. The National Assembly is bound by the result of such referendum.

2 The National Assembly may call a referendum from the preceding paragraph on its own initiative, however it must call such referendum if so required by at least one-third of the deputies, by the National Council or by forty thousand voters.

3 The right to vote in a referendum is held by all citizens who are eligible to vote in elections.

4 A proposal is passed in a referendum if a majority of those voting have cast votes in favour of the same.

5 Referendums are regulated by a law passed in the National Assembly by a two-thirds majority vote of deputies present.

ii Representation and Inclusiveness

Even if there is scope in a new Constitution for the more frequent use of referendums and other forms of popular participation, parliamentary general elections are likely to remain the primary democratic event: the vote that determines who is to govern and the broad outlines of the policies to be pursued during the years ahead. The characteristics of the representative body are therefore vital to the health of the democratic system.

At the time of the establishment of the Scottish Parliament, there was some hope that a 'new politics' would emerge, which would be more open and participatory, and less confrontational and adversarial, than the 'winner takes all' politics of Westminster. Several key innovations were built into the Scotland Act to help support such a change, including Proportional Representation (intended to prevent any single party from having a monopoly of power) and fixed-term elections (intended to deny the executive the right to arbitrarily dissolve Parliament). These reforms, with the addition of stronger committees and a few tweaks to Parliament's internal procedures would, it was hoped, provide an adequate set of checks and balances, protecting us from the careless use and malicious abuse of power. Such hopes, as we know, have not been fully realised. Within the wider question of constitution building, there is an ongoing need for further parliamentary reform if the Parliament of Scotland is to an effective legislative, deliberative and scrutinising forum.

The *Model Constitution* contained several provisions intended to reinforce the role and protect the autonomy of Parliament in the political system. It would enshrine the Mixed Member Proportional (MMP) electoral system, thereby preventing incumbents from taking the damaging retrograde step of reintroducing First Past the Post for reasons of party advantage. It envisaged, additionally, a potential increase in the membership of Parliament to a maximum of 200 members. This would strengthen Parliament by distributing the workload, particularly of committee duties, amongst a wider pool of parliamentarians, while at the same time potentially increasing the chances of minor parties by slightly lowering the threshold of votes needed to win a seat.

The *Model Constitution* also specified a maximum number of Ministers relative to the number of parliamentarians (to reduce the size of the 'payroll vote'), regulated the composition and powers of committees, and made provisions concerning the internal organisation of Parliament (eg the adoption of Standing Orders and the election of the Presiding Officer, the Parliamentary Bureau and the Corporate Body). If we want Scotland to have an active and effective Parliament, not merely one that acts as a sounding board and rubber stamp for the executive, then the powers and rights of the opposition and of minor parties, of the committees and of ordinary members, need to enjoy constitutional status. Although a Constitution cannot regulate everything in detail, these things cannot be left unstated, to be decided by ordinary parliamentary majorities. If they were, the majority would (sooner or later, by sudden usurpation or gradual erosion) use their bloc-voting power to weaken procedural restraints, to the detriment of Parliament as a whole.

Beyond these additional guarantees and minor reforms, however, more substantive changes to the electoral system and to the composition of Parliament were not envisaged. While the most important consideration is that the electoral system should be broadly proportional between parties,[a] the current MMP is generally superior to its main rivals: Single Transferable Vote (STV) or Party Lists. Unless the constituencies are very large, STV is less proportional. Moreover, the need to campaign against other candidates from one's own party often leads to a clientelistic and hyper-local style of politics,[13] in which larger national policy questions are subsumed by the need to provide constituency service in order to build up a personal following.[b] Party Lists, without being balanced by a local constituency element, would conversely break the link between a member of Parliament and a relatively small local area, as to achieve a reasonable degree of proportionality the multi-member constituencies would have to be at least five or six times the size of current single-member constituencies. MMP provides a combination of a proportional result with real, but not overwhelming, constituency link.[c] It also provides room for different

---

a   The advantage of Proportional Representation is not only that it is 'fair' between existing parties, but also that it makes it much easier for new parties to emerge, and thereby encourages parties to continue to pay attention to their voters. In a First-Past-the-Post system, the 'spoiler effect' means that a new party will only harm the chances of its nearest rival and help ideological opponents. The protection against a challenge from the flank offered by FPTP allows parties to become very complacent and to take their supporters for granted.

b   It is notable, for example, that Ireland has seriously considered changing its electoral system from STV to MMP in order to strengthen the national policy focus of parliamentarians and to help reduce the clientelism and local corruption that has plagued Irish politics.

c   Of course, the existing electoral system has imperfections. It allows no preference voting: there is a 'closed' list for the regional seats. This could be changed by allowing

types of member, with different approaches to the role of the Member of Parliament. Some might seek out a constituency seat because they like to be rooted in a local constituency and to devote more of their time to local issues and 'brokerage' work; others, who are more interested in national policy issues, might prefer a regional seat.[d]

Although MMP offers a good combination of party-proportionality and geographical representation, it still structures representation only through these two lenses of party and geography, while ignoring other demographic aspects of representation that might make Parliament look, sound and feel more like the people it is supposed to represent. On this point, there is some room for improvement. A choice between Alice, Bob and Charlie means little unless the outcome of that choice says something meaningful about the public preferences of the choosers. If all three were alike, and yet equally out of touch with the values, attitudes, characteristics, identities and priorities of the majority (or even substantial minorities) of the voters, the election would fail to convey meaningful political information. A Parliament composed of such members, although elected, would have limited representative value, as it would not fully reflect the attitudes of society.

The Scottish Parliament is still an overwhelmingly white, middle-aged and male assembly. Female representation especially has declined slightly from 39.5 per cent in 2003 to just 34.8 per cent in 2011.[14] Even this figure was boosted by the fact that the Labour Party and the Greens decided to 'zip' their regional lists, despite the fact that they are under no legal obligation to do so. A 'zipped list' is a quota system in which candidates are nominated on an alternating basis; in the case of gender-zipped lists, this means that a woman and a man must occupy alternate positions in

---

voters to strike out particular candidates on the list, or to give a preference vote to a particular candidate that would bump them up the ranking (provisions to this effect exist in Sweden and the Netherlands, although only occasionally do they make much difference to the overall outcome). See: Irwin, R. B. & Andeweg, G. A. *Government and Politics of the Netherlands* (3rd edition) (Basingstoke: Palgrave Macmillan, 2009) and Arter, D., *Democracy in Scandinavia: Consensual, Majoritarian or Mixed* (Manchester: Manchester University Press, 2006).

d The relationship between list and constituency members is not, however, without tension. See: Lundberg, T. C. 'Tensions between constituency and regional members of the Scottish Parliament under mixed-member proportional representation: a failure of the new politics', *Parliamentary Affairs*, (67/2, 2014). pp. 351–370.

the ranking order of candidates. A new constitution could, for example, require all parties to use zipped lists for regional seats.[a]

Whether we wish to mandate this at a constitutional level (as opposed to at the level of ordinary electoral law, by voluntary agreement of the parties, or not at all) is a debate yet to be had. Here it is sufficient, without coming down on one side or other of that debate, to note that *if* we wished to use constitutional rules to ensure gender balance in Parliament, then mandating zippered lists would be a relatively simple, tried and tested option that could easily be grafted onto the existing MMP electoral system.[b]

Gender-zipped lists were mandated by law in Italy in 1993, but two years later the Constitutional Court deemed this provision to be contrary to the Constitution's equality provisions; previously, a similar decision of the French Constitutional Council had ruled gender quotas for municipal elections in France unconstitutional.[15] Therefore, even if we do not decide, at this time, to include gender quotas or zipped lists in the Constitution, a provision could be included giving Parliament the right to adopt such rules in the future, in order to protect these rules from being challenged as unconstitutional.

The domination of Scotland's institutions by a relatively small class of professional elites has been well documented.[16] Active policy-making and agenda-setting power is probably in the hands of, at most, a few hundred people: ministers, senior civil servants, senior judges and other powerful individuals such as media barons and those with serious financial power. These few are advised, assisted, supported and constrained by perhaps a few thousand more, including backbench parliamentarians, mid-level political donors, corporate lobbyists, landowners, the senior members of

---

a   This solution is not without flaws. Mandating gender parity for regional list seats, while increasing gender balance, would not necessarily result in 50-50 parity overall. This is because constituency seats would not be affected. Moreover, if there is an unabated tendency to nominate more male than female candidates for the constituency seats, then the gender balance will be skewed between the parties: the parliamentary caucus of the plurality winner, which gains most constituency seats, will be more male-dominated, while that of minority parties, whose parliamentary caucus consists mainly of regional list members, will be more female.

b   It might seem incongruous to combine zipped or quota-based lists with preferential, open lists that allow voters to express a preference between candidates, but it need not be so. Lists could be presented in zipped order, while reserving the right of voters to express a preference vote that would boost a candidate's ranking.

the vast local government and public sector *nomenklatura*, the legal establishment, the Kirk and the staffs of various civil society and campaigning bodies. Thus the inner elite is defined primarily by great wealth, class and access to power, while the outer elite is defined by office-holding, expertise, and social influence, but both tend to exclude ordinary citizens from effective participation and influence. As one contributor to an online discussion on the Constitutional Commission's Facebook group put it: 'Gender and racial balance is excellent. [But] maybe government needs some farmers, postmen, [lorry] drivers, factory workers?'

The fact that day-to-day governance is largely in the hands of a few is not wholly or necessarily a bad thing. A strict and complete equality of political power is impossible. Even if the state were the size of a village, and could be governed by a general meeting of its inhabitants, it would still have to entrust certain preparatory functions to a council or committee, and certain administrative powers to officials with the latitude to make decisions between general meetings. In a country the size of Scotland, democracy must necessarily operate through representative institutions, which must be backed by a professional bureaucratic and judicial apparatus. These people may bring expertise and experience – as well as, in many cases, genuine passion, dedication, and an ethos of public service – to their work. Most of the work, in any case, concerns questions of detail or implementation that are of little interest to the wider public. Moreover, the existence of a 'political class' introduces a useful division of labour. Thanks to the minority who are deeply engaged in matters of government, most of us can spend most of our time contributing to the common good by doing things other than governing: healing the sick, teaching children and keeping the streets clean, the lights on and the shelves stocked.

Despite this, such elites are never fully to be trusted. They necessarily represent a relatively thin section of the population, and their views, interests, experiences and concerns are not always reflective of the whole community. Besides, we cannot pretend that this elite-governed state of affairs is democratic in any but the thinnest sense of the word. Democracy implies a high degree of political equality (equal access to power and equal influence in decision-making), not the unrestricted delegation of power to a specialised political class. In a democracy, nurses, teachers, street sweepers, electricians and shelf stackers are not supposed to 'get on with their lives' or to 'mind their own business', because in a democracy people are not 'private individuals' (economic units of production, consumption and revenue generation); rather, they are citizens, enjoying the status and responsibilities conferred by full and equal membership of the *res publica*. Accordingly, citizens in a democracy have a reciprocal moral duty to use their democratic rights to care for the common good through active participation in public and civic life – and must therefore be given the constitutional tools to enable them to perform this duty.

Most international indices measure democracy in terms of institutional provision: is there a universal franchise, is there an independent judiciary, are freedoms of speech and association respected? Although these measures tell part of the story, they tend to overlook the real disposition of power in the country and to ignore the dynamics of class, wealth and influence on public decision-making. It is becoming increasingly apparent that, while these formal criteria of democracy are met, we are sliding towards oligarchy: the corrupt rule of the rich, privileged, powerful few. Excessive concentrations of private wealth, corporate lobbying, big political donations, the revolving door between politics and directorships, the influence of banks and other financial institutions over economic policy, and the influence of the corporate media, are all part of this worrying trend.

In an oligarchy, the most over-represented people are the rich. In 2012, two thirds of the UK cabinet were millionaires, with a combined wealth of more than £70 million,[17] although millionaires make up only around one per cent of the UK population. A recent study of policy-making in the US showed that average voters have 'only a minuscule, near-zero, statistically non-significant impact upon public policy' while 'the economic elites and organised groups representing business interests have substantial independent impacts on US government policy'.[18] I am aware of no methodologically similar and recent study having been conducted in the UK, but an older study cited by Arend Lijphart showed that the gap between voter policy preferences and government policies, measured on a ten-point, left-right scale, was widest in the UK out of 12 Western democracies surveyed.[19] A YouGov poll conducted on behalf of the Centre for Labour and Social Studies in October 2013 found that the public's preferences were not only a long way from those of the UK Government, but also from those of the main (UK-wide) opposition, with the public being overwhelmingly opposed to privatisation of the NHS and the Royal Mail, and more than two-thirds of those polled being in favour of the renationalisation of railway companies and energy companies.[20] Likewise, it has been argued that:

> the influence that large corporations and wealthy individuals now wield on the UK political system seems unprecedented in the post-war period. There is powerful evidence of politics and business interests becoming increasingly interwoven. The density of connections (directorships, consultancies or shareholdings) between major corporations and MPs is many times greater in the UK than in other established democracies.[21]

In other words, there is a double democratic deficit. The problem is not just that Scotland has been ruled by Westminster governments with no majority in Scotland for 34 of the 68 years since 1945,[22] but also that those governments have pursued their own agenda, dictated by a rich and powerful few, which is not supported even by those who did vote for them. An independence that fixes only one of these problems and ignores the other would not get to the root of what the problem – i.e. government by and for the few.

The oligarchic tendencies of the system we now call 'representative democracy' are, from a historical perspective, hardly surprising. Although we enjoy a wide legal right of political participation (and, crucially, we do not have slaves[a] or legally exclude women), the process through which participation is structured – election – systematically favours the few: professional party politicians,[b] the very rich, the well-connected, the influential, the well-spoken, and the leisured class.[23] Ancient Greeks or medieval Italians would have been quick to grasp that institutions based on the election of a Parliament once every four or five years are barely democratic. Our system would have struck them as, at most, a sort of

---

a   Of course, to our shame, slavery has only been criminalised, not abolished. There are, according to the campaign group Free the Slaves, between 21 million and 30 million people still trapped in slavery around the world: more than half are women or girls, more than a quarter are children, and more than a fifth are in sex-slavery. For more information see: www.freetheslaves.net/

b   Only two per cent of the Scottish electorate are members of a political party, but more than 98 per cent of MSPs are partisans.

'semi-competitive oligarchy', tempered, on quadrennial or quintennial occasions, by one day of weak democracy, where people choose between rival factions of the elite.

If we must accept that there will inevitably be a relatively small number who actively shape government policy on a daily basis, then what do we mean by democracy? How can a state be 'governed by the people' when only a small minority are regularly involved in governing? Niccolò Machiavelli (1469–1527), the Florentine statesman and philosopher, provides useful insight into this problem. Although he is sometimes misunderstood by those familiar only with *The Prince* as an apologist for tyranny and political chicanery, Machiavelli understood the importance of a 'balanced constitution'. In particular, he recognised the need to strengthen the popular element in the constitution, against elites, if oligarchy and tyranny are to be avoided. The essential problem addressed in his *Florentine Histories* and *Discourses on Livy* is one very familiar to us today: how can we stop elites from abusing power, dominating others and, in short, corrupting the state from a 'polity' or 'good government of the many' into an oligarchy or tyranny?

Machiavelli's proposed answer, expressed in his *Discourse on the Reform of the State of Florence*, is to create a robust popular element in the Constitution, chiefly through the institution of randomly selected officials who would have the power to refer decisions to the people for veto or assent. This arrangement, backed up by a citizen army, would force elites, by sharing power with the people (and, indeed, by making themselves dependent on the people), to govern for the common good and not for their own private benefit.[24] The power of the rich would be balanced by the power of the people, such that none would ever be so mighty as to be able to molest or oppress the people with impunity. There might always be a few at the top of the apex of power – not everyone can be Prime Minister – but, if we are equipped with strong institutions, through which we can constrain those who govern and hold them account, and if we are united in refusing to be governed by crooks and shysters, then we might be governed by elites who are forced by the people to be tolerably good, mostly well-meaning, more or less honest and somewhat public-spirited. This is not a utopian vision, but a realist view of freedom.

To achieve this, it is necessary to strengthen the popular element, making politics more inclusive and more participatory. This need is now more urgent and pressing than at any time since the development of modern democratic constitutionalism. The ability of existing institutional models to deliver the 'politics of the common good' has become more elusive and vulnerable than we once thought it to be. Despite the successful spread of what we call democracy – free elections and basic civil liberties – across much of Eastern Europe, Latin America, and parts of Africa and East Asia in recent decades, it now appears that democracy is on the global decline.[25] Many states, after some initial progress in the 1990s, have regressed into authoritarian ways. Others have sustained 'free elections' but never really democratised their societies – power and influence have remained clustered in small, unaccountable elites, breeding the discontent and disillusionment that has been manifested recently in Ukraine, Greece and elsewhere. If we are serious about sustaining a politics of the common good in Scotland, we must have a Constitution that puts the people before the powerful. By establishing the institutional ground rules of inclusive and participatory democracy, it should enable ordinary citizens to share in government and to contest, constrain and compel those who hold office.

Ancient and medieval city-states developed a variety of institutional mechanisms by which non-elites sought to control, or at least to limit the excesses of the ruling class. In Rome, the plebian citizens obtained the right to elect tribunes from amongst their own order, with the right to veto decision; patricians were excluded from this office. In Florence, the minor guilds representing artisan trades fought hard to achieve a fair share of representation in the *Signoria* (executive council). Likewise, in the autonomous chartered towns of northern Europe, such a Liege, Ghent and Bruges, the guilds attempted (with varying degrees of success) to include artisans and tradesmen alongside the great merchants.[26] Modern democracies, being based on universal suffrage, rarely or never make use of these mechanisms. In principle, everyone's vote counts equally, even if in practice, the representative process is distorted in favour of elite interests.[27]

It is possible, however, to imagine institutional mechanisms that could be applied in a modern representative system to increase the presence of social and economic non-elites. If a constitution can prescribe the use of zippered lists based on gender, why could it not also do the same for factors such as wealth or education? Could not the electoral system be designed in such a way that parties would be required to nominate no greater percentage of millionaires than the percentage of millionaires in the country as determined by the latest census? Alternatively, parties could be obliged to place in winnable positions on each list a certain number of candidates who have lived below median household income for the five years preceding the election, corresponding to the percentage of the population in that income bracket.

This might sound far-fetched, but there are some precedents that at least prove the possibility of such an approach. For example, in Egypt before the Arab Spring revolution the constitution required that half the members of parliament be 'workers or peasants'. This was achieved by a system of dual candidacy, whereby each constituency had two members of Parliament, with one place reserved for a worker or peasant, and the other place being open to any qualified candidate. Although Egypt was not a democracy at the time – and therefore elections took place within the constraints of a system that was at most only semi-competitive, 'during the Nasser era Parliament did provide an important channel of access for these elements into national politics.'[28]

The Constitution of India provides a better example, because it combines a system for the representation of marginalised socio-economic groups (defined by caste or tribe) with a functioning pluralistic democracy. Under Article 330 of the Indian Constitution, seats in the lower house of the national Parliament and in the Legislative Assemblies of the 29 states are set aside for 'Scheduled Castes and Tribes'. The scheduled castes were regarded as 'untouchables' by traditional Indian society; they were subject to many forms of discrimination and left to perform the lowest, dirtiest occupations. The scheduled tribes were mainly forest or hill dwellers, dependent on forms of tribal organisation and subsistence agriculture, who claim to be the 'original inhabitants' of India but are excluded from mainstream Indian society. India uses a first-past-the-post electoral system, and there are no regional lists or 'top-up' seats that can be used to promote greater inclusion. Instead, the inclusion of scheduled castes and tribes is achieved by a system of 'reservation', such that only those belonging to a scheduled caste or tribe can be nominated as a candidate for a reserved constituency. First, the number of seats to be reserved in each state is determined in accordance with the proportion of members of the scheduled castes and tribes as a percentage of the population of the state at the latest census.

A hypothetical example will demonstrate how this works. Imagine that a state is entitled to elect, by virtue of its total population, 20 members to the lower house of the Indian Parliament (and is therefore divided into 20 geographical constituencies, each returning one member). Let us presume that 25 per cent of the people of that state belong to 'scheduled castes', and a further 10 per cent to 'scheduled tribes'. In this case, five constituencies in that state (i.e. 25 per cent of 20) will be reserved for candidates belonging to scheduled castes, and two (i.e. 10 per cent of 20) will be reserved for candidates from the scheduled tribes. The remaining 13 seats will be 'general' or unreserved constituencies, in which any eligible citizen may be a candidate. Second, the reserved constituencies must be allocated across the state. This is done in such a way that those constituencies having the highest concentration of inhabitants belonging to scheduled castes and tribes are reserved.[29]

Taking income or wealth as the marker rather than caste or tribe, it is possible to adapt the Indian system to the constituency seats for the Scottish Parliament. If 16 per cent of the Scottish population lives in poverty,[a] then 16 per cent of the constituency seats could be reserved for the poor. With a Parliament of 129 members, this amounts to a reservation of 20 seats. Those reserved would be the 20 constituencies with the highest proportion of poor people living in them. Anyone who is not defined as poor, under whatever robust statutory measure is used, would be ineligible for nomination in those constituencies. Thus the 20 most deprived and impoverished areas of the country would necessarily be represented not by a professional politician but by someone who is expert in the problems of their constituents by virtue of their lived experience.

Various theoretical objections can be raised against such a scheme, or indeed any attempt to broaden the socio-economic base of representation by formal constitutional prescription. It would seem to restrict the choices of voters, in forcing these in reserved seats to cast a ballot for a 'poor' candidate, and of parties, in limiting the pool of potential candidates from

---

a   Based on the Scottish Government's figures from 2012–2013. Source: www.scotland. gov.uk/Resource/0045/00454875.pdf

which they can select nominees. It might, in the opinion of some, lead to a dilution of parliamentary talent.[a]

Even if these objections are refuted, there are many detailed discussions to be had about the best way, practically, of achieving these ends. How should 'poor' be defined for these purposes? What are we to do with those who, being initially poor, are elected to Parliament under this rule and then enjoy a parliamentary salary and all its perks for several years; are these people, whose income is likely to put them above any meaningful threshold, to be denied re-election from the seats reserved for the poor? If so, would this discourage members elected from the reserved seats from remaining close to the needs and interests of their constituents? In other words, would this scheme serve only as a ladder to wealth and influence for a few, who would use it to climb the greasy pole, rather than being a shield for the many? There are also alternatives to consider. Under the mixed-member proportional system, for instance, it might be simpler to rely on quotas for the region's list seats than to use reserved constituencies.

Yet all these objections and difficutlies must be weighed in the balance. If we are to bring democracy back to the people, to reconnect the state with society, to make our representative institutions genuinely representative, and to be governed by our trusted peers and not by a small clique of self-serving politicians, then we should give these ideas serious consideration. If adopted, measures designed to increase the representation of the poor would change not only the face of Parliament but perhaps its heart and mind, too.

---

a   This is true, however, only if we look at talent in a fairly narrow, technical sense. In the words of one activist, 'Not everyone has a college education, nor can even string an eloquent sentence together, but their views and aspirations and their frustrations should be there for us to take on board with our own views, whatever they may be. Surely, we are looking to people from all walks of life, and backgrounds, to join this debate, and exclusivity to the wisdom of words is not going to help us provide the broadest platform possible to achieve this.' There is a case for being led and represented by educated specialists, whose minds have been finely trained; yet, unless hearts have also been finely trained, we risk being governed by mere sophists – people who can sound convincing about things they do not understand, and can argue a position without pausing to consider its real merits. Qualities such as wisdom, integrity, justice, compassion, a sense of public duty and a commitment to the wellbeing of others are obviously not exclusive to well-spoken people in expensive suits and may even be more likely to occur in people who have themselves experienced misfortune or poverty.

iii   Second Chamber: Senate or Tribunate?

Calls for a second chamber in Scotland have so far been subdued and rare, and all hitherto published proposals for a Scottish Constitution have envisaged a unicameral Parliament. The draft interim constitution, published in June 2014, was no exception. As the Parliament of Scotland before 1707 had just one chamber, it is tempting to attribute this apparent preference for unicameralism to historical distinctiveness: unicameralism (more inclusive, egalitarian and comradely than the English practice of separating the ermine-bedecked Lords from the grimy Commons) is the auld Scottish way. However, more proximate 'path dependency' is probably a greater influence. Having been accustomed to a unicameral devolved Parliament since the 1990s, Holyrood politicians see little need for a parallel assembly that could rival their prestige and authority. Moreover, second chambers are today most associated with regionalised or federal states, where they help to protect the identity of cultural or territorial units, and to give them a voice in national law-making;[a] a second chamber may be unnecessary in a relatively small, homogeneous country like Scotland.

Indeed, many of the small states composing northern Europe's great 'arc of democracy' – Luxembourg, Iceland, Norway, Denmark, Sweden, Finland and the Baltic States – do well enough without a second chamber. The absence of a second chamber, however, does not mean that these states concentrate unlimited or unrestrained power in a bare majority of the members of a single chamber. Instead, they make use of constitutional mechanisms that perform the functions of a second chamber – such as facilitating scrutiny, restraining hasty and badly drafted legislation, protecting constitutional rights and representing the diversity of society – in a unicameral system.

In Sweden, to cite one example, any ten members of Parliament may delay for a year any bill that would impose limits on the exercise of

---

a   In Germany, the *Bundesrat* consists of 'delegations' from the governments of the 16 *Länder*. In Australia, the Senate is directly elected, but with equal representation for each of the country's six states. Spain takes a mixed approach, with most of the Senators being directly elected from the country's provinces, and the remainder nominated by the parliaments of the Autonomous Communities.

protected rights and freedoms. This delay may only be overturned by five sixths (84 per cent) of the members of Parliament, giving even a small minority the right to impose a period of reflection and reconsideration on the Government.[30] An advisory 'Council on Legislation' consisting of judges is required to examine bills in order to report on how they 'relate to the Fundamental Laws and the legal system in general', as well as on their internal coherence and technical quality.[31] A special parliamentary 'Committee on the Constitution', which is 'entitled to have access to the records of decisions taken in Government matters and to the documents pertaining to such matters, as well as any other Government documents that the Committee deems necessary', is charged with '[examining] ministers' performance of their official duties and the handling of Government business'.[32]

Sweden is not alone in adopting these check and balances in a unicameral system. Luxembourg has a Council of State that reviews the technical quality of legislation and can impose a three-month delay for reconsideration. In Estonia, Parliament can enact legislation by a simple majority in most cases, but there is a constitutionally-prescribed list of 17 major institutional laws – including the laws on citizenship, elections, referendums, local government, and the organization of the state bank, amongst others – that can be enacted or amended only by an absolute majority;[33] moreover, these laws are not capable of being changed by emergency presidential decrees.[34] In Norway, until recently, the unicameral Parliament would divide itself into two semi-chambers for the separate consideration of bills, before coming together for a final vote[35] – although this experiment was ultimately found to be unsatisfactory, and has since been abolished.

Although many such possibilities of this nature exist, a second chamber does have certain advantages over other ways of limiting and balancing the power of the governing majority. One of these is that it could be constituted on a different representative basis. In a geographically diverse country such as Scotland, a second chamber could, for example, give equal representation to the Western Isles or Clackmannanshire as to Glasgow; although not a 'federal' country, the principle of equal representation – albeit to a chamber with unequal powers – might help to ensure that the interests of remote and rural communities are adequately defended in Parliament.

The use of mandatory candidate quotas or other institutional means to promote the representation of non-elite socio-economic groups, as discussed in the previous section, could be regarded as too far-fetched. In this case, a second chamber could provide a less controversial means of ensuring that people from all walks of life, and not just professional politicians, are represented. With this aim of broadening representation in mind, *A Model Constitution* made provision for a 'Consultative Assembly' as a form of quasi-second chamber, with the right to propose and to review legislation, in which economic and social interest groups would be given balanced representation. Having a bloc of farmers, crofters, trade unionists[a] and third-sector workers sitting in a parliamentary chamber would build on previous experiments, such as the Civic Forum.[b]

Such so-called 'functional' representation might be combined with geographical representation favouring rural areas, as discussed above, to create a workable second chamber that represents the diversity of Scottish life.[c] Given legislative powers at least equivalent to the House of Lords,

---

a   Perhaps the most anti-oligarchic institution of the British system of government, from the 1930s to the 1970s, was the Trades Union Congress. Representing the skilled, semi-skilled and unskilled portions of the working class, it had substantial influence on policy and a virtual veto-power over legislation. However, this informal experiment in economic democracy was limited and ultimately undermined by the self-destructive pressures of a zero-sum, winner-takes-all political system, in which 'them and us' attitudes were dominant.

b   The Civic Forum was a representative body of civil society organisations, created alongside the Scottish Parliament as a quasi-second chamber. It was soon 'choked to death' by politicians and civil servants, because without a firm constitutional basis it could not defend itself or its role. The lesson of the Civic Forum is that if you want an institution to be able to restrain the Government and hold it to account, that institution cannot depend on the goodwill of the Government or the incumbent parliamentary majority. For this reason, all statutory institutions are at best paper guarantees against the abuse of power; only constitutional bodies, whose authority, autonomy and budgets cannot be eroded by Parliament, can be relied upon.

c   For example – and this is merely illustrative – a chamber of 100 members could consist of two members from each of the 32 current local authority areas, elected by the people for six-year terms, with one from each area being elected every third year by Alternative Vote; the remaining members could be elected or nominated for three-year terms by socio-economic and vocational groups (the list of organisations having the right to elect or nominate could be determined by a committee of the chamber, within broad parameters of balance and inclusivity specified by the Constitution; it would include, but not be limited to, the major institutions of 'Civic Scotland').

this would provide a useful scrutinising and revising chamber. If armed with a veto over non-financial legislation that could only be over-ridden by a sufficiently high threshold (eg by referendum, by a two-thirds majority vote in the primary elected chamber, or by an absolute majority in the primary chamber after an intervening general election), such a second chamber could provide an effective check on the absolutism of the Government, and promote a more moderated and balanced politics. In an independent state, this could be achieved without increasing the number of politicians, if the size of such a second chamber were no greater than the number of Scottish MPs and Lords at Westminster.

Fig. 3 Example: Functional Representation – the National Council of Slovenia

---

Constitution of Slovenia, Articles 96–98

96 (Composition)

1   The National Council is the representative body for social, economic, professional and local interests. The National Council has forty members.
2   It is composed of: four representatives of employers; four representatives of employees; four representatives of farmers, crafts and trades, and independent professions; six representatives of non-commercial fields; 22 representatives of local interests.
3   The organisation of the National Council is regulated by law.

97 (Powers of the National Council)

1   The National Council may: propose to the National Assembly the passing of laws; convey to the National Assembly its opinion on all matters within the competence of the National Assembly; require the National Assembly to decide again on a given law prior to its promulgation; require the calling of a referendum [...]; require inquiries on matters of public importance [...].
2   Where required by the National Assembly, the National Council must express its opinion on an individual matter.

98 (Election)

1   Election to the National Council shall be regulated by a law passed by the National Assembly by a two-thirds majority vote of all deputies.
2   Members of the National Council are elected for a term of five years.

A more radical alternative is the selection of a second chamber by 'sortition', or random lot. This is the so-called 'Athenian option', after the use of random lot in ancient Athens, although random lot was also widely used in other classical as well as medieval republics; it might just as well be known as the 'Florentine option', the 'Venetian option', or even the 'Great Yarmouth' option.[a]

Random lot is an inherently democratic device, since (provided the pool from which prospective candidates may be drawn is not restricted to particular nominees or groups) it ignores considerations of wealth, fame, popularity, status, education, connections and ability. The lot, compared with elections, allows for a more equal distribution of offices, rewards, burdens and honours, and prevents the rise of cliques and factions. The one with many friends and clients, who has plenty of money to buy partisans, has a great advantage in elections, but is on a level with the poor, obscure, humble citizen in the drawing of (fair) lots.[36] If lots were drawn from a list of volunteers, on an opt-in basis,[b] the effect would be less democratic, since the wealthy, educated and leisured would tend to predominate; nevertheless, the selectees would still represent the 'ordinary citizens of the community', as members of the public, distinct from the elected party-politicians.

It would not be sensible to choose the members of the sole or primary chamber of Parliament by lot, since in a parliamentary democracy these members are part of the chain of democratic delegation and accountability which runs from the people, through Parliament, to the Government.[37] Selection by lot would break this chain, denying the people an active choice in who should govern them and making responsibility difficult to enforce.[38] However, it is possible to apply sortition to a second chamber, which has no role in the formation or removal of governments, but instead performs an ancillary role as a chamber for further deliberation, reflection and scrutiny.

Imagine, for example, if there were to be a second chamber of one hundred citizens, randomly selected from the electoral register. The lorry drivers, the plumbers, the car salesmen, the receptionists, the street stall

---

a   Random lot was used to select town officials in the East Anglian town of Great Yarmouth until the 1835 Municipal Corporations Act, see: Dowlen, O., *The Political Potential of Sortition: A study of the random selection of citizens for public office* (Exeter: Imprint Academic, 2009), pp.138–142.

b   For example, there could be a tick-box on the electoral registration from 'Do you wish to be included in the selection list for the second chamber, Yes or No?'

vendors, the apprentice joiners and the kitchen porters, the teachers, the doctors, the advocates and the architects, would all be in the mix together, without any distinction. Such an institution would not be a 'Senate', but a 'Tribunate'.[a] There would be no 'party hacks' and no professional politicians. A one-year term of office would be long enough to give members of the Tribunate a feel for the task, without becoming institutionalised. After having served for a year, reselection would be prohibited for at least five years (the odds are very much against it anyway), and ex-members would not be able, during that five years, to stand for election (so that the institution which is supposed to be a shield for the common man and woman does not become a ladder by which a few are recruited into the elite). A few necessary exceptions, similar to those that apply to jury service, might be necessary, as well as an option to defer service, if selected, on personal or compassionate grounds. There would also have to be clear rules, similar to those concerning maternity leave, to ensure that people's jobs were held open for them and that their salary would be covered by the state while performing their duties.[b] Equipped with the power to veto laws, to conduct enquiries and to force a referendum, such a Tribunate could overturn oligarchic politics and radically revitalise democracy.

There are less radical alternatives, stopping short of a randomly selected second chamber. In a unicameral system, a sprinkling of randomly selected members of the public might make a useful addition to parliamentary committees. The numbers involved would be relatively small – perhaps, for instance, a panel of six members for each parliamentary committee – but the difference to the quality of deliberation, which would

a   The Roman Senate was the council of the 'great and good', of the rulers and the ruling class. The Tribunate, in contrast, was – until the final corruption and destruction of the Republic – the self-defence institution of the non-elite plebian order.

b   An alternative to covering people's existing salary would be to pay only the median family wage, but to give those selected indefinite rights of deferral; this would make service attractive to the poor, and inconvenient – but avoidable – for the rich. The principle is simple: give the poor the opportunity to be heard in the making of laws, and watch how fast things change for the better. To pay the poor to attend, not compel the rich to do so, is, according to Aristotle, the basis of democracy. This would be a step too far, away from a healthy balance, were it not for the fact that such a chamber would be counter-balanced by an elected body in which elites are systematically favoured.

have to play closer attention to public interests and not just party political ones, could be substantial.

Another possibility is to establish randomly selected mini-assemblies in each of the parliamentary constituencies: not a second chamber, but a series of mini-chambers up and down the country. The function of these mini-chambers would be to advise, question and scrutinise the elected parliamentarians, to debate bills before Parliament, to propose bills, and to vote on non-binding resolutions. Their role would thus be merely deliberative and consultative, but they would provide a deliberative forum for public opinion, and as such their resolutions would carry a certain degree of weight – more so if the resolutions passed in each mini-chamber were aggregated into a national straw poll that could be reported to Parliament.[a] Meeting perhaps on a monthly basis in the constituency, those randomly selected to participate in mini-chambers would not have very far to travel, and would not have to dedicate themselves continually to public affairs. The barriers to participation would be low; those who might not be able to move to Edinburgh for a year in order to serve as a tribune might be able to give up one evening a month to attend their constituency mini-chamber in their local town hall. In comparison to a Tribunate, the number of participants in mini-chambers could also be much higher. In a given year, only a hundred citizens could be selected to a national Tribunate, but (assuming a Parliament with the current number of constituency and list members) more than seven thousand people a year could participate if there were to be a mini-chamber of a hundred citizens in each constituency. Over time, most people would know someone who is serving, or has served, in such a mini-chamber; people would expect to be chosen – as realistic a prospect, say, as being chosen for jury service – and, as such, would have an incentive to stay informed and engaged in public affairs.

a   This idea is a transposition to the Scottish context of the proposal for a 'Virtual National Assembly', presented by Kevin O'Leary in *Saving Democracy: A Plan for Real Representation in America* (Stanford University Press, 2006).

iv Local Democracy

There are two problems with local democracy in Scotland: it is not local and it is not very democratic. The Reid Foundation's *Silent Crisis* (2012) identified the scope and severity of the problem, and there is little to add here that would not merely echo its conclusions.[39]

The near-absence of local democracy has profound consequences for the quality of our democracy and civic life at the national as well as the local level. Writers concerned with the socio-cultural dynamics of power in Scotland, such as Lesley Riddoch,[40] have identified that the problems flowing from Scotland's centralised system of government are social and psychological as well as administrative. Lack of real control at the hands-on local level makes people passive: waiting for the distant, faceless council to do things, rather than taking initiative and responsibility through local action.

In other words, local democracy is important not only as an instrument for ensuring good local administration ('meeting needs as a cost-effective enabler of public services', as those who see through the narrow lens of neo-liberal managerialism might put it), but, more vitally, as place of participation where politics can be brought down to the scale of the park bench, the youth club and the pensioners' bus service. Centralised power teaches people to be subjects; local democracy teaches people to act as citizens, and to think in concern with fellow-citizens on a local scale. As Noam Chomsky put it:

> To be effective, democracy requires that people feel a connection to their fellow citizens, and that this connection manifests itself though a variety of non-market organizations and institutions. A vibrant political culture needs community groups, libraries, public schools, neighbourhood organisations, cooperatives, public meeting places, voluntary associations, and trade unions to provide ways for citizens to meet, communicate, and interact with their fellow citizens.[41]

Professor Antonella Valmorbida, Secretary General of the European Association for Local Democracy, notes that 'a participatory community is a successful community, not the other way around'. The practice of public participation in decision-making at the local level helps to create a community in which the common good is deliberatively discovered and co-operatively realised. In other words, *folkric* is conducive to *folkweal*, at the local as well as the national level. While it is true that participatory institutions and processes have a cost, since they may be time-consuming and difficult to organise, these costs, according to Valmorbida, should be considered 'as an investment'. Participation has beneficial effects on civic character and culture, lifting people out of apathy, 'learned powerlessness', and disregard for communal affairs. As Valmorbida puts it, 'when you participate, you care'.[42] The experience of meaningful participation shakes off the debilitating notion that public affairs are someone else's business. Participation also has other, less ethereal, benefits. When the public are widely involved in policy-making, fewer policy mistakes are made, and the misuse of public resources is minimised.[43]

There are several ways in which a new Constitution – whether for an independent Scotland, or for an autonomous Scotland within the United Kingdom – could recognise, strengthen and democratise local government. First, it could formally enshrine the role and existence of local government in the Constitution, thus giving local authorities the added legitimacy, status and protection of a constitutional rather than merely statutory foundation.[a] Second, it could define and guarantee certain powers of local authorities, either in terms of a specific list of policy areas that are devolved to them, or by a commitment in principle to subsidiarity. Third, it could deepen local government by the creation of 'burgh' and 'community' level institutions below the level of the existing 32 local authority areas. This is a measure that would do much to revitalise local community life, even if these hyper-local councils were only given, at the outset, the powers of an English civil parish. Fourth, it could give constitutional protection to the use of proportional representation in local elections, preventing a return to the one-party fiefdoms of the past, and so strengthening the democratic legitimacy of local authorities.

The internal structures of local democracy could also be strengthened

---

a   Constitutional recognition is enjoined by the European Charter of Local Self Govern-ment, 1986. As a result of ratifying this Charter, Malta and Ireland, amongst others, have amended their Constitutions to give local democracy constitutional status.

through the institution of directly elected chief executives with a leadership role. These could have broadly similar powers, in relation to cities like Glasgow and Edinburgh, Dundee and Aberdeen, as the Mayor of London has in relation to that city. The question of whether directly elected executive mayors improve local policy making and service delivery is an open one, and evidence appears to be inconclusive; their contribution to local *government*, in the strict sense of running the administration, may be limited. However, elected mayors do seem to have a more active role than indirectly elected 'council leaders' as civic leaders, spokespersons, and 'champions' of their community, and their contribution to local *governance*, in the wider sense of engagement with the private and third sectors, with the community, and with other public bodies, is substantial and beneficial. They also put a name and a face on local government, which may help promote local political engagement. It is telling, for example, that Ken Livingston and Boris Johnson are household names, even in Scotland, despite being mayors of London, while very few Scots would be able to name the Lord Provost of Scotland's capital city.

The various techniques discussed in this book for strengthening the popular against the privileged elements of society, and for shifting power from entrenched elites to ordinary citizens, can also be applied at local level, such that local democracy leads the way for reform at a national level. For example, there could be constitutional provision for local referendums, on any matter within the competence of the local authority, to be held on the proposal of the elected mayor, or by a decision of the council, or even at the request of a certain number of voters.

More radically, the idea of a mini-chamber selected by random lot could be incorporated into the Constitution's local government provisions. There could be, for example, a Citizens' Assembly in each local authority area, selected by random lot, and responsible for overseeing the decisions of the council. The Citizens' Assembly might have the authority to propose by-laws, to decide on neighbourhood budgets, or to put controversial council decisions to a referendum. This is a speculative idea, and the effect creating randomly selected Citizens' Assembly, in terms of improving the quality and performance of local government and in terms of promoting democratic participation, can only be guessed at. Yet there are precedents, in some South American cities, that suggest that such bodies, if properly established and resourced, can have a beneficial effect, particularly empowering the poorest communities that are otherwise likely to be ignored.[a]

v Democratising Parties

In a well-functioning democracy there are many channels through which the people's voice and influence might be directed: at the ballot box in elections and referendums, in court, on the streets in demonstrations, through trade unions, through the engagement of civic, social and religious institutions, by means of petitions, at hustings, and now also online through social media. In a parliamentary democracy, however, political parties are major conduits of public opinion, which perform vital roles as forums for political debate, the formation of policy, the aggregation of interests and the representation of the people.

The organisation of political parties, therefore, ought not to be left to chance; in a democracy, the internal structure and ethos of parties must themselves be democratic. The 'personal party', which is dominated by its sole founder-leader-financier, is a particularly destructive force. Such parties, having no principles other than the ambition of their leaders and the private interests of their funders, are not proper instruments for public participation or deliberation. The members of such a party do not join in order to serve a principled vision of the common good in what small way they can, but to gain preferment. In effect, such a party is merely a corrupt faction, and quite incompatible with the ideals of a civic democracy.[b]

In recognition of this, constitutional provisions regulating the duties and internal structures of parties are now found in several Constitutions, especially in those of countries newly emerging from authoritarian rule. Germany is a pioneer in this field. In order to prevent a resurgence of the one-party rule that had destroyed the Weimar Republic, the post-war

---

a For a discussion of 'participatory budgeting' in the Brazilian city of Porto Alegre and for information on the use of random lot to select Citizens' Assemblies in Canadian Provinces, see: Smith, G. *op. cit.*

b The rise of the 'personal party', which is little more than an electoral machine for its leader, has had a deleterious effect on the quality of democracy in several European nations. For a discussion on the effect of Berlusconi's party in Italy, see: Viroli, M. and Bobbio, N. *The Idea of the Republic* (Polity Press, 2003).

Constitution acknowledged the role of political parties in 'the formation of the political will of the people', permitted their free formation, required them to adhere to 'democratic principles' in their internal organisation, and required their assets and sources of funding be open to public scrutiny. Parties 'that, by reason of their aims or the behaviour of their adherents, seek to undermine or abolish the free democratic basic order or to endanger the existence of the Federal Republic of Germany' could be banned on the grounds of unconstitutionality by a decision of the Federal Constitutional Court.[44] Other, more recent Constitutions have gone even further in recognising the need for the regulation of political parties. For example, the 1997 Constitution of Poland requires the state to 'ensure freedom for the creation and functioning of political parties' while demanding that their financing be open to public inspection. Parties that are totalitarian in purpose, or secretive in their membership and methods, are expressly prohibited.[45]

Fig. 4 Example: Recognition and Restriction of Political Parties

Basic Law of the Federal Republic of Germany: Art. 21

1   Political parties shall participate in the formation of the political will of the people. They may be freely established. Their internal organisation must conform to democratic principles. They must publicly account for their assets and for the sources and use of their funds.

2   Parties that, by reason of their aims or the behavior of their adherents, seek to undermine or abolish the free democratic basic order or to endanger the existence of the Federal Republic of Germany shall be unconstitutional. The Federal Constitutional Court shall rule on the question of unconstitutionality.

3   Details shall be regulated by federal laws.

Constitution of Poland, Arts. 11 & 13

11(1) The Republic of Poland shall ensure freedom for the creation and functioning of political parties. Political parties shall be founded on the principle of voluntariness and upon the equality of Polish citizens, and their purpose shall be to influence the formulation of the policy of the State by democratic means.

2   The financing of political parties shall be open to public inspection.

13   Political parties and other organizations whose programmes are based upon totalitarian methods and the modes of activity of nazism, fascism and communism, as well as those whose programmes or activities sanction racial or national hatred, the application of violence for the purpose of obtaining power or to influence the State policy, or provide for the secrecy of their own structure or membership, shall be forbidden.

The effect of such constitutional rules is to change the nature of the party from an essentially private organisation – a select club, which just so happens to include people who are in, or contending for, high public office, but which does not have to be publicly accountable in terms of its structures, financing, or aims – to a quasi-public institution whole role, where duties and internal organisation are to a greater or lesser extent regulated by the state. The prohibition of parties in particular opens up difficult questions of political theory; by limiting the range of ideological choice available to both parties and voters, it could be seen as an inherently undemocratic mechanism. However, provided that proper safeguards are in place, such as a trustworthy and non-partisan judicial authority to enforce the ban, it can be justified on covenantal grounds. The German Constitution has excluded anti-democratic forces from the political system in order to give effect to its covenantal commitment to certain primary normative values, such as human dignity and democracy, that are binding upon all. To exclude opponents of democracy is not, therefore, to limit democracy, but to protect it from self-destruction. Likewise, the rule that funding must be publicly accounted for, and sources of funding acknowledged, is not an invasion of the right to privacy, but an expression of a very public covenantal commitment to a democracy in which secret payments cannot buy parties or politicians.[a]

A basic degree of internal party democracy might be guaranteed by requiring that parties, in order to be registered with the Electoral Commission, must select their leaders by one-member-one-vote. Party leadership elections (the closest that a parliamentary system usually gets to a 'primary' election for the Prime Minister) might also be subject to funding rules designed to protect party leaders from reliance on rich, powerful donors.[b]

It would be harder to apply internal party democracy to candidate

---

a   Beyond donation limits, transparency rules, bans on foreign or corporate contributions, equal access to the media, and other means of reforming campaign finance, there is the option of public funding. Although there are some very attractive arguments in favour of public funding, great care must be taken, if this route is considered, not to go too far in making parties agents of the state; they should be agents of society for the control of the state, not agents of the state for the control of society.

b   One major difference between a party leadership election and a primary is that primaries are often open to all *supporters* of a party, or even to all registered voters, whereas the norm in leadership elections is to limit the electorate to paid-up *members* of the party.

selection, but if the constitution or electoral law were to mandate parties to nominate a 'balanced ticket' of candidates for Parliament, as discussed in the third section of this chapter, the parties would have to consider such factors in their candidate selection processes. This might at least encourage parties to adopt more open processes, and to cast the net a little wider in the search for suitable talent.

The inclusion of such provisions in a Scottish Constitution – while obviously not a complete or flawless solution – could help to prevent the domination of the political system by corrupt, personalist or anti-democratic parties. The constitutional regulation of party funding and accounting, coupled with a constitutional mandate to the effect that Parliament has the right to enact laws in pursuit of such ends (for example, by limiting donations or banning foreign or corporate donations) would assert the primacy of the public interest in these matters, and prevent the courts from declaring such regulations unconstitutional. The *Model Constitution*, for example, gives the Electoral Commission a specific mandate to ensure compliance with the laws regulating campaign spending and political donations, as well as ensuring the regular auditing of the parties' accounts.

While on the subject of internal party democracy, something must be said about discipline. Some Constitutions, including those of South Africa, India, Bangladesh and Fiji, contain rules against 'floor crossing'. Party discipline is enforced by a constitutional sanction that punishes members with the loss of their seat if they vote against the party line. Such a provision undermines the role of backbenchers in holding the Government to account; it weakens Parliament by weakening the discretion and integrity of individual members. It removes from the political scene that most important character: the slightly awkward, idiosyncratic, rebellious back-bencher who is willing to ask difficult questions and to put principle before party. This is not to say that party discipline is unimportant, or that there should be no party whip; party discipline provides the unity of purpose that is essential to the proper functioning of parliamentary democracy. Its absence would lead to confusion, corruption, and a lack of accountability for the policy and performance of the Government. However, informal forms of party discipline are already strong enough, and there is no need for constitutional reinforcement; if anything, a constitutional rule to guarantee the right of members to vote according to conscience would be more beneficial.

CHAPTER FIVE

How can the Constitution promote good governance and accountability?

THIS BOOK IS ORGANISED around the central theme that *folkric* and *folkweal* are intimately and necessarily connected. Reason and experience show that the common good is more likely to emerge from a broad, inclusive and participatory political process than from one dominated by narrow, elite and partisan interests. The Constitution has a vital role to play in structuring and defining that participatory process, and in preventing it from being captured or distorted by incumbents or by powerful groups or individuals.

The previous chapter introduced some ways in which a Scottish Constitution could use alternative forms of representation and public participation – from adjustments to the electoral system to the creation of a Tribunate chosen by random lot – to increase the inclusivity of the political process. This chapter examines ways in which a combination of constitutionally prescribed checks, both inside and outside of Parliament, could make those who exercise power more accountable to the people and more responsible for their actions. It also discusses how the Constitution could improve processes of deliberation and decision-making within and between the institutions of the state, so as to filter out bad decisions.

i Parliamentary Scrutiny and Fourth Branch Institutions

The usual pattern of policy-making in the United Kingdom is for decisions to be taken by small groups of Ministers, partisan advisors, senior civil servants and lobbyists, meeting behind closed doors.[a] For the most part,

---

a   For an analysis of this tendency, and its ill-effects, see King, A. & Crewe, I. *The Blunders of Our Governments* (Oneworld Publications: London. 2014).

these decisions are presented to Parliament, to the public, and often even to the Cabinet itself, as done deals. Tony Blair introduced the notion of 'sofa government', which gave this long-standing practice of secretive decision-making a benign, cosy, spin-doctored glow. We should not be so easily deceived. Whether we are governed from the sofa of Downing Street or the dining table at Claridge's (or, for that matter, the Edinburgh New Club), such informal and private decision-making is a sure sign of a corrupt state. Whenever policy decisions can be taken in private, without public scrutiny and without effective opposition, misgovernment is the evitable result.

Constitutional government is the antithesis of sofa government. By structuring political institutions and regulating decision-making processes, a Constitution can ensure that decisions are arrived at through a process that is public, inclusive, deliberative and non-arbitrary. Moreover, the constitution can ensure that these processes are stable, formal, and dependable, and never dependent for their existence or effectiveness on the good will or indulgence of particular persons.

In a parliamentary democracy (even one that contains important elements of direct and participatory democracy), the preeminent site of such discussion, deliberation and decision-making will be Parliament. Some critics of constitutionalism have argued that a Constitution undermines the position of Parliament. This is not (or need not be) the case. A good Constitution, in upholding the sovereignty of the people, and in recognising a role for the judiciary as a protector of procedural and substantive rights, necessarily limits the absolutism of Parliament. However, it will also establish the centrality of Parliament as the great public council of the realm and protect Parliament in the performance of its duties. One of the most important of these duties is to ensure that power is at all times subject to the gaze and scrutiny of the people, and that those who wield power have to give a regular public account of their stewardship. Many of the detailed rules about how Parliament makes use of its capacity must necessarily be determined by Parliament's own Standing Orders, but certain basic provisions should be set out in the Constitution.

In particular, a good Constitution can define Parliament's composition, internal structures, and rules of procedure, in a way that protects the autonomy of Parliament vis-à-vis the Government and strengthens the capacity of Parliament as a legislative, scrutinising, deliberative and representative body. The constitutional status of such basic rules ensures that they cannot be set aside by a parliamentary majority that seeks to limit the role or influence of the opposition. The *Model Constitution* proposed various measures in this vein, such as: (i) reserving a certain portion of parliamentary time for Opposition business and Private Members' business; (ii) granting investigatory powers to committees; (iii) ensuring proportional representation on committees; (iv) maintaining the non-partisan status of the Presiding Officer; and (iv) placing agenda-setting and timetabling powers in an all-party Parliamentary Bureau.

These measures – none of which are very radical, and most of which already exist in the Scottish Parliament as a matter of law or practice – are simply the constitutional guarantees necessary for Parliament to protect itself from incumbent manipulation, authoritarian backsliding and corruption, and so, in turn, to protect the people from these evils. They ensure constitutionally recognised roles for the opposition, minor parties, backbenchers, and committees, in scrutinising and overseeing the Government. Members of Parliament, shielded and empowered by these constitutional rules, would be able to ensure that public decisions are thoroughly debated and considered in an open, publicised forum, and that power is always publicly held to account.

In addition to parliamentary mechanisms of scrutiny and accountability, most modern constitutions establish extra-parliamentary bodies, of an independent and non-partisan nature, to protect the *res publica* from authoritarian backsliding, incumbent manipulation and corruption. These bodies, which are sometimes collectively known as 'fourth branch' institutions, typically possess regulatory, supervisory quasi-judicial or appointive powers, but do not fit into the traditional *trias politica* (legislature, executive, judiciary). Thus a modern democratic Constitution will typically include institutions such an Ombudsman, to whom complaints of maladministration can be brought, an Auditor-General to oversee the administration of public finances, bodies such as an Electoral Commission to ensure the integrity and impartiality of the electoral process, perhaps a Public Service Commission to maintain the professionalism and neutrality of the civil service, and a Judicial Appointments Commission to ensure the independence of the Judiciary. Some Constitutions also include a

Broadcasting Commission to oversee the administration public broadcasting, an Anti-Corruption Commission to maintain integrity in public life, a Human Rights Commission, and, in some federal countries, a Finance Commission to ensure an equitable fiscal distribution between different parts of the country.

Fourth branch institutions, with the notable exception of an Electoral Commission and a Broadcasting Commission, are not absent in Scotland. In the case of the judiciary, for example, the Judicial and Courts (Scotland) Act 2008, places the Judicial Appointments Board for Scotland on a statutory basis. Likewise, although there is no Public Service Commission for Scotland, there is a Public Appointments Commissioner, appointed by Parliament on a statutory basis, who performs some of the functions that a Public Service Commission might typically perform. The problem, rather, is that these institutions and mechanisms, being dependent on ordinary laws, lack constitutional protection. There is nothing – except perhaps self-restraint – to defend them from a reckless Government in command of a loyal parliamentary majority. If they are to perform their functions properly, fourth-branch institutions should enjoy constitutionally guaranteed autonomy: members should be appointed in a cross-partisan or non-partisan way, with involvement, where practicable, from the opposition parties, so that the Government cannot pack these institutions with their own appointees. Their members should have security of tenure and quasi-judicial guarantees of independence. They should be excluded from all party-political activities. None of these rules should be dependent on statutory provisions that the governing majority could change at will.

This raises a more general point. Constitutions do not necessarily have to change things: sometimes, the best they can do – and all they need to do – is to protect what exists from being undone. When a new Constitution is adopted in a newly democratising country, it must establish democracy; when a Constitution is adopted in an existing democracy, it might attempt to improve and deepen democracy but, above all, it must defend democracy. Therefore, in so far as fourth-branch institutions exist in Scotland on a statutory basis, a future Constitution should recognise and consolidate their autonomy. Where they do not exist, the Constitution, and not ordinary statutes, should establish them on a secure, independent and non-partisan basis, such that they have substantial autonomy from the Government and from the parliamentary majority.

Fig. 5 Example: The Electoral Commission in Malta

1   There shall be an Electoral Commission for Malta.

2   The Electoral Commission shall consist of a Chairman, who shall be the person for the time being holding the office of Chief Electoral Commissioner and who shall be appointed to that office from the public service, and such number of members not being less than four as may be prescribed by any law for the time being in force in Malta.

3   The members of the Electoral Commission shall be appointed by the President, acting in accordance with the advice of the Prime Minister, given after he has consulted the Leader of the Opposition.

4   A person shall not be qualified to hold office as a member of the Electoral Commission if he is a Minister, a Parliamentary Secretary, a member of, or a candidate for election to, the House of Representatives or a public officer.

5   Subject to the provisions of this section, a member of the Electoral Commission shall vacate his office –

   a   at the expiration of three years from the date of his appointment or at such earlier time as may be specified in the instrument by which he was appointed; or

   b   if any circumstances arise that, if he were not a member of the Commission, would cause him to be disqualified for appointment as such.

6   Subject to the provisions of subsection (7) of this section, a member of the Electoral Commission may be removed from office by the President acting in accordance with the advice of the Prime Minister.

7   A member of the Electoral Commission shall not be removed from office except for inability to discharge the functions of his office (whether arising from infirmity of mind or body or any other cause) or for misbehaviour.

8   If the office of a member of the Electoral Commission is vacant or if a member is for any reason unable to perform the functions of his office, the President, acting in accordance with the advice of the Prime Minister, given after he has consulted the Leader of the Opposition, may appoint a person who is qualified to be appointed to be a member to be a temporary member of the Commission; and any person so appointed shall, subject to the provisions of subsections (5), (6) and (7) of this section, cease to be such a member when a person has been appointed to fill the vacancy or, as the case may be, when the member who was unable to perform the functions of his office resumes those functions.

9   In the exercise of its functions under this Constitution the Electoral Commission shall not be subject to the direction or control of any other person or authority.

An objection may be made that the members of such boards and commissions are not representative of society. They are usually recruited from the ranks of the great and good, with a preponderance of retired judges and former senior civil servants, with perhaps ex-politicians whose careers never quite peaked and occasionally a few safe academics thrown into the mix. Although intended to be neutral and non-partisan, it is inevitable that these members will bring into their positions certain values, attitudes and assumptions that reflect their place in society and their experience in life. To a greater or lesser extent, such objections can be countered by ensuring that the mode of appointment to fourth branch institutions is fair and transparent, and that political biases are at least balanced out. The Model Constitution recommended, for example, that three members of each independent commission be appointed on a bi-partisan basis on the joint nomination of the Prime Minister and the Leader of the Opposition, while four be elected by Parliament by proportional representation. This is not the only, or even perhaps the best, way of constituting such bodies, but it seems a satisfactory one.

Constitutions also can prescribe measures intended to broaden participation by marginalised groups in fourth branch institutions. For example, the Judicial Service Commission of Kenya, under the constitution of 2010, includes provisions to ensure gender balance, while the South African Judicial Service Commission is required by the constitution to consider the need to represent the racial balance of the country in making appointments to the judiciary. It would not be difficult to introduce similar provisions, if required, into the design of fourth branch institutions in a future Scottish (or even UK-wide) Constitution.

In contemporary constitution-making around the world there is perhaps a tendency to create too many independent fourth branch institutions. It is as if, having recognised the usefulness of such institutions, constitution-makers have come to regard them as a panacea, adopting a 'the more the merrier' approach. But in this regard, as in most other aspects of consti-tutional design, there is a need for balance and moderation. Too much constitutional engineering can be almost as bad as too little. As well as adding to the costs of administration, an over-proliferation of fourth branch institutions may weaken elected legislatures as the proper institutions of public accountability and, rather than protecting and reinforcing the demo-cratic process, weaken it. To guard against this tendency, it is possible to establish, if not a firm principle, at least a good 'rule of thumb' in determining whether an independent fourth branch institution is required.

The purpose of such institutions is to insulate the 'state as such' from the government of the day, and thereby to prevent the government from using the supposedly neutral instruments of the state for partisan or corrupt ends. As such, the use of fourth branch institutions should, in general, be limited to situations in which they have an appointative, administrative or regulatory function that needs to be separated from the general exercise of executive power, particularly in relation to the judiciary, the civil service (including, where this is not a local function, the police) and the electoral process. Where a fourth branch institution is being considered simply to perform a monitoring or scrutiny role, without any independent appointative or administrative function, it would probably be better, in most cases, to rely instead on a parliamentary committee.

A final consideration is to provide for the retrospective accountability of those who have left office.[1] In this respect, some of the classical, medieval and renaissance republics were more advanced than contemporary democracies. In Athens, for example, it was customary to conduct a 'scrutiny' of a former magistrate after the end of their term of office.[2] In the Roman Republic, 'censors' were elected once every five years, whose duties included performing a retrospective scrutiny of senatorial conduct, and expelling from the Senate those whose behaviour rendered them unfit for office.[3]

Inspired by the Roman example, a scrutiny tribunal called the 'Council of Censors' was created by the 1776 Constitution of Pennsylvania.[4] This body possessed a range of judicial and quasi-judicial functions related to the retrospective scrutiny of public officials, the protection of the Constitution, and the auditing of public finances. Two unique features distinguished it from other scrutiny institutions: its popular election, and its sporadic existence. The Council was directly elected the people once every seven years, to serve for a term of one year. Its members, therefore, stood outside of ordinary politics, acting upon the political system, but not being a regular part of it. The year of electing the Censors would be a fallow year for the harvesters of corruption, and a year of jubilee for the people. The *res publica* would at the end of every seven years be set free from its bondage to corruption, and liberty would be proclaimed throughout all the land unto all the inhabitants thereof. According to the account of James Madison in The Federalist Papers (No. 48), it was quite effective at bringing corruptions, infringements of rights, and abuses of power to light, although less effective at rectifying these problems.[5] In any case, this fascinating experiment did not last long enough to establish its position or to prove its worth, as it was abolished by a conservative reform of the Pennsylvania Constitution in 1790.

A less radical provision (but one more easily adapted to Scotland's circumstances) exists in the Constitution of Sweden. This establishes a 'Committee on the Constitution' with a broad remit to scrutinise the legality and propriety of ministerial conduct. What distinguishes this committee from other forms of parliamentary scrutiny, is its power to bring charges against both serving and former ministers for criminal acts committed by them when in office. The constitutional existence of such an institution might have changed Tony Blair's calculations in the lead up to the 2003–2011 Iraq war. If he had known even after leaving office he could be subject to a public investigation that might lead directly to criminal charges, perhaps he might have conducted himself differently.

Fig. 6 Examples: Scrutiny Tribunals – Actual and Historical Models

---

Swedish Instrument of Government (Constitution), Chapter 13

1 The Committee on the Constitution shall examine ministers' performance of their official duties and the handling of Government business. For its examination, the Committee is entitled to have access to the records of decisions taken in Government matters and to the documents pertaining to such matters, as well as any other Government documents that the Committee deems necessary for its examination. Another parliamentary committee or a member of the Parliament is entitled to raise in writing with the Committee on the Constitution any issue relating to a minister's performance of his or her official duties or the handling of Government business.

2 Where warranted, but at least once a year, the Committee on the Constitution shall communicate to the Parliament any observations it has found worthy of attention in connection with its examination. The Parliament may make a formal statement to the Government as a consequence of this.

3 A person who is currently, or who has been previously, a minister may only be held accountable for a criminal act committed in the performance of his or her ministerial duties only if he or she has grossly neglected his or her official duty by committing the criminal act. A decision to institute criminal proceedings shall be taken by the Committee on the Constitution and the case tried before the Supreme Court.

> **Constitution of Pennsylvania, 1776, Section 47**
>
> ... there shall be chosen by ballot by the freemen in each city and county respectively... in every seventh year... two persons in each city and county... to be called the Council of Censors;
>
> And whose duty it shall be to enquire whether the constitution has been preserved inviolate in every part; and whether the legislative and executive branches of government have performed their duty as guardians of the people, or assumed to themselves, or exercised other or greater powers than they are entitled to by the constitution:
>
> They are also to enquire whether the public taxes have been justly laid and collected in all parts of this commonwealth, in what manner the public monies have been disposed of, and whether the laws have been duly executed.
>
> For these purposes they shall have power to send for persons, papers, and records; they shall have authority to pass public censures, to order impeachments, and to recommend to the legislature the repealing such laws as appear to them to have been enacted contrary to the principles of the constitution.
>
> These powers they shall continue to have, for and during the space of one year from the day of their election and no longer.

ii Recall and Popular Dissolution

A recall vote is a direct vote that enables the people to remove an elected representative or official between scheduled elections. The recall mechanism is usually directed against a representative who has exhibited unsatisfactory conduct or lack of integrity in office. It strengthens public control over the behaviour of our elected representatives, and thereby acts as a popular check against actions that are contrary to the common good.

In response to the 2009 parliamentary expenses scandal, and in a climate of increasing distrust between people and the political establishment,[6] a commitment to the introduction of a statutory recall mechanism for the House of Commons was included in the coalition programme of the Conservative-Liberal United Kingdom Government formed in 2010. The recall bill was eventually passed into law, but in such a diluted form as to be almost meaningless as a means of public control.[7] Under the Recall of MPs Act, a recall petition can be launched only if a Member of Parliament is given a prison sentence or is suspended from the House for at least 21 days, meaning that the initiative to trigger a recall vote rests, not with the people, but with the judiciary or with the House itself. The effectiveness of such a recall mechanism, as a deterrent against misbehaviour and as a means of enabling popular control over the conduct of representatives, is therefore likely to be minimal.

What follows is a sketch of a stronger, more effective and more genuinely popular recall mechanism that could be adopted in a Scottish Constitution (whether for an independent Scotland, or for an autonomous Scotland within the United Kingdom). A certain number of registered electors could initiate the process for the recall of a Member of the Scottish Parliament by means of a petition to the Presiding Officer. This threshold number of signatures could be set at ten per cent of the total electorate in a constituency seat, or five per cent in the more geographically dispersed regional list seats: a percentage large enough to discourage frivolous petitions, but not so large as to make the process prohibitively expensive or time-consuming. The petition would have to claim constitutionally permissible grounds for recall, but these should be considerably wider than those envisaged in the House of Commons' bill (they might include, for example, breach of the Code of Conduct or other misbehaviour, even if this does not lead to criminal prosecution or suspension from Parliament). The Presiding Officer would then be required to verify the petition. If she or he finds it to be in order, the member concerned would be formally notified, and would then have an opportunity to challenge the recall petition as malicious or vexatious. Such challenge might be decided by the Electoral Commission, with the possibility of an appeal to the Supreme Court. If the recall petition is unchallenged, or if the challenge is rejected, the Presiding Officer would then set a date for the recall vote to take place in the constituency or region concerned.[a]

There would have to be a relatively high threshold for the removal of a sitting member – say, an absolute majority of the total electorate in the constituency or region, or perhaps, a little less rigorously, an absolute majority of votes cast amounting to not less than 40 per cent of the

---

a   The main difference between this proposal and that outlined in the (unenacted) Recall bill presented in the Westminster Parliament is that parliamentarians would not decide on the admissibility of a recall petition. In the event of a challenge by a sitting member, the decision of whether a recall petition has demonstrated sufficient grounds would rest with an external and independent body.

electorate. This would indicate that the member has forfeited the trust of a substantial proportion of the community. In the case of constituency members, such a majority voting for recall of the member would lead automatically to a by-election. In the case of regional list members, the next available candidate from the same party on the list presented at the most recent general election would accede to office.[a]

In a parliamentary democracy, where Ministers are members of Parliament, there is an additional complication. What happens if a recalled member is a Minister? In that case, their recall from office is not simply a matter of a local community removing its representative; it has national implications. The simplest solution is to make Ministers, or at least the Prime Minister and Deputy Prime Minister, immune from recall votes, although one might argue that this immunity would limit, to some extent, the power of the recall mechanism as a way of controlling and restraining political leaders. Another possibility is to make recall votes concerning a Minister into national votes; the petition might be started and submitted by the voters in the Minister's constituency or region, but the vote would take place on a nationwide basis. This would certainly be a powerful, if rather blunt, weapon in the hands of the people. Depending on how wide or narrow the criteria for recall are set, this could be used as a sort of popular veto power to throw Ministers out of office.[b] A further possibility would be to state in the Constitution that a recall only affects a person's membership of Parliament – and, not, if they happen to be a Minister, their Ministerial office. This would need the rule requiring Ministers to be Members of Parliament to be slackened, such that it would be at least theoretically possible (if politically difficult) for them to continue as a Minister even if recalled from Parliament. The *Model Constitution* envisaged up to a third of the Council of Ministers being appointed from outside of Parliament,[c] while in several countries a

---

a   Recall need not be restricted to members of Parliament. The same principles, and a similar process, might apply to members of local councils.

b   There are more than a few people, I should imagine, who would like to do this to George Osborne or Iain Duncan-Smith, and there are probably also more than a few who would like to do this to Alex Salmond.

c   *Model Constitution*, Art. IV, Sect. 8: 'The Ministers shall be appointed from amongst the Members of Parliament; provided, however, that up to one-third of the Ministers may be appointed from outside Parliament, on account of their specialist knowledge, experience, and qualifications.'

Minister may hold office for a limited period without being a Member of Parliament.[a]

There is another form of recall – which might be better termed 'popular dissolution' – that differs in two ways from outlined above: (i) it is directed against Parliament as a whole, and not a particular member; (ii) it may be invoked on grounds of general policy, as a way of bringing Parliament before the people for a vote on its record and conduct, without having to demonstrate any misconduct on behalf of any particular member. In Latvia, for example, one tenth of the electorate may initiate a petition for a referendum on the dissolution of Parliament. This then leads to a referendum on the question of dissolution. If a majority of the voters support dissolution, on a turnout of at least two thirds of the number who voted in the last parliamentary election, then Parliament is dissolved and a general election is held. In the Latvian case, this provision is subject to several temporal safeguards: it may not be activated during the first year or the last year of the Parliament's four-year term, nor may it be activated during the last six months of the (mostly ceremonial) President's term of office.[b] It may not be activated twice during a period of six months.

Fig. 7 Example: Popular Dissolution procedure in Latvia

Constitution of Latvia: Art. 14

Not less than one tenth of electors has the right to initiate a national referendum regarding recalling of the Parliament.

If the majority of voters and at least two thirds of the number of the voters who participated in the last parliamentary elections vote in the national referendum regarding recalling of the Parliament, then the Parliament shall be deemed recalled.

The right to initiate a national referendum regarding recalling of the Parliament may not be exercised one year after the convening of the Parliament and one year before the end of the term of office of the Parliament, during the last six months of the term of office of the President, as well as earlier than six months after the previous national referendum regarding recalling of the Parliament.

---

a   In Australia, for example, this period is three months (Constitution of Australia, Sect. 64).

b   The Latvian President has similar right, under Article 48 of the Constitution, to initiate a referendum on the dissolution of Parliament. To prevent its abuse, this comes with the catch that if the people vote against dissolution, the President is thereby

A popular dissolution provision would make Parliament accountable to the people at all times, and not merely once every few years. If the parliamentary majority were to pursue an unpopular course of policy, the people could do something about it without having to wait for the next election; a petition for dissolution could be organised, a referendum on dissolution held, and then, if the people so decide, an extraordinary election could take place. The usual practice whereby a party reneges on its promises once elected, secure in the knowledge that their terms of office are longer than voters' memories, would be much harder to get away with. However, popular dissolution is a very extreme measure. It has an 'all or nothing' effect, which could escalate political crises. A right to recall individual parliamentarians coupled with an abrogative or minority-veto referendum mechanism could achieve the same result in a less disruptive way.

iii Prime Ministerial Term Limits

The accumulation of power in a few hands, however popular, skilled or well-meaning, is always potentially dangerous. When that power is kept in the *same* few hands, over a long period, the risk becomes greater. There are very few people in history who have long held high office without becoming arrogant, distant, and obsessed with their own power and survival. Those long in high office gradually lose touch with reality. Their world consists of ministerial meetings, secret exchanges, diplomatic maneuvers and fawning courtiers. Too often, they turn their backs on the people, and ignore the grievances that they were chosen by the suffrage of the people to redress.

Enforced 'rotation' is the classical solution to this problem. Terms of office should be short and re-election restricted. In its most thorough form, rotation in office approaches the ideal of democratic equality: ruling and being ruled in turn. In the Florentine Republic, for example, members of the highest ruling council, the *Signoria*, held office only for two months,

---

automatically removed from office. Unlike petition-initiated popular dissolution, which would be easily adaptable to Scottish conditions, it is difficult to see how this presidential power could be adapted to a system in which the head of state is hereditary, and therefore lacks even an indirect democratic mandate. One of the arguments for replacing the monarchy with a *mostly ceremonial* president is that they need not be *solely ceremonial*; they might also possess such 'balancing' powers.

and were thereafter ineligible for immediate re-election.[8] The Chartist reformers of the 19th century demanded annual parliamentary elections for much the same reason: to prevent the accumulation of power in the same hands for long periods.

Such very short terms, however, while consistent with a system based on sortation, would be inconsistent with the stability of policy in a representative system based on election. Those in office must be given a sufficient lease of power to enable them to fulfil their election promises, and near-constant electioneering would be a distraction from governing. Because of this, terms of office in all contemporary democracies are measured in years rather than months.[a] Most European and Commonwealth democracies hold regular general elections on a four-year or five-cycle; Australia and New Zealand are exceptional in having three-year terms.[b]

However, the principle of rotation in office still survives, albeit in a modern and attenuated form. In many presidential democracies, the president cannot be re-elected for more than a set number of terms (usually two, in some cases only one). It could be argued that to deny an incumbent leader the chance of re-election, on the basis of a blind constitutional rule, is a restriction on the people's choice, and is therefore undemocratic. However, a living democracy requires more than just a free, regular and popular choice of leaders; it also requires that leaders be limited and balanced in such a way that the dominance of particular persons over the state cannot be established. The enforced rotation of office by means of term limits prevents the personalisation of power and puts temporal restraints upon its exercise. Term limits send a message that the *res publica* is a 'public thing', and that no person, regardless of how great their poll-ratings, their pride or their ambition, is indispensable.

A periodic change of chief executive also has other, pragmatic, advantages. Almost every first-term incumbent brings at least some energy,

---

a   The tiny Republic of San Marino, which elects its two captains-regent for six-month terms, is an insignificant – although glorious and fascinating – exception.

b   One sleight of hand to be aware of is that Westminster extended the life of the Scottish Parliament elected in 2011 from four years to five, mainly for reasons of its own administrative and political convenience (to prevent 2015 Scottish and Westminster elections being held on the same day). This *ad hoc* change should not be allowed to set a precedent for the extension of the normal parliamentary term from four to five years.

drive, fresh ideas and new vision to the office. By their third term, most leaders are exhausted, out of touch, barren of ideas, haunted by their mistakes and dogged by scandals and corruption. A forced circulation in office prevents such stagnation: it pumps oxygenated blood around the body politic.

In parliamentary systems, however, such limits on re-election were traditionally seen as impracticable. By the conventional rules of parliamentary government, Prime Ministers, being formally appointed by the Head of State, do not serve for a 'term of office', but continue in office for as long as they maintain the support of a majority in Parliament. Nevertheless, if the Prime Minister is formally appointed after each parliamentary election – as has been the case with the First Minister of Scotland since 1999 – then term limits are both possible and consistent with the system of government as a whole. In the Cayman Islands, for example, the Premier is formally chosen after each legislative election, on the basis of the election results, and no one may be renominated as Premier who has served as such for two previous consecutive terms.

Fig. 8 Example: Prime Ministerial Term Limits in the Cayman Islands

---

1 The Premier shall be appointed by the Governor as follows.

2 Where a political party gains a majority of the seats of elected members of the Legislative Assembly, the Governor shall appoint as Premier the elected member of the Assembly recommended by a majority of the elected members who are members of that party.

3 If no political party gains such a majority or if no recommendation is made under subsection (2), the Speaker shall cause a ballot to be held among the elected members of the Legislative Assembly to determine which elected member commands the support of the majority of such members, and shall record the vote of each member voting; and, where such a ballot is held, the Governor shall appoint as Premier the elected member who obtains a majority of the votes of the elected members.

4 Notwithstanding subsections (2) and (3), the Governor shall not appoint as Premier a person who has held office as Premier during two consecutive parliamentary terms unless at least one parliamentary term has expired since he or she last held that office; and for the purposes of this subsection a parliamentary term shall be deemed to be a period commencing when the Legislative Assembly first meets after being constituted under this Constitution or after its dissolution at any time, and terminating when the Assembly is next dissolved.

The constitutional limitation of a Prime Minister to two terms of four years should be given serious consideration in a new Scottish Constitution, whether for an independent state or an autonomous Scotland within the United Kingdom. It would offer a simple, practical and safe way of preventing the personal domination of the polity. It would also give Prime Ministers an honourable way to retire without losing an election, and might therefore discourage them from clinging to office when they really should make way for fresher minds and cleaner hands.

It might be argued that a Prime Minister in his or her second and final term would have no incentive to remain responsive to the people, since the greatest prize – that of re-election – would be barred to them. However, the hope of leaving a well-respected legacy and of being succeeded by a colleague of their own party, rather than losing the election to an opposition party, should be a sufficient incentive. Party colleagues, too, wishing to retain their own seats, would be sure to exert a beneficial pressure on a final-term incumbent.

If combined with a rule requiring the election of party leaders by one-member-one-vote (discussed in the previous chapter), a two-term limit would also allow for the periodic renewal of parties. If a Prime Minister is near the end of his or her second – and constitutionally last – term of office, there would have to be a leadership election before the forthcoming general election in order to select the Prime Ministerial candidate who will lead the party into that election. This would end the practice whereby new leaders are invariably chosen only after an electoral defeat, at a time when a party is focused on its internal problems, and not before an election, when public issues are more prominent.

iv Guarding the Guardians: Supervision of the Military and Security Services

Democratic thinkers have long recognised that there is a close relationship between 'good arms' and 'good laws'.[9] The essential question is how can a democratic country defend itself, through organised military force, without allowing that organised military force to dominate and undermine the essence of the democratic order that it is supposed to protect? The military must be sufficiently effective to secure peace and political liberty against foreign invasion, but without exposing the state to the risks of military coups. The right regulation and democratic control of the armed forces, including intelligence and security services, is not, therefore, a mere matter of military convenience, but one of vital constitutional significance. This is particularly so in our age, as the creeping 'securitisation' agenda – characterised by the centralised control of modern military technology, global and national surveillance networks, 'extraordinary rendition', outsourced torture, drone strikes, and a pervading air of fear and paranoia – poses a grave threat to democracy and civil liberties.

From antiquity to the 19th century, the preferred system of military organisation amongst supporters of political liberty was one in which the people would be directly responsible for the defence of the *res publica*.[10] The citizen-body as a whole, or a major part thereof, would be armed, trained and equipped for defensive actions: every citizen would be a soldier, and every soldier a citizen first and foremost. In principle, such a citizens' army would ensure, first, that the distribution of political power guaranteed by the Constitution would be reinforced by a distribution of military force, and second, that the army would reflect the state's democratic values and ethos. The idea was that a citizens' army, being one with the people, could not be used as an instrument of repression and would not be capable of launching a coup.

In Scotland, these principles were expressed by Andrew Fletcher of Saltoun (1655–1716), who, in opposing the Union of the Parliaments in the early 18th century, made a series of constitutional proposals intended to secure the liberty of Scotland under a loose Union of the Crowns. He proposed that 'no regiment or company of horse, foot or dragoons, be kept on foot in peace or war, but by consent of Parliament' and that 'all fencible men of the nation, between 16 and 60, be with all diligence possible armed with bayonets, and firelocks all of a calibre, and continue always provided in such arms with ammunition suitable'.[11] Similar views were expressed by a fellow Scot, David Hume, in his *Idea of a Perfect Commonwealth* (1752). Hume proposed a militia based on that of Switzerland, but this was apparently so well known to his contemporaries that he felt no need to go into further detail on the subject, except to say that an army of 20,000 should be called upon every year for training purposes.[12] In William Hodgson's *Commonwealth of Reason* (1795), a more complete plan for a militia is laid down: he recommended that every citizen should be required to keep a firelock and bayonet ready for immediate use, that one day in every two months should be set aside for military training, and that in times of war or invasion, forces should be mobilised from this general pool by the drawing of lots.[13]

Such notions may be consigned to the era of the musket and dismissed as fanciful in a contemporary Scottish context. Even if a citizens' army, such as that of Switzerland, were theoretically preferable on democratic grounds, and practicable on grounds of military feasibility, there is unlikely to be any political or public appetite for a system of universal service that would be resented by many as a heavy and unconscionable burden. However, the basic argument that a democratic state needs to be defended by democratic armed forces, which are loyal to the Constitution and based on civic, democratic values, still stands. Likewise, without restructuring our armed forces on Swiss lines, we may recognise the inherent danger of concentrated military power, and take steps to constrain and control that power by democratic means. The role of the Constitution is to ensure that such force remains under civilian and democratic control, and that it is not misused. The *Model Constitution* (Art. v, Sect. 11) included three provisions. First, the supreme command of the armed forces would be vested in the Council of Ministers, meaning that key decisions would have to be taken in a full meeting of the cabinet, not privately or secretly by the Prime Minister.[a] Second, the armed forces are to be regulated only 'subject to the Constitution and laws', meaning that the organisation and structure of the armed forces would be determined by Act of Parliament. Third, declarations of war and the decision to deploy troops on active service would require the prior consent of a two-thirds majority in Parliament, except if Scotland is under 'actual or imminent enemy attack'. The requirement for a two-thirds majority would give the opposition an effective veto over the commitment of troops, raising the threshold of decision-making to ensure that any such commitment reflects a political consensus, not a snap, personal or narrowly partisan decision.[b]

---

a   Art. II, Sect. 4 also gave the role of 'commander-in-chief' to the monarch as Head of State, but this office is mainly ceremonial, and is to be exercised, as stated explicitly in the *Model Constitution*, only on the binding advice of the Council of Ministers.

b   An alternative to the two-thirds majority rule would be to require a referendum on

It would be possible to go further in ensuring the civilian and democratic oversight of the armed forces. Members of the armed forces, like other public officers, should pledge allegiance not to the Crown or the Government, but to the people in accordance with the Constitution and the laws. It might be beneficial to include a constitutional rule specifying that laws regulating the armed forces remain in effect only for a maximum period of four years from the date of their enactment (i.e. the life of a Parliament). This would ensure that the armed forces are always dependent on parliamentary consent for their continued existence, and that Parliament has an opportunity to renew that consent in each session.

Another possibility would be to specify the roles of the armed forces in the Constitution in order to make any use of the armed forces outside of those specified roles unconstitutional. Such legitimate roles may include: (i) protecting Scotland from enemy attack in time of war or threat of invasion; (ii) contributing to international peacekeeping and security forces in accordance with international law; (iii) contributing to collective defence in accordance with treaty commitments; (iv) ensuring the protection of essential infrastructure and the safety of civilian populations in event of a natural disaster, epidemic, attack, or other calamity; (v) providing assistance to Fire and Rescue services, ambulance services, and other civilian emergency services when required and authorised according to law; (vi) the defence of Scotland's territorial waters and coasts; (vii) fishery protection; (viii) the protection of off-shore assets; (ix) air-sea rescue; (x) meteorological services; (xi) the prevention of smuggling, trafficking by sea, and piracy; and (xii) associated duties specified by law.[14] This is a broad scope, but it contains important limitations. For instance, the duty of 'contributing to international peacekeeping and security forces in accordance with international law' implies that there is no permission to contribute to activities in contravention to international law.

---

military deployment or declaration of war, thus giving ultimate responsibility to the people. This was even proposed in the United States, with the so-called 'Ludlow Amendment' (discussed in the US Congress between 1937 and 1939, but never adopted). This would provide a stronger and more democratic check against military adventurism than a mere parliamentary vote – even one requiring a two-thirds majority for approval. However the practical difficulties (not least the inevitable time-delay in organising a referendum, particularly at times when the military and diplomatic situation is rapidly changing) may be insurmountable.

Finally, the role of the security services cannot be ignored. Many contemporary democracies, convincing themselves that they are under siege from terrorism, political violence, organised crime, and other threats to their security, have increasingly sought to establish the kind of surveillance mechanisms that were once a unique feature of authoritarian states or an exceptional expedient of democracies in times of war. Such concentration of broad, secretive, often unaccountable, power in the security services poses a real challenge to the maintenance of a free, civic, democratic order, entailing great loss of liberty and privacy for a small gain in security. Any constitutional project that takes liberty and democracy seriously must not ignore this challenge. It might be advisable to make explicit constitutional provision for the existence of security services, and, in so doing, to strictly regulate their scope, role and powers in the Constitution, to provide effective institutional oversight at both ministerial and parliamentary levels, and to ensure their actions are subject to judicial review.

Most of the comments made in this section are directly applicable only to the Constitution of an independent Scotland with its own armed forces and its own foreign policy. Scotland in the Union, even a sovereign and very autonomous Scotland in a loose, equal and confederal Union, is unlikely to have direct control over its own military institutions or defence policy. Yet the need for democratic accountability in the organisation and use of the armed forces is just as great on a United Kingdom-wide as on a Scottish scale, and if Scotland is to remain as part of a reconstituted United Kingdom then securing robust constitutional guarantees against the use and misuse of military power should be part of Scotland's constitutional demands; we cannot simply insist on 'more powers' without also challenging the ways in which the powers kept by Westminster and Whitehall are used.

Fig. 9 Example: Constitutional regulation of the Armed Forces
in the Netherlands

Article 96

1 A declaration that the Kingdom is in a state of war shall not be made without the prior approval of the States General (Parliament).

2 Such approval shall not be required in cases where consultation with Parliament proves to be impossible as a consequence of the actual existence of a state of war.

3 The two houses of the States General shall consider and decide upon the matter in joint session.

4 The provisions of the first and third paragraphs shall apply *mutatis mutandis* to a declaration that a state of war has ceased.

Article 97

1 There shall be armed forces for the defence and protection of the interests of the Kingdom, and in order to maintain and promote the international legal order.

2 The Government shall have supreme authority over the armed forces.

Article 98

1 The armed forces shall consist of volunteers and may also include conscripts.

2 Compulsory military service and the power to defer the call-up to active service shall be regulated by Act of Parliament.

Article 99

Exemption from military service because of serious conscientious objections shall be regulated by Act of Parliament.

Article 99a

Duties may be assigned for the purpose of civil defence in accordance with rules laid down by Act of Parliament.

Article 100

1 The Government shall inform the States General in advance if the armed forces are to be deployed or made available to maintain or promote the international legal order. This shall include the provision of humanitarian aid in the event of armed conflict.

2 The provisions of paragraph 1 shall not apply if compelling reasons exist to prevent the provision of information in advance. In this event, information shall be supplied as soon as possible.

CHAPTER SIX

How can the Constitution reflect public values and identities?

THIS CHAPTER CONSIDERS several themes relating to 'covenantal' aspects of constitutional design: the preamble, religion-state relations, and the monarchy and national identity. These concern the role of the Constitution in expressing our values and identity – rather in organising and regulating the institutions of government. Throughout this chapter, emphasis is placed on the need for compromise if we are to build a Constitution that reflects the common good. A good Constitution – whatever else it might also be – is one that as many citizens as possible can unite around. An imposed blueprint, meeting only the aspirations of a committed few, while alienating the majority, has no future: one that speaks only for the majority, and ignores the claims of minorities, offers little freedom.

i   The Preamble and Para-Constitutional Covenants

Most constitutions are preceded by a preamble – a statement of purpose and intent, in which the 'needs, idioms and aspirations' of the community, as well as the authority of the people as both the 'creators and subjects of the constitutional order' are expressed.[1] A preamble is different from the rest of the Constitution (the 'operative' text) in several ways. In content, the operative text defines how state institutions work; the preamble explains whom and what the state is for. In purpose, the operative text is an instrument of civic governance, intended to distribute and restrain powers of government, to settle points of order, and to resolve questions of rights and competences. The preamble is an instrument of nation-building, intended to legitimate, to inspire and to unite. In style, the operative part is prosaic and often written in dense legalese; the preamble may be poetic, rhetorical and memorable. In effect, the operative text is legally binding and regulatory; the preamble usually only morally persuasive and declaratory.[a] In audience, the operative text is addressed principally (although not exclusively) to those who must use the constitution in a professional capacity – to lawyers, civil servants and politicians; the preamble is addressed primarily to ordinary citizens, and to the watching wider world.

It would be a little too neat and artificial to say that the preamble embodies the 'Constitution as Covenant', whilst the operative text embodies the 'Constitution as Charter'. Covenantal elements may also be present, even if only in an implied way, throughout the operative text – for example in provisions relating to socio-economic rights. Nevertheless, it is in the preamble that the essence of the national covenant – in terms of the *teleos* and *ethos* of the community, is most directly proclaimed.

The Constitutions of India (1950), South Africa (1996) and Kenya (2010) provide illustrative examples of covenantal preambles from countries that have a history of British rule. Each contains certain features: (i) an invocation of the people as source of authority and as subjects of the Constitution; (ii) a brief 'autobiographical' statement of the nation's history, identity and values; (iii) a substantive description of the national covenant itself, in terms of the teleological purposes of the Constitution and of the state; and (iv) a formal adoption clause, establishing the operative text of the Constitution as the legal and political instrument by which these purposes are to be achieved. The South African and Kenyan preambles also include a religious invocation, connecting popular sovereignty in civic and temporal matters to the ultimate supremacy of God in human affairs.

In some countries, documents which are external to the constitution, and usually predate the constitution, may perform a symbolic, nation-defining function, and may stand in place of, or alongside, a preamble. In Israel, for example, the Declaration of Independence (1948) proclaims that:

> The State of Israel will be open for Jewish immigration and for the ingathering of the exiles; it will foster the development of the country

---

a   In some countries, courts have held that preambles do have legal effect. The Constitutional Council in France, for example, has ruled that the Declaration of the Rights of Man and of the Citizen, 1789 and the Preamble of the Constitution of the Fourth French Republic, 1946 are integral to the constitutional law.

for the benefit of all its inhabitants; it will be based on freedom, justice and peace as envisaged by the prophets of Israel; it will ensure complete equality of social and political rights to all its inhabitants irrespective of religion, race or sex; it will guarantee freedom of religion, conscience, language, education and culture; it will safeguard the Holy Places of all religions; and it will be faithful to the principles of the Charter of the United Nation.[2]

Fig. 10 Examples: Preambles in three Constitutions

India (1950, as amended)

We, the people of India –

Having solemnly resolved to constitute India into a sovereign socialist secular democratic republic and to secure to all its citizens:

JUSTICE, social, economic and political;

LIBERTY of thought, expression, belief, faith and worship;

EQUALITY of status and of opportunity;

and to promote among them all FRATERNITY assuring the dignity of the individual and the unity and integrity of the Nation;

In our Constituent Assembly this twenty-sixth day of November, 1949, do hereby adopt, enact and give to ourselves this Constitution.

South Africa (1996)

We, the people of South Africa –

Recognise the injustices of our past;

Honour those who suffered for justice and freedom in our land;

Respect those who have worked to build and develop our country;

And believe that South Africa belongs to all who live in it, united in our diversity.

We therefore, through our freely elected representatives, adopt this Constitution as the supreme law of the Republic so as to –

• Heal the divisions of the past and establish a society based on democratic values, social justice and fundamental human rights;

• Lay the foundations for a democratic and open society in which government is based on the will of the people and every citizen is equally protected by law;

• Improve the quality of life of all citizens and free the potential of each person; and

---

• Build a united and democratic South Africa able to take its rightful place as a sovereign state in the family of nations.

May God protect our people.

Nkosi Sikelel' iAfrika. Morena boloka setjhaba sa heso. God seën Suid-Afrika. God bless South Africa. Mudzimu fhatutshedza Afurika. Hosi katekisa Afrika.

Kenya (2010)

We, the people of Kenya—

Acknowledging the supremacy of the Almighty God of all creation:

Honouring those who heroically struggled to bring freedom and justice to our land:

Proud of our ethnic, cultural and religious diversity, and determined to live in peace and unity as one indivisible sovereign nation:

Respectful of the environment, which is our heritage, and determined to sustain it for the benefit of future generations:

Committed to nurturing and protecting the well-being of the individual, the family, communities and the nation:

Recognising the aspirations of all Kenyans for a government based on the essential values of human rights, equality, freedom, democracy, social justice and the rule of law:

Exercising our sovereign and inalienable right to determine the form of governance of our country and having participated fully in the making of this Constitution:

Adopt, Enact and give this Constitution to ourselves and to our future generations.

God bless Kenya.

Leaving aside, for the moment, many valid questions about the extent to which the State of Israel actually lives up to these commitments, in particular with respect to its Palestinian population, the relevance of this declaration lies in its covenantal character. David Bar-Rav-Hai, a leading Labour (*Maipai*) politician and a member of the Constitution, Law and Justice Committee in the First Knesset, argued that the Declaration performed the functions of a preamble, providing shared principles on which the state could be built.[3] Crucially, Israel is one of very few countries, other than the United Kingdom, that does not have a codified and entrenched Constitution. Instead, it relies on a series of Basic Laws, which are distinguished from ordinary laws, but can be changed without a super-majority, referendum, or other higher hurdle to amendment. This means that the Declaration of the Establishment of the State of Israel is a rare example of a national constitutional 'covenant' without a corresponding 'charter'.

In Ireland, the Republic Proclamation of 1916 has been claimed by some as a para-constitutional, covenantal document.[4] Although it is still a politically contentious text and its covenantal or foundational status is by no means universally accepted, it remains 'an enduring point of reference for those calling for fidelity to its ideals or a renewal of Irish national life based on its principles [and] has often been treated as a touchstone for existing or possible future constitutional arrangements'.[5] There is a curious tension between, one the one hand, the Proclamation's popular rhetorical commitment to 'cherishing all children of the nation equally' (which, although originally referring to equality between Protestants and Catholics, has often been re-interpreted through a lens of left-wing republicanism to refer to social justice more generally, including economic equality), and on the other hand, the Irish Constitution's 'cautious, measured, anodyne and stilted' Directive Principles of Social Policy, which have explicit (although non-justiciable) constitutional status.[6]

The *Model Constitution* did not include a preamble. Instead, it opened with a simple declaratory provision, defining the state as a 'parliamentary democracy based upon the sovereignty of the people, social justice, solidarity and respect for human rights'.[7] In this respect, it followed from the 1964 SPCA text and the SNP's 2002 text, both of which were without a preamble. The intention was to provide a form of words that would act as a relatively uncontroversial frame for the substantive and structural provisions of the text. The inclusion of a preamble in the Constitution of an independent or autonomous Scotland would, however, provide an opportunity for the people to form a unifying democratic national covenant that gives authoritative voice to the nation's highest aspirations and ideals, breathing spirit into the dry bones of the constitutional text. Indeed, the desire for such a statement of values, principles, ethics and identity seems stronger, in some quarters, than a desire for the operative, institutional, parts of a Constitution. Angus Reid's *Call for a Constitution*, for example, can better be understood as a 'Call for a Preamble'. It refers to the need 'to respect and to care for the sacred', 'to respect and to care for freedom of conscience', 'to recognise the gift of every individual, to respect it care for it, nourish it', 'to care for and protect communities', and 'to care for the land and wherever the land has been abused to restore it so that it can support all forms of life', but says nothing about institutions, processes, or forms of government.

The form of words recommended by Angus Reid, with its strong invocation of 'the sacred', may be too spiritual and theistic (or perhaps pantheistic) for some tastes. If the preamble is to express a genuine national covenant – one that unites and does not divide – it must reflect the values and identities that are truly common. It should neither echo the voice of the dominant mainstream majority, to the exclusion of minorities and social non-conformists,[a] nor impose the worldview of an enlightened few, whose liberal and cosmopolitan values may fail to resonate with the traditional *mores* of many people. Agreeing a workable preamble therefore requires balance, moderation compromise, as well as aspiration, vision and idealism. Most of all, it requires a deep listening exercise and a far-reaching public conversation through which we can identify and define the things that we as 'the whole community of the realm' hold in common.

People with very different ideological or cultural perspectives may find it easier to agree on institutional provisions, which are amenable to pragmatic negotiation, than on the statements of values and identity that would typically go into a preamble. Given the highly visible, symbolic and declaratory nature of a preamble, it is often better to say nothing than to say something that alienates or causes controversy. Some Constitutions avoid this problem by doing without a preamble, or by restricting it to a simple and non-controversial introductory statement to the effect that the Constitution is adopted in the name and on behalf of the people. That is not to say that these Constitutions lack covenantal provisions, only that their covenantal content is perhaps thinner, less visible, less-well defined, and more open to different forms of interpretation.

---

a The Hungarian Constitution of 2011 has been condemned for reflecting a conservative, nationalist ideology that is alienating to many Hungarians. See: Toth, G. A. *Constitution for a Divided Nation: On Hungary's 2011 Fundamental Law* (Budapest: Central European University Press, 2012).

With respect to the preamble, as to the other parts of the Constitution, the extent to which we can make covenantal commitments of purposes and ethics, and the extent to which we must be content with a prosaic charter that upholds an open, pluralistic, democratic political order, will depend on the extent and depth of the social consensus; to what extent do we agree, and to what extent must we agree to disagree? This calls for pragmatism, compromise and moderation. Even a covenantal constitution cannot impose the ideology of one party without the risk of undermining the whole Constitution. It is great to have a preamble that is a transformative rallying cry, but only if it comes from the whole chorus, and not a soloist. Therefore, to discover the values and principles that will command the support of a broad swathe of Scottish society – or, in the case of a federal Constitution for the United Kingdom as a whole, British society – will require people from across the land, and from all ideological perspectives and all walks of life, to be heard if the preamble is to be reflective of that which we have in common.

Without attempting to prescribe particular outcomes, and without negating this need for genuine public participation, it is possible to identify certain principles and values that are likely to enjoy broad support in Scotland and which could provide a basis on which to construct a preamble for a future Scottish Constitution.[a] In this process we are aided by the work of the Constitutional Convention and the Consultative Steering Group in the 1990s. The latter identified four founding principles in its 1998 report, which became the basis for the Scottish Parliament's structures and standing orders. These were: (i) sharing the power – between the people, Parliament and the Government; (ii) accountability – of the Government to Parliament and of the Government and Parliament to the people; (iii) access and participation – particularly with regard to the development, consideration and scrutiny of policy and legislation; (iv) the need to promote equal opportunities. These principles are perhaps rather institutional in nature. They speak more to how structures of government

---

a   Crafting a preamble that reflects 'Scottish values' would be a much easier task than crafting on that reflects 'British values', if only because Scotland is a much more homogenous and unified society than the UK as a whole. It seems that a Federal Constitution for the United Kingdom would have to be much less 'covenantal' than a Constitution for Scotland alone (be that an independent or an autonomous Scotland).

should operate than to the values we would wish to see embodied in those structures. The Mace of the Scottish Parliament takes a slightly different approach. The words engraved upon it, 'Wisdom', 'Justice', 'Compassion' and 'Integrity', speak to aspirations and ideals that many of us would like to hold dear.[8] Together, these eight principles might at least provide a reasonable and relatively uncontroversial starting point. To these could be added some statement of universal democratic values and human rights invoking, for example, the UN Universal Declaration of Human Rights, the European Convention on Human Rights and the International Covenants on Political and Civil Rights and Economic, Social and Cultural Rights.

Another potential source of common ground from which inspiration might be drawn is the Commonwealth Charter. This document sets out the values and principles of the Commonwealth. It encapsulates the best aspirations of that family of nations of which Scotland would continue to be an integral part, either by virtue of its membership of the United Kingdom or in its own right as an independent Commonwealth Realm. The Charter speaks in glowing terms of democracy, human rights, environmental protection, freedom of expression, rule of law and of the valuable contribution made by small independent states.[9] The advantage of the Commonwealth Charter as a source of principles is that it has been signed by the Queen and the British Prime Minister. It would, therefore, have legitimacy in the eyes of those who are strongly attached to a British identity and would provide a certain degree of mutual acceptability between Nationalists and Unionists.

ii   Religion and State

Just as the Constitution forms the apex of the legal and political systems, and the nexus of the state and society, so also a Constitution usually regulates the relationship between the state and religion. This relationship between the state and religion can take many forms. Most Constitutions – and all that are derived from the Western, liberal tradition – establish religious freedom, protect people from religious compulsion and discrimination, and uphold the rights of religious minorities and of dissenters. Many Constitutions also formally recognise the place of a particular religion in a nation's culture, history and identity, or proclaim the allegiance of the state to particular religious values. Some Constitutions – especially those in Muslim-majority societies – establish religion as a source of law, and often mark out particular fields of human activity where religious law, which is adjudicated in religious courts, prevails. In a few countries, such as Iran and the UK, there is even an established state religion, such that the leaders of a particular privileged religion are publicly appointed and hold high office in the state.[10]

Finding a solution to the problem of how to constitutionally regulate relations between religion and the state in an increasingly pluralist society, in a way that is conducive to the common good and neither alienates minorities nor exacerbates sectarian divisions, is critical to the success of the constitutional project. This is one of the most delicate problems facing constitutional designers around the world, even in societies that are relatively homogenous in culture and religion. Although not as difficult as in places such as Lebanon or Northern Ireland, where religious tensions have produced violence and a breakdown of democracy, the current situation in Scotland is not easy, given the lingering problems of sectarianism in parts of the country, as well as more recent tensions over certain issues of domestic policy.[a]

The constitutional provisions relating to religion must therefore be considered very carefully if a broadly acceptable Constitution is to be produced. In this section, the aim is simply – without being directly prescriptive – to set out the available constitutional options, and to reflect on their viability and acceptability in our context. Because religion expresses core internal values and communal identities, it can be very difficult to reach a workable compromise between adherents of different religious communities and worldviews. The intention, nevertheless, is to try to find constitutional formulations that will be as broad and inclusive as possible, and that will alienate as few as possible of our fellow-citizens.

In an earlier age, a general deference to religion and religious values,

---

a   An non-exhaustive current list of these issues would include, in no particular order: (i) religiously-segregated education; (ii) prayer in schools or 'time for reflection'; (iii) the reservation of one-third of the seats on local authority education committees for unelected clerics; (iv) same-sex marriage; (v) adoption; (vi) abortion; (vii) euthanasia; (viii) chaplains on the public payroll in institutions such as hospitals; and (ix) the symbolic role of religion in public ceremonies.

together with a privileged position for the Church of Scotland, could be assumed. The SPCA's draft Constitution of 1964, for example, contained the provision (Art. 4) stating that:

> The national church is the Church of Scotland by law defined in the Act for the Security of the Protestant Religion and Presbyterian Church Government in the Kingdom of Scotland, 1707, and the Articles Declaratory of the Constitution of the Church of Scotland in Matters Spiritual, 1921.[a]

At the time, this was unremarkable. The kirk was one of the great conduits which connected Scotland to its earlier pre-1707 statehood, and its General Assembly was, for 300 years, the closest thing Scotland had to a representative body of public opinion.[b] Today, the Church of Scotland is no longer in the position of cultural dominance that it once was, and to insist on such a constitutional status for the Church of Scotland in particular, or Christianity in general, would be highly controversial. Although some still insist that the state should be tied, in some more or less formal way, to Christian values and institutions, this has been met by a growing secular lobby, which promotes the separation of church and state, and seeks to diminish the institutional (although not necessarily the social or cultural) influence of religion in public life. When in April 2014 a consortium of church groups issued a joint statement demanding that any future Scottish Constitution should give recognition to Scotland's Christian heritage and should explicitly protect manifestations of religious belief,[11] the Scottish Secular Society responded by arguing that the Constitution should confine itself simply to giving equal rights of religious freedom to all, without granting established status or institutional privileges to any religion.[12] The Scottish Government, for its part, has tried to avoid being drawn into this debate; in the run-up to the independence referendum it simply re-affirmed its commitment to the European Conv-

---

a   The full text of the SPCA's draft is available from http://www.constitutionalcommission.org/resources.php

b   The often-repeated view that the General Assembly acted as a sort of 'substitute Parliament' between 1707 and 1997 requires qualification; although clearly in touch with every parish in the land, the kirk, even in its heyday, never claimed the active allegiance of more than a bare majority of the people.

ention on Human Rights and insisted that it had no plans to change the existing legal position of the Church of Scotland in the Interim Constitution.

The European Convention on Human Rights is indeed an excellent starting point. It upholds the foundations of religious freedom and religious equality as now generally understood, through the accumulated experience of an often bloody history, across the Western world. Article 9 of the European Convention guarantees freedom of conscience, thought and religion, including freedom of religious worship, teaching, practice and observance. These rights may be enjoyed alone or with others, and in private or in public, subject only to such limitations 'as are prescribed by law and are necessary in a democratic society in the interests of public safety, for the protection of public order, health or morals, or the protection of the rights and freedoms of others'. Article 10 protects freedom of expression: this includes religious expression, including expressions of religious dissent. Article 14 protects people from discrimination in the exercise of their Convention rights. These fundamental rights help ensure that we maintain a free, open, pluralist society. They keep us safe from religious wars, pogroms, inquisitions, burnings, racks, dungeons, and other such diabolical instruments of over-zealous devotion. They are necessary not only for the sake of public peace, but also out of principled respect for individual conscience and for the sacred right of private judgment in matters of religion.

Such fundamental rights would rule out both the establishment of a theocratic state in which laws and institutions are wholly based upon and subordinate to religious norms and, equally, of an anti-religious state in which religious beliefs and activities are actively suppressed. Between these parameters, however, the European Convention on Human Rights does not regulate the institutional relationship between the state and religion, nor try to define the religious identity of society; these things fall into the wide 'margin of appreciation' which states enjoy to order their own affairs in their own ways. Indeed, a variety of approaches can be observed across the set of European and other Western democracies. These can be treated under four general categories: (i) *laïcité*; (ii) secularism-as-neutrality; (iii) pluralist accommodation; and (iv) religious establishment.

Laïcité (also known as 'strong secularism') is, in principle, the most stridently anti-clerical approach that is consistent with religious liberty.

While respecting the right of consenting adults to practice religion in the privacy of their own churches and homes, it seeks actively to exclude religion from public life, and most of all from public education. 'Secularism-as-neutrality' (also known as 'weak secularism') in contrast, simply insists on the non-activity of the state in religious matters. The neutral state protects freedom of religion and ensures there is no discrimination on religious grounds, but it makes no religious claims, does not attach any religious dimension to the state's identity, and neither encourages nor discourages any form of religiosity. The difference between *laïcité*, as practiced in France, and 'secularism as neutrality', as practiced in the United States, can be seen by examining their different approaches to the wearing of religious insignia by pupils in publicly funded schools. A child in a French public school cannot wear a cross, because the school is a *laïc* institution, a temple to the universal values of the Republic: Liberty, Equality and Fraternity. A child in a US public school can do so, because the state does not use the school to enforce either religious or non-religious values: it simply maintains a careful and delicate neutrality.[13]

Another common model of religion-state relations is 'pluralist accommodation', as practised in countries such as Canada, India, South Africa and Germany. According to this model, the state accommodates religious practice, on a pluralistic and non-discriminatory basis, while respecting personal freedom of religion, and not actively favoring or encouraging any particular religion to the exclusion of others. In Canada and South Africa, there is a reference to God in the Constitution, albeit in a very generic sense. The public funding of religious schools would be unconstitutional in the USA, but is permitted in Canada – or at least in certain Provinces of that highly decentralised country, where the Constitution mandates separate Protestant and Catholic school boards. In Germany, pluralist accommodation even has a fiscal dimension, with various officially recognised religious institutions having the authority to collect a 'church tax'.[14]

The final approach to consider is that of religious establishment. This means that the state – again, while protecting freedom of religion and the rights of minorities – does actively support, endorse or recognise a particular religion, which has the status of the 'national' or 'established' religion. Provisions to this effect are found in the Constitutions of several

Nordic democracies, including Norway, Denmark and Iceland. The extent of establishment can vary. In Norway, for example, a constitutional reform in 2012 freed the Church from official control, while retaining a specifically religious identity for the state. The old text (Art. 16) read: 'The King ordains all public church services and public worship, all meetings and assemblies dealing with religious matters, and ensures that public teachers of religion follow the norms prescribed for them.' The new text of this article reads: 'All inhabitants of the realm have the right to free exercise of their religion. The Norwegian Church, an Evangelical-Lutheran Church, remains Norway's Church and supported as such by the state. Specific provisions on the organisation thereof are laid down by law. All religions and religious groups are supported equally'. In other words, Norway still has a religious establishment, but it is 'weaker' than before, and is balanced by a degree of pluralist accommodation that recognises other religions.

These categories can be used to understand Scotland's current position. Unlike the Church of England, the Church of Scotland has no bishops for the Crown to appoint, and no representation in Parliament, and this causes some to argue that the Church of Scotland is not 'established'. However, the Church of Scotland is formally recognised and privileged by law. It is connected to the state through the Lord High Commissioner, who attends the General Assembly of the Church as the delegate of the Head of State.[15] The Queen, in Scotland, takes an oath to defend and uphold the Church of Scotland and the Protestant religion.[16] Ministers of the Church of Scotland have a privileged position with regard to leading religious observance in supposedly 'non-denominational' public schools, and sit as unelected members of local education authorities. No Roman Catholic can inherit the throne. In comparative terms, this must be defined as 'weak establishment'.

The situation in Scotland is complicated by the fact that the state's involvement in religious affairs cuts two ways; the religious privilege extended to the Church of Scotland is balanced by a degree of pluralist accommodation extended to other Christian groups, chiefly in the form of public funding for Roman Catholic schools and in the presence of clerics from various churches on local authority education committees. This hybrid arrangement has continued mostly by tradition and pragmatic inertia. Until the recent emergence of the constitutional debate, there has been little public or political appetite to discuss it, let alone to change it. If we are to establish a new Constitution, however, in which certain principles and ground-rules are to be written down, then these issues will have to be brought to light, alternatives calmly considered, and acceptable choices made.

Some religious groups have argued for a provision defining Scotland as a Christian nation, through the constitutional establishment of a national church, or by explicitly claiming a Christian religious identity for the state in the Constitution. Such proposals are unlikely to be broadly acceptable in today's Scotland. To tie the state to one religious identity in that way would send an unavoidably triumphalist and exclusionary signal. Those who belong to other non-privileged religions, or who do not profess or practise any religion, would have their second-class status embedded in the Constitution. This would negate the principle of open, inclusive, civic nationalism rooted in equal citizenship.

A constitutional commitment to Christianity as a national or established religion would also reduce the label 'Christian' to a marker of national or cultural identity, shorn of any transformative personal commitment to the way, truth and life of Jesus of Nazareth. Seen from this perspective, ritualistic state-sponsored religion, of the sort foisted upon primary school children in assemblies, or paraded in royal pomp on state occasions, far from strengthening Christian witness, makes a mockery of it. It dresses up Caesar in the ill-fitting robes of Christ.

For these reasons, many Christians have embraced the separation of church and state, the strict neutrality of the state in religious matters, and the widest possible religious liberty, as principles which are not opposed to, but rather follow logically from, their deepest theological convictions.[a] According to this view, the *ecclesia* is the gathered community of followers of Jesus, united in love and faith under the leading of the Holy Spirit, for the worship of God and the service, healing and restoration of the world. The *res publica*, meanwhile, is the covenanted community of citizens, united by their Constitution, for the establishment of peace, order and

---

a   This is especially true of those Christian expressions that originated in the radical reformation, such as the Baptists, Unitarians and Quakers.

justice and for the collective management of their temporal affairs for the common good. Although there may be some incidental overlap in membership, these two communities differ in purpose, nature and extent. It is on appreciation of these differences that the Christian case for constitutional secularism is rightly based.

It should be noted that this does not prohibit the practice of a religiously motivated politics. Some people are impelled by their religious convictions to engage in politics, in respect of issues ranging from prostitution and human trafficking to poverty, debt, and the environment. So long as they do not attempt to do so by compulsion, or by capturing the state as the instrument of religious enforcement, this poses no danger to liberty in a plural society:

> A 'religious state' must be distinguished from 'religious politics'; while the former is often dangerous for democracy, the latter need not be. Politicians may enter the lists [i.e. stand for election] inspired by their religious faith, and may even appeal to their religious identity in the search for votes; and parties may claim to be based on the principles and values of a particular religion. So long as the state itself treats all religions (and non-religious currents) equally, no harm comes to democracy from this religiously-inspired activity in the political life of the country.[17]

If the distinction between *ecclesia* and *res publica* is eroded by too close and cosy an association between church and state, then corruption and oppression are likely to result. The church will cease to be a dispenser of salt and light and will become instead a comfortable and privileged defender of the established order. It will preach up *passive obedience*, abandon itself to the solace of otherworldly Gnosticism, and cease to perform its prophetic function. Despite all its temporal power and influence, it will be impotent in spirit, losing its voice and true authority. The state, for its part, will cease to protect and serve the common good of all citizens, regardless of their belief or lack thereof, and will favour the dominant religious group while oppressing dissidents and minorities.

Nevertheless, this is not to say we should insist on a self-consciously secular Constitution. Constitutional secularism, like constitutional establishment of religion, is likely under present circumstances to be highly divisive, and therefore difficult to justify in a Constitution that is supposed to be an instrument of unity and agreement. For many who maintain a religious identity, secularism in any form has negative connotations; it is often perceived as an exclusionary attempt to deny the legitimacy of religious values and institutions, to prohibit religious people from expressing the most precious aspects of their identity, and to silence religious voices in the public square. 'Secular', in such a mental landscape, smells suspiciously sulfurous. Such hostility to secularism may well be a reasonable response to French-style *laïcté*, especially in its more vigorous manifestations. It is important to recognise, however, that 'secular' is not a synonym for 'non-religious' or 'anti-religious'. Secularism-as-neutrality would not to the slightest extent diminish the rights (as distinct from the privileges) of religious people or religious institutions as equal participants in a free, open, pluralist society. Crucially, secularism-as-neutrality only seeks to separate religion from the state at a legal-institutional level, not to drive religion out of society. It would not limit the charitable, social or cultural role of religion, which many secularists acknowledge to be broadly positive, nor would it prohibit religious people from bringing their faith fully to bear on public and civic life. Indeed, it would protect their full and equal right to do so.

Yet even US-style 'secularism-as-neutrality', if consistently applied in a Scottish constitutional context, would have some very controversial consequences. As well as severing the remaining institutional and legal ties between the state and the Church of Scotland, it would also demand that Scotland's system of religiously segregated education be replaced by integrated schools. Such changes would harm the institutional interests of both the Church of Scotland, which would lose its privileged 'national church' status, and the Roman Catholic Church, which, in giving up segregated education, would lose one of the mainstays of its influence. Even if that were desirable (and there are some strong 'social cohesion' arguments to suggest that it might be) it is almost certainly too contentious and divisive an issue to be included in a Constitution that is intended to reflect a broad, settled, national consensus.

There are some ways, however, in which this apparent impasse between those who wish to see explicit religious recognition in the Constitution and those who wish for a secular Constitution can be overcome. One possibility is through the constructive power of constitutional silence. The SNP's 2002 draft Constitution limited itself to protecting freedom of religion and freedom from discrimination, in accordance with the provisions of the European Convention, and omitted all mention – positive or negative – of a national religion. By focusing on the structural institutions of democratic government and on generic fundamental rights, the 2002 draft would have left the question of religion-state relations and of national religious identity open. These questions could be resolved at the sub-constitutional level pragmatically and contingently, and in response to changing public desires, through the ordinary processes of parliamentary politics and by ordinary law. Under this scheme, the Constitution is silent on the public funding of religious schools, but law need not be; the Constitution specifies no Accession Oath, but the law may. The 2002 text maintained a similarly non-prescriptive stance on questions such as abortion and euthanasia, on which similarly intense religious divisions may be manifest.

A Model Constitution set out to do the same thing, but for the avoidance of doubt, and to make its impartial position more explicit, certain clarifying provisions were added to the text, stating that nothing in the Constitution would affect the existing legal status of the Church of Scotland. In other words, the Model Constitution would not render the Church of Scotland Act 1921 unconstitutional. This is a fine distinction that has often been misunderstood. The Model Constitution would not have constitutionally entrenched the position of a national religion, but neither would it have rendered existing statutory establishment unconstitutional. That is to say that the existing patterns of religion-state relations would be undisturbed – so the Constitution could not be regarded as an attack on any existing arrangement in this regard – but would not be protected against sub-constitutional change by statute or convention. Likewise, the provisions relating to the Head of State's duty to attend the General Assembly of the Church of Scotland (in person or through the Lord High Commissioner as her representative) was intended simply as a reflection of present reality, which would have allowed current practices to continue under the Constitution but would not have made them constitutionally binding.

This studied silence on religion-state relations (which also appeared to have been replicated in the 2014 draft Interim Constitution) removes a contentious, divisive issue from the agenda of constitution making and pushes it into the future, where it must be dealt with under constitutional rules that are equally acceptable to both clericalist and secular lobbies.

This is an example of how the procedural, charter-type constitutionalism discussed in Chapter Three can help a society which is divided on ultimate questions of value or identity to live together in peace, and to pragmatically and discursively realise the common good. In a Scottish context, this may well turn out to be a wise compromise.[a]

Another possible route to compromise may be described as 'recognition without establishment'. To understand this, it is necessary to make a distinction between the prescriptive and descriptive roles of a Constitution. This distinction can be seen in the contrasting provisions of the French Constitutional Charters of 1814 and 1830.[b] The 1814 text read: 'Every one may profess his religion with equal freedom, and shall obtain for his worship the same protection. Nevertheless, the catholic, apostolic and Roman religion is the religion of the state.'[18] After the liberal revolution of 1830, the revised and re-promulgated Charter removed all reference to a 'religion of the state', and described Catholicism merely as the religion 'professed by the majority of the French'.[19] The first is a prescriptive statement of religious establishment, which defines the state in religious terms; the second is a descriptive statement of religious recognition, which describes society as it is. Such a descriptive statement could easily be dismissed as meaningless verbiage. Certainly, the inclusion of such recognition in a Scottish Constitution would add very little in concrete legal terms to the meaning of the text.[c] However, we must always remember that a Constitution is much more than a legal charter; it is also a political and a social covenant which reflects the nation to itself. While denying the privileges of constitutional establishment and refusing to define the state in exclusive religious terms, a descriptive recognition of the historical, social and cultural role of Christianity in Scotland may go some way to reassuring the faithful that they, too, are members of society, and that religious voices need not be marginalised or ignored.

It is also possible to frame such descriptive provisions in non-exclusive

---

a I draw this argument primarily from Hannah Lerner's discussion of constitutional provisions in religiously divided societies. See: Lerner, H. *Making Constitutions in Deeply Divided Societies* (Cambridge: Cambridge University Press, 2011).

b These were written when France was still a constitutional monarchy, and before the republican doctrine of *laïcité* assumed its present pre-eminence.

c Although it might be relied upon by Parliament and the courts as a non-binding guide to interpretation.

terms, which while recognising the central importance of a particular religious tradition, do not make adherence to that tradition a condition for full membership of the nation or polity. The Constitution of Poland is instructive on this point. Its preamble refers to:

> We, the Polish Nation – all citizens of the Republic, both those who believe in God as the source of truth, justice, good and beauty, as well as those not sharing such faith but respecting those universal values as arising from other sources, equal in rights and obligations towards the common good.[20]

These approaches are not mutually exclusive. It is possible to maintain a careful and deliberate constitutional silence on the religiosity or secularity of the state, such that issues like the legal status of the Church of Scotland or religiously segregated schools can be handled at the sub-constitutional level within a broad framework of rights, while also granting a limited symbolic and descriptive recognition to the role that religion – and Christianity in particular – has played in national life. A Constitution produced on such lines would not challenge the *status quo* with regard to issues such as the status of the Church of Scotland or the role of religion in education, but neither would it insulate present practices from future democratic challenges.

This combination, although not without the faults that are inherent in any messy and pragmatic compromise, seems to offer the most practical solution, which would alienate as few people as possible. The advantage of such compromise is that it would enable constitution building (which is the best chance we have for a democratic renewal of Scottish society, for the common good of all citizens, regardless of their faith) to proceed without being sidetracked by disagreement on the religious orientation of the state.

iii   Monarchy and National Identity

The SNP's constitutional policy is, and always has been, to keep the monarchy in an independent Scotland – until and unless the people vote to abolish it in a future constitutional amendment. This gives rise to much confusion. How, it might be asked, could the sovereignty of the people be reconciled with the retention of a hereditary Head of State?

The answer is very simple: although there would be the same Queen, the monarchy in an independent Scotland, under a Scottish Constitution, would not, constitutionally speaking, be the same monarchy as that now existing, or that which might continue to exist south of the border. To understand this, a distinction must be made between the person of the Queen and the institution of the Crown. The Queen of the several Commonwealth realms is the same physical person from Australia to Tuvalu, but the Crown in each realm is distinct, and each separate Crown has its own powers and constitutional status under each national Constitution. That is to say, the same monarch would be both Queen of Scots and Queen of the 'United Kingdom of England, Wales and Northern Ireland', but there would be two entirely separate Crowns, with different powers and functions, deriving from different constitutional principles.

In other words, an independent Scottish monarchy need not necessarily be the old British-imperial Protestant monarchy, which derived its position from the religious and dynastic struggles of the 17th century. Instead, we could have a Scottish democratic monarchy, deriving its legitimacy from a Constitution endorsed by the sovereign people.

To reiterate, it is in the right of the people to adopt and amend the Constitution that their sovereignty is most clearly manifested; the sovereignty of the people is upheld not by the substitution of a hereditary for an elected Head of State, but by ensuring that only the people have the authority to make fundamental changes to their fundamental (that is, constitutional) laws. That is not to say, necessarily, that the monarchy should be retained in an independent Scotland. It is simply to suggest that keeping the monarchy, under proper constitutional rules, is not inherently incompatible with democratic principles. It is significant that the 2002 draft Constitution and the draft interim Constitution never referred to the Queen as 'sovereign' but only as 'Head of State'; the word 'sovereign' is reserved only for the whole people acting in its constituent capacity. The Queen, under that Constitution, would hold the public office of 'ceremonial ribbon-cutter' in a state that is, for all practical purposes, a democratic republic. She wouldn't 'reign' as Elizabeth II of the United Kingdom, but instead would 'hold office' as Elizabeth I, Queen of Scots.

Whether we decide to keep the monarchy or not will depend on the good character and good conduct of the monarch, and this is a matter for the Parliament and people of Scotland to judge. If it were to be discovered, for example, that the Queen had tried to use her considerable influence to block Scottish independence, or that the heir to the throne had been writing letters to Ministers seeking to sway public decisions, then some might conclude - citing the Declaration of Abroath as a guiding principle - that such a monarch had violated their position of trust and should, for breach of the conditions of kingship, be driven out.

Moreover, the Parliament of an independent Scotland would be able, subject to the Constitution, to determine the law of succession to the office of Head of State and the qualifications and exclusions surrounding the office. The conventions recognised in the Statute of Westminster (which anticipates commonwealth realms passing similar legislation in parallel on matters concerning the royal succession) might be accepted as voluntarily binding, so long as the monarch is well behaved, but they would not bind us in law, and if required for the safety, liberty or good reputation of Scotland then we could, short of abolishing the monarchy, simply transfer it to another, better, candidate.

Whether in an independent Scotland or in a reformed democratic United Kingdom, the adoption of a new written constitution provides an opportunity for the uncertain boundaries of royal power to be more narrowly circumscribed. Although the Scotland Act regulates the nomination of a First Minister and the procedure for dissolving Parliament, and thereby curtails royal prerogative in these areas, it is still unclear whether the Queen may refuse assent to legislation, and if so under what circumstances this could occur. This is not merely a point of academic interest. The fact that assent has not been refused in the past does not mean that it could not be refused in the future. In both Belgium and Luxembourg it was assumed that royal or grand ducal assent was a technicality and would not be refused, and yet in both of those countries, the Heads of State exercised their long-dormant power of refusal when confronted with legislation that they opposed on religious grounds: an abortion bill in Belgium and a euthanasia bill in Luxembourg. In the Belgian case, the Cabinet invoked its constitutional right to suspend the King from office for the day and then promulgated the law in his absence. In Luxembourg, the constitution was swiftly amended to deprive the Grand Duke of his right of absolute veto, transforming it into a mere

90-day delay, after which the law would come into effect without requiring the Grand Duke's approval. To address this issue, the *Model Constitution* outlined a procedure that would make the granting of royal assent subject to the advice and counter-signature of the Presiding Officer, who would be able to refer bills to the Supreme Court for a ruling on their constitutional validity. This would deny personal discretion from the monarch, and so remove any potential threat that a future King or Queen of Scots might seek to obstruct democratic processes, whilst providing an effective brake on the passage of egregiously unconstitutional legislation.

Provided the constitutional powers and functions of the Head of State are precisely and narrowly defined, the question of whether the office should be filled by a hereditary figurehead, as in Norway and Sweden amongst many others, or by an elected president, as in Latvia, Ireland or Malta, is symbolic, not structural. The difference between a King or Queen whose only task is to smile, wave and cut ribbons and a non-executive elected President with the same job description, is that they emphasise different aspects of the nation's identity. A monarch embodies a continued connection with a wider British and Commonwealth community, as well as referencing historical continuity with the pre-1707 Kingdom of Scots. A president would represent the severance of those connections, and would present a newer, less 'British', more egalitarian, national image to ourselves and to the world. A figurehead elected president would not be more *democratic* than a figurehead monarch, but would be more *demotic*; in other words, a presidency would not give more power to the people, but it would speak to the people in their own voice.[a]

Likewise, provisions regulating a country's coat of arms, the site of its capital city, its flag, anthem, national holiday and even the names of its

---

a   Some have suggested that we do not need a Head of State at all, and that the functions of the Head of State should be performed by the Head of Government. This would, in my view, be a very dangerous step. Maintaining a separation between the symbolic and ceremonial representative of the state-as-such, and the leader of the Government of the day, even if the former has little or no power, sends an important signal; it shows that the *res publica* is bigger than the Government, and that the head of Government is not a ruler, but a public servant. There are also pragmatic considerations: separating the offices allows for a division of labour (one can open community centres, while the other reads important cabinet papers), and provides for formal continuity during the moment of transition of power from one Head of Government to another.

Fig. 11 Examples: Defining and limiting the powers of the monarch

---

Constitution of Tuvalu, Sections 50–52

50 (The office of Head of State)

In addition to the other functions of the office, the office of Head of State is a symbol of the unity and identity of Tuvalu, and the Head of State is entitled to proper respect accordingly.

51 (Functions, etc., of the Head of State generally)

1 The only privileges and functions of the Head of State are those prescribed as such.

2 Subject to this Constitution and to any Act of Parliament, the privileges and functions of the Sovereign as Head of State may be had and performed through a Governor-General appointed in accordance with Division 3 (the Governor-General) and, except where the context requires otherwise, references in any law to the Head of State shall be read as including a reference to the Governor-General.

52 (Performance of functions by the Head of State)

1 Subject to section 17 (impracticability of obtaining advice, etc.) of Schedule 1, in the performance of his functions under this Constitution or any other law the Head of State shall act only in accordance with the advice of (a) the Cabinet; or (b) the Prime Minister or another Minister acting under the general or special authority of the Cabinet, except where he is required to act- (c) in accordance with the advice of any other person or authority (in which case he shall act only in accordance with that advice); or (d) after consultation with any person or authority, including the Cabinet (in which case he shall act only after such consultation); or (e) in his own deliberate judgment (in which case he shall exercise an independent discretion), or where this Constitution obliges or specifically permits him to act in a particular way.

2 When the Head of State is required or permitted by this Constitution or any other law to act in accordance with the advice of, or after consultation with, any person or authority, no question- (a) whether he received the advice; or (b) whether he has the consultation and the nature of the consultation; or (c) what advice (if any) he was given; or (d) by whom he was advised or whom he consulted, shall be considered in any court.

Constitution of Spain, Articles 56 & 64

56 (Head of State)

1 The King is the Head of State, the symbol of its unity and permanence. He arbitrates and moderates the regular functioning of the institutions, assumes the highest representation of the Spanish State in international relations, especially with the nations of its historical community, and exercises the functions expressly attributed to him by the Constitution and the laws.

> 2 [...]
>
> 3 The person of the King is inviolable and is not subject to responsibility. His acts shall always be in the manner established in Article 64 and shall lack validity without that countersignature [...].
>
> 64 (Countersignature)
>
> 1 The actions of the King shall be countersigned by the Prime Minister and, when appropriate, by the competent ministers. The nomination and appointment of the Prime Minister and the dissolution provided for in Article 93 shall be countersigned by the President of the Congress of Deputies.
>
> 2 The persons who countersign the acts of the King shall be responsible for them.

major institutions might be irrelevant to the constitutional structure,[a] but highly relevant to the symbolic function of the Constitution as a nation-building and state-defining instrument. These things affirm for domestic constituencies, and declare to foreign audiences, who we are and what sort of nation we wish to be.[b]

There is an interesting difference between the SNP's 2002 text and the draft Interim Constitution in this regard. The former, except for a very inclusive definition of rules of citizenship, a demarcation of the national territory and recognition for Scots and Gaelic alongside English as official languages, contained remarkably little 'constitutional nationalism'.[c] It specified no flag or anthem. The latter had a slightly more 'nationalist' tone: it moved away from the establishment of basic structures of government (about which it said almost nothing of substance, but instead would rely on a few tweaks to the existing Scotland Act) and towards the formal proclamation of national identity. Its purpose seemed to be to assert Scottish statehood, rather than to regulate its government.

---

a For a very narrow view of this argument see: King, A. *Does the United Kingdom still have a Constitution?* (London: Sweet and Maxwell, 2001).

b It is striking, for example, that in Ireland, Irish names for institutions and offices were adopted, whereas in most other countries with British-influenced parliamentary institutions, the names and styles were taken directly from Westminster; structurally, there is no difference between a Prime Minister and a Taoiseach – symbolically, there may be.

c The term 'constitutional nationalism' is used here to describe attempts to assert and proclaim particular national identities through the Constitution, or to privilege particular ethno-cultural national identities amongst the citizen-body of the state.

National identity in Scotland has become politicised and even partisan. If there is to be an independent Scottish state in the future, and if it is to be a stable, inclusive and harmonious state, it cannot be a state of and for Scottish Nationalists. It has to be a state for everyone, including those who feel strongly that they are British as well as Scottish. The nature of Britishness in an independent Scotland would change. It would no longer be a state identity, but instead an affinity to a cultural, historical and geographical entity. If a Scottish cultural identity can be maintained in a British state for 300 years, why cannot a British cultural identity – for those who wish it – be maintained in a Scottish state? It might be beneficial to frame the 'identity defining' portions of the Constitution in a relatively open and non-prescriptive way, such that these multiple, overlapping, non-exclusive identities are protected, thereby helping to overcome any feeling of loss or dislocation occasioned by a transition to independence.

How can the Constitution help us to achieve social justice, tackle poverty and reduce economic inequalities?

i Social and Economic Rights

AS DISCUSSED IN Chapter Three, the fundamental rights provisions of a constitution, by protecting the rights of citizens to freely speak, associate and assemble, provide a framework within which democratic political action can take place. The space necessary for political discourse and contestation is protected against those in power who might wish to stifle criticism, opposition, or the expressions of alternatives. Likewise, procedural rights, such as those guaranteeing equality before the law and the right to a fair trial, ensure that people are not persecuted on account of their political views, while privacy rights and the right to freedom of information, if sufficiently robust, will preserve an open society and protect citizens from the potentially authoritarian consequences of mass surveillance coupled with paranoid secrecy. All these rights belong to the charter aspects of the constitution. They can be sustained by a relatively thin but broad political consensus that is compatible with many different competing and contrasting notions of 'the good' within the general rubric of a pluralist and democratic political order. Indeed, a society that did not guarantee these rights would be regarded, correctly, as not only falling short of democratic standards but also as falling short of humane standards.

The function of the European Convention on Human Rights (ECHR) is to prevent the recurrence of the grotesque human rights abuses that took place under Nazism and other forms of brutal, totalitarian rule. Its role in providing a minimum baseline for a free society is widely recognised and its provisions are already binding on the Scottish Parliament, so it is unthinkable to imagine a future Constitution for Scotland that did not embody these rights. The provisions of the ECHR have also been influential beyond Europe as they have been incorporated, often at the insistence or with the approval of the British Colonial Office, into the post-independence constitutions of the Caribbean, Africana and South Pacific states. In other words, there is an established jurisprudence from Commonwealth countries where courts have been applying these rights for several decades.

However, the ECHR includes only civil, legal and political rights. These rights, while necessary, have become increasingly recognised as insufficient. A free, flourishing, humane and democratic society needs more than just protection from gross authoritarian abuses of power. It also requires a certain distribution of material prosperity and opportunity, some restrictions on the arbitrary power of employers and landlords, and a safety net that protects the poor and vulnerable. A democratic Constitution, in a humane and civilized society, should be good news for the poor.

This means that the state has a positive obligation to secure social and economic rights, including rights to employment, decent wages and working conditions, housing, health care, education and financial support for those who need it, such as those who are unable to work, the sick and the old.

The exclusion of citizens from these social goods will not only diminish their quality of life and undermine their ability to share in the common good, but also poses a threat to democracy itself. As Franklin Roosevelt, President of the United States during the Great Depression, noted: 'Necessitous men are not free men. People who are hungry and out of a job are the stuff of which dictatorships are made.' This need for democracy to be grounded on a reasonable degree of economic security and equality has been observed around the world:

> Poverty and democracy in the contemporary world are therefore strange bed-fellows. A hungry stomach has an angry mind that has no time for popular participation in decision-making. The concern of a hungry stomach is not how decisions are made but whether the decisions made will put something in it. [...] There will be loss of the 'voice' in order to gain access to the essential need.[1]

Roosevelt's response was to articulate a 'second Bill of Rights' that would provide a degree of economic security, including the rights to a decent home, medical care, pensions, sickness and unemployment benefits and education.[2] Yet although Roosevelt was able to establish many of these rights on a statutory basis through his New Deal program, no constitutional recognition of these rights was achieved in the United States. The lack of constitutional recognition made these rights precarious; they were not only dependent on political majorities in an unrepresentative legislature, but also never fully legitimated or accepted into the 'covenant' of American citizenship. Consequently, they could be attacked as 'un-American' by right-wing politicians from Reagan onwards.

In other parts of the world, however, the role of the state in addressing social and economic needs was recognised on a constitutional basis. The Constitution of Australia, for example, was amended in 1946 to empower the federal government to make provision for 'maternity allowances, widows' pensions, child endowment, unemployment, pharmaceutical, sickness and hospital benefits, medical and dental services… benefits to students and family allowances'.[3] This grant of power (and implied responsibility) does not directly guarantee any right to these benefits, but it does at least legitimate their existence, creating certain expectations and indicating to all concerned that these forms of social mutuality are now integral to Australia's constitutional covenant.

Likewise, in the democratic re-foundation of Western Europe after 1945, after the turmoil of the Depression, dictatorship, and war, the desire for a humane and democratic political order was extended, at a constitutional level, into social and economic life.[a] The post-war constitutions of France and Italy, which were produced from a fusion of Christian democratic and social democratic principles, included social and economic directives as well as civil and political rights.[b] In Germany, the new 'Basic Law' guaranteed the dignity of the individual while presupposing, in its allocation of federal and concurrent powers, an active role for the democratic state in securing to all citizens the necessary material conditions for a just and flourishing society.[4]

---

a   Although social and economic provisions have become more prominent and more widespread since the middle decades of the 20th century, earlier constitutions were not always silent on the subject. For example, the Dutch Constitution, as early as 1815, made provision for education and for the care of the poor, accepting the state's duty to ensure that these social goods were adequately provided.

b   The French Constitution of 1946 (the Fourth Republic) expressed these rights only in the form of a non-justiciable (but politically salient) preamble.

In addition to these developments in Western democracies, social and economic rights achieved wider global legitimacy and recognition, including in the global south, through international instruments such as the Universal Declaration of Human Rights (1948) and the International Convention on Economic, Cultural and Social Rights (1966). Today, the need to secure better material conditions of life for ordinary citizens is, in many countries, central to the politics of constitutional change. In parts of Africa and Latin America, where people have become disillusioned with the ability of politicians to break their election promises, citizens have looked to constitutional rules as a way of forcing those in power to pay attention to their concerns for improved public services and better living and working conditions.

The social and economic provisions of a constitution embody the promises and undertakings that we, as citizens, make to one another. The inclusion, scope and extent of social and economic rights in a constitution is an important statement of who we are, what our common ground is, and what values we want our country to be based upon. Social and economic rights are constitutional in the deepest sense of the word because they concern the distribution of power, influence, wealth, prestige and opportunity in society. An extensive commitment to social and economic rights implies a thicker social covenant and a deeper commitment to mutuality. We are agreeing, by assenting to such constitutional provisions, to live in a society where we share resources and in which we each contribute for the benefit of all. To be a citizen in such a society is to belong to a national fellowship or fraternity in which risks and rewards are, to some extent, pooled and managed co-operatively for the benefit of all members. In the words of J. William Fulbright, a Democratic us Senator from 1945 to 1975:

> In ... democratic societies higher income people provide the bulk of tax money to finance public services of which the poor are the principal beneficiaries; the redistribution of wealth has become a normal and accepted function of democratic government. The rich pay not as a private act of *noblesse oblige* but in fulfillment of a social responsibility; the poor receive benefits not as a lucky gratuity but as the right of citizens.[5]

Because social and economic rights express these relatively deep mutual commitments, they can be regarded as covenantal in nature. They go beyond mere procedural rules to prescribe certain outcomes, and in so doing, they elevate certain values and principles to constitutional status: that no child should be unable to get an education, that no one should be driven into penury by illness or old age, and that no one should be denied the medical treatment they need on grounds of cost. Despite the fact that Scotland does not always live up to its cosy myth of social democracy, there would probably be sufficient consensus to establish such rights in the constitution. Opinions may differ across the political spectrum on how to fund and deliver public services, but the general principles of universal education, universal healthcare, social security and help to those in need command sufficiently widespread support to be constitutionally recognised.

ii *Judicial or Political Enforcement*

The main question is *how* to recognise social and economic provisions. There are two broad approaches. The first is to express them as justiciable rights, enabling the courts to annul legislation that contravenes these rights, and providing judicial remedies by which citizens can claim these rights through the courts. This approach can strengthen the enforcement of such rights, making it harder for governments to evade their obligations. This is found, for example, in the Constitution of Kenya (2010), which places rights to the highest attainable standard of health, which includes the right to health care, adequate housing, reasonable standards of sanitation, freedom from hunger, access to clean and safe water, social security and education, as well as the right to a clean and healthy environment, and the right of workers to fair remuneration, reasonable working conditions, the right to join a union and the right to strike.[6] The Constitution grants these alongside rights such as freedom of expression and association and gives them the same authority, providing the same enforcement mechanism: 'Every person has the right to institute court proceedings claiming that a right or fundamental freedom in the Bill of Rights has been denied, violated or infringed, or is threatened'.[7] Court proceedings to vindicate these rights may be instituted not only by a person acting in their own interest, but also by 'a person acting on behalf of another person who cannot act in their own name; a person acting as a member of, or in the interest of, a group or class of persons, a person acting in the public interest; or an association acting in the interest of one or more of its members'.[8] The courts are mandated by the Constitution to play an active role as 'guardians of the covenant' in ensuring governments do not betray the people. For those concerned by the tendency of constitutionalism to transfer power away from elected legislatures to courts, this (far more so than the role of courts in upholding the ECHR) would be an unacceptable overreach of judicial power.

The second approach is to include social and economic rights not as enforceable and justiciable rights, but simply as 'Directive Principles', which the state is morally and politically bound to uphold. This approach was pioneered by the Constitution of Ireland in 1937 and has been adopted in other jurisdictions where the influence of English common law has been strong, including India (1950) and Malta (1964). Social and economic rights are listed, but only in the form of objectives that the state must pursue; the decision of how to pursue them is left entirely to the Government and Parliament, and the courts have no say in the matter. Chapter Two of the Constitution of Malta, for example, recognises *inter alia* the right to work, guaranteed holidays and days of rest, equal pay for equal work, a minimum wage, protection of minors, the equality of women, the right to education, and social assistance for those unable to work due to accident, illness, disability or involuntary unemployment. The Constitution then goes on to state: '[These provisions] shall not be enforceable in any court, but the principles therein contained are nevertheless fundamental to the governance of the country and it shall be the aim of the State to apply these principles in making laws'.[9] In other words, these provisions are not legally binding or directly enforceable: they depend, for their effective realisation, on ordinary laws enacted by Parliament.

Those who view the constitution solely as a legal document and as a charter of rights may dismiss such 'Directive Principles' out of hand as an irrelevant, rhetorical distraction from the main business of the Constitution. If, however, we recognise that the constitution is a social and political document as well as a legal one, and that its function is to declare and express the national covenant as well as to guarantee judicially enforceable rights, then the value of such Directive Principles becomes clear. They declare aims and objectives. They set a measure against which the performance of institutions can be judged. They provide campaigning groups with a 'hook' on which to hang their campaigns for the realisation of the promised rights. Most of all, these Directive Principles make it evident – to the public, to Parliament, and to the courts – that the state has an active duty to the common weal that includes, but goes beyond, the mere protection of individual rights. A Constitution including such provisions holds before our eyes a national covenant that says: 'Yes, we *are* our brother's keeper, and we acknowledge a public, civic responsibility to bear one another's burdens'. In India, in particular, the transformative intent of the Constitution has given the Directive Principles a special resonance:

> [...] the Directive Principles of State Policy are constantly referred to in political debate, social agitation and academic research and at least a basic awareness of what they contain is part of the civic knowledge of even moderately educated Indians.[10]

The *Model Constitution* adopted an ambiguous solution whereby provisions relating to social and economic rights began with the phrase 'Parliament shall be responsible for ensuring by legislation [that the following right is realised]' but would not have been expressly excluded from judicial review. This would place the primary responsibility for realising social and economic rights upon the Parliament, but could potentially allow the courts to decide on the compatibility of legislation with constitutional provisions. For example, an Act to abolish the NHS might be deemed unconstitutional, because it would be inconsistent with the constitutional duty of Parliament to provide for universal healthcare. How this would develop in practice would depend on the future interactions between Parliament and the courts, although my expectation (remembering, of course, that this is speculation about a hypothetical Constitution for a state that does not yet exist) is that the courts would defer to Parliament, and that the effect of these provisions would be, except perhaps in extraordinary instances, mainly declaratory and symbolic.

Perhaps a better – that is to say, less ambiguous – alternative is to adopt systems of political, rather than judicial, enforcement. This would require the Government to respect the social and economic principles of the Constitution, and would give Parliament a specific role in the enforcement of these provisions while shielding social and economic policies from judicial policy-making. Taking the idea of 'Directive Principles' as a starting point, this approach would require a Minister introducing the Bill to signify that it complies with the Directive Principles, a procedure not unlike that contained within the UK's Human Rights Act, 1998 (although without the wriggle room of being able to proceed without making such a statement). In addition, the constitution could require Ministers to conduct 'impact assessments' through consultation with social partners (trade unions, employer's associations, the third sector and local authorities) on the effect of social and economic legislation on the working poor, the unemployed and other vulnerable groups, as well as the environment and future generations. The courts, for their part, would be able to issue a 'statement of incompatibility' if they determine that an Act of Parliament goes against the Directive Principles without, however, annulling the act or limiting its application. It would then be up to Parliament to respond to that statement.[a] A constitutionally defined all-party parliamentary committee, convened by an opposition member, could be required to oversee the process and to report annually to Parliament on the Government's record with regard to compliance with the Directive Principles. Such an arrangement would enable Parliament to decide on social and economic policies, and leave plenty of room for 'ordinary politics' in the balancing of ideas, interests, budgets and priorities, while still underlining a clear public intent that these constitutional principles are too important and fundamental to be ignored.

iii   Beyond Rights: Empowering the People

The need for social and economic rights to be included in a Constitution is now more important and urgent than ever, because such rights have been subject to sustained attack from an oligarchic state intent on their

---

a   This is, in essence, the system adopted for the protection of European Convention rights under the Human Rights Act. While this is insufficient, in my view, for the protection of civil and political rights (which are part of the Charter-provisions of the Constitution), it might provide a pragmatic compromise for the protection of social and economic rights (which are Covenantal, and thus stand in a different relationship to the democratic process). The former are essential for procedural democracy; the latter, a product of it.

destruction. However, tackling poverty is not the only priority. If we seek
to maintain a democratic and socially just society we must also tackle the
problem of excess wealth. The neo-liberal policies enforced during the last
30 years have resulted in an inverse redistribution of wealth from the poor
and the middle class to the very rich. This has consolidated vast wealth in
the top 'one per cent' of society. Andy Wightman, looking solely at
property wealth according to figures from the Office of National Statistics,
notes that:

> The median value for household net property wealth is £90,000 (i.e.
> half of households have less than this and half have more). To be in
> the top 10% requires net property wealth of over £314,500 whilst
> 32% of households have nothing. The top 1% of the population has
> net property wealth of up to £15,040,000.[11]

According to Oxfam, in 2013 85 families had more wealth than the total
wealth of the bottom 3.5 billion people.[12] Just five families in Britain have
more wealth than 12 million people.[13] Such concentrations of wealth are
dangerous to the existence of a democratic state; money is power, and the
distribution of power in the hands of the rich few is the very essence of
oligarchy. Although the immediate political landscape has, so far, changed
only at the margins, one of the beneficial results of the financial crisis of
2008 is a renewed focus on social and economic justice, and a deeper
questioning of neo-liberal orthodoxies. After 30 years of 'growth' (as
measured by GDP), many people's real quality of life – in terms of housing,
household debt levels, working hours and economic security – is worse than
that of their parent's generation. In response, many are now once again
questioning the distribution of wealth in society, and are realising that the
gross concentration of wealth and the coexistence of excessive wealth and
poverty are harmful to all of us and incompatible with the common good.[a]
We are also, to a greater extent, questioning the nature of wealth, with a
renewed emphasis on 'enough' rather than 'more', and on happiness and
wellbeing rather than the accumulation of possessions. As GDP gains
cannot be eaten, worn, sat on or lived in, then increasing real wealth

---

a   The current authoritative work on this subject is: Wilkinson, R. and Pickett, K., *The
     Spirit Level: Why More Equal Societies Almost Always Do Better* (London: Allen
     Lane, 2009)

might mean working fewer hours to spend more time in the garden growing vegetables or looking after children or elderly relatives.[a]

There is also a growing awareness that the class lines have been redrawn. The class system as it existed during the industrial age divided the working class against the middle class. Neo-liberalism has changed all that. As well as promoting the rise of the super-rich, it has resulted, first in an increase in the size of the underclass and a return to the levels of absolute poverty which a generation ago we thought we had put behind us forever, and second, in an expansion of the precarious lower middle class with university degrees but little economic security. In this context, the difference between the working class and the middle class falls into insignificance compared to the difference between all of us and the very rich. The Occupy movement, although it failed in its immediate objectives, at least introduced into our lexicon the notion of 'the 99 per cent' against the 'one per cent'. The distinction that matters politically is no longer between the lorry driver and the dentist or the cleaning lady and the headmistress, but between all of these and a small, super rich elite which has embedded itself parasitically into the financial and governmental systems and is using the state for its own benefit.

If the Constitution is to achieve social justice and is to enable us, as free and equal citizens, to seek the common good, then we need more than social and economic rights. We also need stronger democratic institutions, as outlined in the foregoing chapters, enabling power to be transferred from the few to the many – from the one per cent to the 99 per cent. Such institutions will enable us to prevent policies that are opposed to the common good, while promoting those that are seeking to achieve the common good.[b]

---

a The Reid Foundation's *Time for Life* (2014) provides some interesting insight into this possibility.

b If arrangements such as a randomly selected Tribunate or the right of the people to trigger an extraordinary dissolution and general election are deemed too radical, then at least certain specific prohibitions could be incorporated into the Constitution. Just as several Constitutions require the use of a referendum for certain specified decisions, such as the decision to delegate powers to an international organisation, so a Scottish Constitution could, for example, forbid the privatisation of a public service or asset, unless the decision is endorsed by the people in a referendum.

CHAPTER EIGHT

How can the Constitution promote public ethics?

IN RECENT YEARS, a growing number of political scientists, theorists and practitioners have put a renewed emphasis on the role of the active, virtuous, ethical citizen in public life.[a] According to this view, a 'mechanical republic', whose finely balanced powers would work 'like clockwork' to protect against tyranny and corruption, and to bring good laws and policies out of passive and indifferent citizens,[b] has been shown to be incapable of sustaining a lively, principled democratic life. Such a system may protect individual rights, but it is disempowering and demoralising all the same, because it does not allow sufficient scope for citizens' voices.[1] Drawing on a rediscovery of civic traditions with roots in antiquity and in the city republics of medieval Italy, citizenship is increasingly viewed as more than a legal status; it is a state of being. A citizen, in this sense of the word, is expected to *act* as a citizen, to take part in government, and to care for the common good. Institutional structures are important, because without them citizens cannot act effectively, but even the best institutional tools are not sufficient, unless there are good citizens to work them.

Just as a monarchy depends largely on the character, excellence and

---

a   For a general introduction to this tradition see: Bellamy, R. *Citizenship: A Very Short Introduction* (Oxford: Oxford University Press, 2008); Honohan, I. *Civic Republicanism* (Abingdon: Routledge, 2002); Petit, P. Republicanism: *A Theory of Freedom and Government* (Oxford: Oxford University Press, 1997); Viroli, I. *Republicanism* (Hill & Wang, 2001); White, S. and Leighton, D. (eds) *Building a Citizen Society: The Emerging Politics of Republican Democracy* (Lawrence & Wishart, 2008).

b   James Harrington (1611–1677) made an analogy between the Constitution and cats cooking. As a well-designed machine would enable cats on a treadmill to perform all the operations of a kitchen, turning the spit and basting the meat, without having any idea or will of their own, so a well-designed Constitution would enable the citizens, even if lacking in passion, virtue and will, to govern the state. See: Pocock, J. A. G. (ed), *The Political Works of James Harrington* (Cambridge: Cambridge University Press, 1977) p. 744.

public spirit of the monarch, so the quality of democracy (be its institutional forms and written Constitution ever so excellent) ultimately depends, in large part, on the character, excellence and public spirit of the people. The foundational assertion that constitutional democracy (*folkric*) will best serve the common good (*folkweal*) depends on the people – or at least most of the people, most of the time – having a passion to seek the good, the knowledge and wisdom to discern it, and the courage and steadfastness to insist upon it.

In the absence of honest and courageous citizens to care, to think, to argue and to act, the best we can hope for will be a shrill and shallow populism, in which the self-gain and vainglory of ambitious politicians will prevail over honourable public service, and special interests will prevail over the good of the community. The best electioneer, not the best candidate, will be chosen, and policy will follow the best-placed bribe, not the best course of action.

As noted in Chapter Two, questions of virtue and corruption – that is, whether the state serves the public or private interests – are at the heart of the distinction between good and bad forms of government. If the Constitution is to promote the common good by establishing political liberty and by guarding the 'res publica' from authoritarianism, manipulation and corruption, then it must be concerned not only with the structures and processes of power, but also with the character, behavior and ethics of those in power. The process of reconstituting Scottish democracy must consider, alongside institutional questions, the 'constitution of character' that our public institutions proclaim and embody. The question of how to develop the ethos of democratic citizenship, through the covenantal provisions of the Constitution or otherwise, should be taken as seriously by constitution-builders as, say, the design of the electoral system or the rules for protecting judicial independence.

i The need for Good Citizenship

At its best, a democratic Constitution elevates humanity from the arrogance of mastery and the shame of servility. As members of the *res publica*, we are not dependent upon the arbitrary will of anyone. We do not have to bow, scrape, grovel or flatter, for we are protected by equal participation in public institutions and universal rules that embody the authority of all, applied for the protection and wellbeing of each. It has long been recognised that if we wish to sustain such a *res publica*, and to enjoy this free and civic way of life under the equal protection of its Constitution and laws, we must bear the easy yoke and light burden of citizenship.[a]

If we wish to savour the full fruits of liberty, we must cultivate civic virtue, and equip ourselves with the habits and character of good citizens. This idea of good citizenship should be neither slavish nor hedonistic. It should reject, as unworthy of the status and duties of a citizen, both passive obedience to the power of the state and the immediate gratification of unreflective personal desires. Good democratic citizens will stand up for their rights, and also for the rights of others. They will take part in public life, not only voting in elections and referendums, but also learning about the issues and the candidates, thinking about public concerns, and trying to discern what is just, good, and beneficial for society. Democratic citizens should understand, respect and defend the Constitution, regarding it as the cornerstone of public life, but never treat it as an idol, or as something that is absolute in itself. They should be willing to resist power, through demonstrations and even civic disobedience, when it breaks its lawful and constitutional bounds, yet freely support it when it acts according to the laws and Constitution. They will understand that opinions differ, and whilst seeking to convince others of the views they hold to be correct, will also be open to having their views challenged and corrected by others through lively – and at times testy – public discourse. They should have the ability to discern truth from falsehood, to resist flattery and intimidation, and to speak boldly but with gentleness, avoiding the vices of both arrogance and cowardice in their conversation. In all things, good citizens should have a sense of connectedness to their fellow citizens and as sense of responsibility for the common good. In sum, good citizens will exercise *caritas rei publicae*, or 'loving care towards public things'.[2]

---

a   We find this point being made, with subtle variations, by Aristotle the Greek philosopher and by Cicero the Roman statesman, by Machiavelli the urbane Florentine and by Rousseau the rustic Genevan, by John Milton the prophetic poet and by Giuseppe Mazzini the poetic prophet, by Jim Wallis the political preacher and by Vaclav Havel the anti-political President.

There are two lurking threats to such democratic citizenship. The first is the neo-liberal idea of liberty, popularised by the right-wing politics since the 1970s, according to which liberty is reduced to the expression of shallow, individual, utility-maximising choices. Neo-liberalism, in treating all human interactions as 'bargains' in a marketplace, rather than as 'deliberations' in the public square, undervalues public, collective and democratic decision-making.[3] 'Freedom', according to these debased notions, is found in consumer capitalism, not a Town Hall meeting, Parliament or voting booth. In placing private gain above the common good, the 'every man for himself' mentality of neo-liberalism erodes the habits of solidarity and civic activity, and weakens the ethos of community and public service that is necessary to sustain democracy.[4]

The second threat comes from the fact that the UK establishment's view of 'good citizenship', much in vogue during Gordon Brown's premiership and having a miserable renaissance under David Cameron, is essentially authoritarian. People must be seen (owing to a secretive surveillance state), but rarely heard (because of a weak and poorly functioning democracy). In economic life, we are supposed to be productive 'strivers', without asking too much in return; in public life, we are to be obedient. 'Good citizens', in this oligarchic state, are supposed to hold down a job, obey the law, pay their taxes, keep out of trouble, get excited about the Olympics and wave the flag. There is nothing wrong with any of those things, but they are not a sufficient basis for democratic citizenship.

These two influences combine to promote a society in which we actively work and consume in our private and economic lives, and obey the state in public, without ever, as citizens, taking effective control of either. As it was expressed by Benjamin Constant, a leading (although not an uncritical) 19th-century theorist of liberal modernity:

> The danger for modern liberty is that we, absorbed in the enjoyment of our private independence and the pursuit of our particular interests, might surrender too easily our right to share in political power. The holders of authority encourage us to do just that. They are so ready to spare us every sort of trouble except the trouble of obeying and paying![5]

We should articulate a deeper view of 'good citizenship' – one that is consistent with a democratic Constitution, and builds on the best aspects of our civic traditions. Such a view of good citizenship is not utopian or monolithic. Civic virtue in a democratic state does not demand that we should neglect our proper economic occupations, our family and personal obligations, our social and cultural activities or our spiritual life. Rather, it requires us to hold all these different spheres of life in a right balance with the common good and with our public and civic obligations. This model of citizenship is not only for an elect few, but one that ordinary men and women can mostly be expected to achieve.

ii Education for Citizenship

Freedom is its own apprenticeship. The experience of acting as a citizen trains us for the responsibilities of citizenship. When citizens of democratic societies take part in public debates, sign petitions, go on marches, cast votes in elections and referendums, write to representatives, serve on juries or even share a news story with friends, they are not only contributing – however marginally and indirectly – to the development of public policy and the conduct of public affairs, but also learning to think as a citizen thinks. The process of participation teaches us how to listen to others, to form alliances, to discern truth and reasonable argument from spurious soundbites and to consider the common good in addition to our own needs. Thus a democratic constitution is an important spur to the encouragement of the values by which it is sustained. The existence of constitutional rights and the challenge and responsibility of democratic self-government will, in time, help the people who have previously learned only to cajole or supplicate, as subjects, to speak as citizens ought – treating none as subordinate or superior, but all as friends, brethren and fellow citizens. Conversely, if there are no public forums in which to freely debate issues and no effective, accessible means by which to influence policy in light of such debates, then civic spirit will atrophy.

The public square, the jury room, the voting booth and the hustings, therefore, are the 'finishing schools' of citizenship, in which we learn by practice how to live the life of freedom. There is also a need, however, for preparatory education, so that young citizens are aware of their responsibilities and equipped to handle them. Historically, the school system has been one of the most important means of promoting civic virtue in democratic societies. Considered in its broadest sense, education helps people to develop the skills, knowledge and traits of character that citizens need in order fully to enjoy their rights and to perform their duties.

A commitment to public education ought therefore to be treated as an integral part of the state's foundation. To enshrine the principle of free and universal education in the constitution is to recognise that education is not merely an investment in an individual's future employability (although that might be an important aspect of it), but also a public good, intrinsically linked to overall wellbeing of society and to the quality of citizenship. A constitutional commitment to the public funding of universities, likewise, shows that universities are not intended to be feeder institutions for the lower managerial rungs of corporate capitalism, but to be public institutions with a clearly moral and civic purpose: namely, the creation of a broadly educated, morally mature, civically conscious citizenry.

Beyond a general commitment to the principle of public education, it would not be proper, or even possible, for a Constitution to go into details of educational structures or the curriculum. Nevertheless, three brief comments on education for citizenship might be excused. First, there is a strong case for compulsory civics classes in school, in which children should study their Constitution, learn how their public institutions work, and understand their rights and duties as citizens. Second, a visit to Parliament should be organised, as part of the civic curriculum, for every child. In the Netherlands, there is an organisation called Pro Demos, attached to the Parliament's visitor centre, which every day hosts classes of school children from across the country: they have a tour of the Parliament and take part in workshops, games and quizzes designed to teach them about the Constitution and the democratic principles on which it rests. The exercises include one in which young people representing different political parties take part in coalition-formation negotiations, and one in which children playing the part of local councillors have to make town planning decisions. In exercises such as these the young citizens not only learn about how their institutions work, but also how to work their institutions. Third, without ignoring the need for technical and vocational education, there is much to be said for a traditional liberal arts education, and, in consequence, for sustained public investment in the arts and humanities. A broad foundation in classics, history, philosophy, modern languages and literature not only teaches intellectual precision, but also trains people to deal with ethical questions: Was Brutus right to kill Caesar? Did Antigone do well to insist, against Creon's wishes, that her brother be given a proper burial? How should we act when faced with those who would corrupt the republic for their own ambitious ends? What should we do when confronted with unjust orders? An education that trains children to engage in such questions is one that also trains citizens to lead without dominating, to obey lawfully without being obsequious, to argue without shouting, to listen without being fooled, and to co-operate without compromising their integrity.

Besides the public education system and the universities, another public body with responsibility for promoting a civic ethos and well-informed, civilised public debate is the broadcasting service. The pursuit of *folkweal* through *folkric* puts faith in the people to discern the common good through argument, negotiation, deliberation, discussion and voting. If democracy is to succeed in its promise of realising the common good, even in a pragmatic and contingent way, the quality of public discussion must raise above the sort of shrill invective that only divides and enrages the people; it should proceed instead along more civil, rational and generous lines. A genuine 'public service' broadcaster, with a constitutional mandate to educate and inform, which takes seriously its role in refining our minds and elevating our hearts (and not simply catering to our most base desires, as commercial channels are forced to do), can do much to set the right tone, and is therefore of inestimable benefit to a democratic society.

In decades past, the BBC did for the most part an admirable job; its cultural, news, educational and documentary output did much to broaden the public mind. In recent years, however, its political independence (always, as ever in the British system, a matter of convention and unspoken understanding, rather than firm and clear rules) has been eroded, and its credibility and political impartiality, especially on the monarchy, the armed forces, religion, and matters concerning Scottish news, politics and current affairs, has been undermined. In broadcasting, as in other areas, it is becoming clear that informal, conventional restraints against abuses of power are insufficient.

To preserve the independence and integrity of a public service broadcaster, it must be protected both from the corrosive tendency of the market to drive down standards and quality for the sake of ratings and revenue (which means it must be publicly funded), and from the influence of the Government and the political parties who might seek to use it as their mouthpiece. To this end, the *Model Constitution* proposed the creation of an independent, non-partisan Broadcasting Authority. It was envisaged that this body, enjoying guaranteed constitutional autonomy, would have responsibility for supervising public service broadcasting in a way that would protect its editorial independence from commercial or party-political influences, while ensuring accountability to the highest standards of professional conduct and ethics. The establishment of such a body is vital to the health of democracy, and any Constitution without one would be incomplete.

iii   Principles of Public Life and Codes of Conduct

Good citizenship, in the general sense described above, is a moral obligation on all members of the *res publica*, which we owe to our fellow citizens on a reciprocal basis. Some citizens, however, have a stronger sense of calling to public life, and are blessed with talents and resources (such as vision and initiative, leadership or organisational ability, or the ability to communicate well) that give them greater opportunities for public service. These are the natural and suitable leaders of a democratic society. The importance of such leadership cannot be underestimated. It is impossible to do without leaders. Even the most egalitarian human organisation requires certain people to carry out facilitating, co-ordinating, preparatory or implementing functions that place a duty of leadership upon them. So, if we do not have good leaders, motivated by a sense of civic duty and public service, then we will have bad ones, motivated by ambition and greed.

> [The] paradox is that egalitarian democracy actually requires a hierarchy both of values and of persons of excellence. Otherwise, money and sophistry co-conspire to destroy it, as they have in recent years. Democracy can only be sustained when there is a parallel, non-democratic concern with *paideia* – the formation of good character – which links talent to virtue and both to positions of appropriate social influence. Without the extra-democratic inculcation of character, democracy cannot enter into the debate about the good, which is the only legitimate and non-corrupt debate that can be held.[6]

In a corrupt state, the absence of principled and trustworthy democratic leadership at the top inhibits the practice of good citizenship throughout society. The citizens will in most cases follow the tone set by national leadership on points of ethics and behaviour; a corrupt leadership and venial, hypocritical political class will soon corrupt the rest of society, making renovation difficult to achieve. It is, for example, difficult to convince people that paying taxes is an honourable and worthy contribution to the common good, when they see the rich and powerful evading tax. It is difficult to cast a good, well-informed, public-spirited vote if there are no good candidates from which to choose.[a]

Amongst those active in public life, a variety of 'humours', or temperaments, can be found. Some are statesmen, who bring vision and leadership to bear on public affairs. They contend for civic righteousness and seek the wellbeing of their country and of the world, now and for future generations. In their conduct, they think of the precedents that might be set by their example, and recognise the transcendent need for rectitude in public life. Some are honest if less inspiring representatives, who might lack the vision, leadership and historical bearing of statesmen, but are honest defenders of the public good as they see it. They care about the lives and livelihoods of their constituents, and are conscientious in pursuing particular issues of concern to them. Some are ideologues. They are motivated by ideas and policies. Often they are innovators and passionately committed to achieving specific reforms. Unfortunately, their zeal is trapped inside narrow ideological bonds, which can make them inflexible and can cause them to go beyond legitimate means in the pursuit of what they believe to be supremely important ends. Some might best be described as conscientious objectors. They may share the purism of the ideologues, but they are less focused on holding power and changing policy; rather, they prefer to act like gnats, pricking the public and parliamentary conscience, asking awkward but necessary questions, and exposing the false certainties of others.

---

a   As a frustrated anonymous American correspondent wrote of the mayoral election in his city, 'Seriously, who cares about [our city's mayoral election] when the choices are between a corporatist, a loudmouth douchebag and a dish-dog at a hipster downtown restaurant? At this point I'd actually prefer the racist homophobe who's not running, and that's pretty sad.'

All these humours, in balance, have a part to play in maintaining the good temper and health of democratic institutions. Yet these four humours are easily overbalanced by a noxious but pervasive fifth humour: that of the careerists. Careerists see politics as a trade to be entered into for profit. They treat the *res publica* as if it were a private estate to be farmed, not a public trust to be nurtured. Having no point of principle to orientate them, other than their own advancement, they seek favours from those at the top of the party structure. They become toadies to those above them, and bullies to those below.

If not purged regularly by an active public conscience, through the rough surgery of the ballot box, an excess accumulation of careerists in the system can poison democracy. An abundance of careerists can reduce public deliberation to an exchange of sterile platitudes and insults between scripted talking heads, turn parliamentary proceedings into a ritualized theatre of confrontation between mass ranks of 'lobby-fodder' who do not even bother to read the bills on which they are required to vote, and turn accountability to an attempt to attain advantage by exposing the faults of others while covering up one's own.

Recognising this, a good constitution must – through the institutional mechanisms discussed in earlier chapters – empower the people to exercise control over the state. But it is also necessarily to put rules and guidelines in place so that both those in office and the citizens who are supposed to hold them to account know what is expected of them. A written constitution can provide an authoritative and publically endorsed statement of what principles and virtues should guide our public life, and what sort of conduct is acceptable.

Some steps have already been taken. The Nolan Report of 1995 (the First Report of the Committee on Standards in Public Life),[7] issued in response to political 'sleaze' during the premiership of John Major, identified seven principles of public conduct: selflessness, integrity, objectivity, accountability, openness, honesty and leadership.[8] These, with some minor alterations of wording and ordering, formed the basis for a Scottish set of principles, applied to devolved institutions, and issued by the Commission for Ethical Standards in Public Life in Scotland.[9] However, these statements of principles are merely *official* and not *public*; they are the result of administrative acts, not of a covenantal agreement of the people. They

Fig. 12 The Key Principles of Conduct in Public Life

(From the Commission for Ethical Standards in Public Life in Scotland)

Duty and Public Service	Holders of public office should uphold the law and act in accordance with the law and the public trust placed in them. They should act in the interests of the body they serve.
Selflessness	Holders of public office have a duty to act solely in terms of the public interest. They must not act in order to gain financial or other material benefit for themselves, family or friends.
Integrity	Holders of public office must not place themselves under any financial or other obligation to any individual or organisation that might reasonably be thought to influence them in the performance of their duties.
Objectivity	Holders of public office must make decisions solely on merit when carrying out public business.
Accountability & Stewardship	Holders of public office are accountable for their decisions and actions to the public. They have a duty to consider issues on their merits, taking account of the views of others and must ensure that resources are used prudently and in accordance with the law.
Openness	Holders of public office have a duty to be as open as possible about decisions and actions they take, giving reasons for their decisions and restricting information only when the wider public interest clearly demands.
Honesty	Holders of public office have a duty to act honestly. They must declare any private interests relating to their public duties and take steps to resolve any conflicts arising in a way that protects the public interest.
Leadership	Holders of public office should exhibit these principles in their own behaviour. They should actively promote and robustly support the principles and be willing to challenge poor behaviour wherever it occurs.

speak to officials, not to citizens, and they can be found only in obscure official publications, where, for the most part, only those who have a vested interest in evading or misconstruing them are aware of their existence.

Putting these principles into a Constitution that can be read by every adult and taught to every child would increase their status and visibility, transforming them from official guidelines to foundational principles of the state. This would send an important signal of intent to repudiate corruption and self-interest and to embrace an ethos of public service. No one should be so naïve as to suppose that articulating general principles, even in so august a document as a Constitution, will solve the problem of public integrity. However, giving explicit public endorsement to such principles can shape the direction and boundaries of public discussion, and can provide a common model of good behaviour that has an important normative and educational purpose.

If these principles are to be taken seriously, they must be more than just educational guidelines. They must also be translated into a form that can be enforced. For this reason, the statement of principles should be backed up by a code of conduct. Statements of principles set the goal; codes of conduct, the rules. Principles offer general guidelines of behaviour, providing a model of 'excellence' to which citizens and officials should aspire; codes of conduct regulate or prohibit specific actions in particular circumstances. Principles are upheld by public sentiment; codes are backed by the threat of sanction. The principles must inform the codes of conduct; the codes of conduct help to implement the principles (but cannot replace them, since it is possible, for example, for one to conform outwardly to the letter of the law and to codes of conduct, while undermining their spirit).[a] As it states in current the Code of Conduct for MSPs:

> The key principles, as compared to the ethical standards set out in the Code itself, are aspirational in nature. Their intent is to guide and inspire members toward the very highest ethical ideals. The key principles, in contrast to ethical standards, do not represent obligations and do not form the basis for imposing sanctions.[10]

---

a   The relationship between the Statement of Principles and the Code of Conduct reflects, in some ways, the relationship between a preamble and the operative text of a Constitution, or between its covenantal and charter-like provisions.

At present, under the Ethical Standards in Public Life (Scotland) Act 2000, Codes of Conduct relating to local councils and other public bodies are drawn up by the Scottish Ministers, while under Rule 1.6 of the Parliament's Standing Orders, Parliament adopts its own Code of Conduct for members. These essentially self-regulatory arrangements place too much responsibility in political hands, with too little visibility and independent oversight. It would be better for this function of transforming general principles into a specific and enforceable code of conduct to be vested in an independent commission with a non-partisan composition and guaranteed constitutional autonomy from the executive and legislature.[a]

Ethical responsibility does not cease when one leaves office. Consideration should also be given to the retirement and future employment of former high officers of state. If former ministers can walk into well-paid jobs in the private sector, perhaps in the very firms whose activities they might previously have been responsible for regulating, or whose contracts they might previously have had a hand in awarding, then they will, in effect, be accountable to those firms, and not to the public. To help prevent this, a constitutional rule could forbid any minister from holding any private employment or consultancy which may give rise to a conflict of interest. This ban should of course apply when in office, but should also be extended, after they leave office, for a term long enough to close the 'revolving door' between government and business interests. The Public Service Commission could be responsible for enforcing this rule, with the right to censure under the Code of Conduct any ex-minister who acts improperly in this regard. A generous pension on leaving office, to encourage former ministers to retire, or devote themselves to non-remunerative but socially useful work, might also help to reduce such conflicts of interest.

iv Public Honours

Another way of promoting civic virtue and good citizenship is through the right ordering of the honours system. Public honours, in principle, are a way of recognising and rewarding those who have served the public good with merit and distinction. In practice, however, the honours system

---

a The *Model Constitution* proposed (Art. X., Sect 5) that this duty be vested in the Public Service Commission.

in the United Kingdom often falls short of that objective, because it is used in a selective and subjective way to reward friends and placate rivals. The sale of peerages was a scandal when Lloyd George did it in the early 20th century, and it remains a scandal today. It is not a system of honour, but of patronage (money is enough to bribe poor people; to bribe rich people you might need a gong). The honours system in the UK thus provides many alluring opportunities for corrupt and dishonourable actions.

Scotland, whether independent or in an autonomous Home Rule or loosely federal arrangement, could have its own honours system. If so, however, it must reward genuine merit and public service, and not be a vehicle for patronage and corruption. To ensure this, the award of honours must not depend on the secretive or arbitrary decisions of the Scottish Government. One possible approach is to establish an all-party parliamentary Honours Committee with sole constitutional responsibility for advising the Head of State on the award of honours. Ministers, to avoid conflicts of interest, would be excluded from the committee. If this committee were bound by rules of transparency and were required by the Constitution to base its nominations on stated meritorious criteria and on public (not partisan) service, this might go some way to making the honours system live up to its name. A further possibility is to require parliamentary approval, by plenary vote, for the award of honours, meaning that the honours list would be subject to a ministerial statement and general debate before it can be approved.

Fig. 13 Example: Reform of the honours system
(Scottish Provisional Constituent Assembly text, 1964)

Article 40

The Sovereign shall confer decorations for distinguished services on the advice, or with the consent, of the National Assembly.

No rank or title shall be conferred other than that which each office carries with it. The title Lord shall cease to be used in relation to all offices within the nation.

No personal or hereditary titles or privileges shall be recognised other than those of Princes and Princesses of the blood royal within the immediate succession.

There shall be no party-political honours or decorations.

No citizen shall accept rank, title, or privilege from the head of any other State or from the government of any other State without first securing the sanction of the National Assembly. Awards for humane achievements may be awarded and accepted without sanctions.

CHAPTER NINE

How can we build a new constitutional settlement?

CONSTITUTION BUILDING has been likened to 'rebuilding a ship at sea'.[1] The state has to be kept afloat – taxes collected, laws enforced, schools and hospitals kept open – even while its structures are being refashioned, as it were, from the keel up. Constitution building is also (to quote the famous words of Ron Davies, the former Secretary of State for Wales, uttered in relation to devolution) 'a process, not an event'. There is much preparation to do before the actual moment when one constitutional order gives way to another (the point, to continue the analogy, where the flag is struck from the old ship and hoisted on the new) and much implementation work to do after that moment has passed.

The process of constitutional transition therefore requires careful planning over a period that may extend over several years. Such planning cannot prevent the failure of the process, but it can do much – especially if broad and inclusive agreements are made at an early stage – to avoid stalemate, delays, boycotts, and subsequent illegitimacy. If we are committed to the democratic reconstitution of Scotland, either as an independent state or as a largely autonomous state within a federalised or otherwise 'loosely United' Kingdom, then we must pay attention to the process, as well as to the aims, of change.

In this final chapter, two basic questions are addressed. First, does the process actually matter in the sense of there being a relatively clear link between process and outcome, and certain common criteria by which we can distinguish good processes from bad ones? Second, what might a good process look like in our context, in terms of practical stages?

i   Does Process Matter?

For a long time, the connection between constitution building processes and democratic outcomes was under-researched. The success or failure of democratic constitutionalism was generally attributed not to anything inherent in either the design of the constitution or the processes by which the constitution was adopted, but to general levels of political, social and economic development, or to deeply ingrained cultural traits. Briefly put, an industrialised and literate society, having a broadly Western culture and a tradition of representative government and the rule of law, with a relatively homogenous population and a dense civil society of non-state organisations, would be fairly assured of democratic success. Meanwhile, a pre-industrialised and mostly illiterate society, with a non-Western culture, a tradition of absolutist rule, a thin civil society, and deep ethno-linguistic or cultural divisions, would be very likely to revert to dictatorship. Without necessarily discounting the effects of these background preconditions of democracy, scholars from the 1990s onwards expressed a renewed interest in the independent effect of institutional design, based predominantly on the study of new democracies in Latin America and Central and Eastern Europe, as well as on democratic transitions in parts of Africa. This sparked a lively debate on the relative merits of parliamentary and presidential forms of government, on electoral systems, and on different ways of accommodating or integrating diversity. Yet the influence of the process of constitution building, as distinct from the content of the constitutional text, was still mostly ignored.

The experiences of European constitutionalism after the Second World War suggest that there is no simple and direct connection between the degree of participation in the constitution building process and the success of the Constitution that emerges from it. In France, the people voted first in a referendum held in October 1945 to adopt a new constitution, and, at the same time, elected a constituent assembly. The draft proposed by that assembly was then submitted to the people, who rejected it in May 1946. Another constituent assembly was elected, and another draft constitution – modified to address the concerns that had led to the rejection of the first draft – was submitted to the people in October, which they narrowly adopted. Thus the process of adopting the Constitution of the Fourth French Republic took, in total, two constituent elections and three referendums over the course of a year: a hearty dose of democratic participation and deliberation.[2] The resulting Constitution, although technically sound in many respects, lasted just twelve years before collapsing in disarray. In

Italy, there was an initial referendum on the abolition of the monarchy and the simultaneous direct election of a Constituent Assembly. The Constitution was adopted by the Constituent Assembly, on behalf of the people, without direct recourse to the people in a referendum.[3] It has remained in effect to this day, and to that extent can be deemed a success. It has never, however, lived up to its promises; implementation has been patchy, and its provisions have not been sufficient to fully protect Italy from instability, failures of governance, systemic corruption, and periods of personalist rule.[4] The German Constitution (Basic Law of the Federal Republic of Germany), in contrast, was drafted by a parliamentary conference made up of delegates from the various *Länder*, without much public involvement. It was neither endorsed by an elected body nor put to the people in a referendum. Yet it quickly gained legitimacy, provided a stable basis for a workable, effective democracy, and is still widely respected.

Likewise, most of the Constitutions adopted by former British colonies when they became independent were produced by a relatively closed, elitist and non-participatory process. For the most part, these Constitutions were negotiated by a small conference of the main political parties in each country, assisted by legal and political experts. These conferences based their work on a limited number of tried and tested constitutional templates that could be minimally adapted to particular circumstances. The resulting Constitutions could be criticized on many levels – for the most part, they offer little scope for direct democracy, establish majoritarian electoral systems that limit political competition, and are written in an impenetrable style that diminishes their impact as instruments of national unification or civic empowerment. Many of these Constitutions have succeeded, however, in providing for the peaceful and democratic transfer of power, backed by the protection of human rights, even in several places where democracy might have seemed unlikely.

While there is a limit to what can be inferred from these examples, the experience of both Europe and the Commonwealth does seem to indicate that extensive and direct public participation (however desirable it might be in principle) is neither necessary nor sufficient to produce a workable, legitimate and enduring Constitution. When *A Model Constitution* was written, my inclination – drawn from these and other similar cases – was to be wary of extensive public participation in constitution-building. My concern was that public participation could lead to a poorly drafted, inconsistent and over-ambitious Constitution that would fail in the essential task of consolidating a democratic system.

Now, however, I would place greater emphasis on the need for public participation and political agreement in the constitution building process. As a general principle, a democratic Constitution should begin with a democratic Constitution building process. The Roman law principle of *quod omnes tangit debet ab omnibus approbari* ('that which touches all, should be approved by all', or in plain terms, 'nothing about us, without us') demands that the Constitution should be the product of widespread public participation. This is because the design of the process reflects the distribution of power, and results in the inclusion or exclusion of interest groups who may be inclined to influence outcomes in their own favour. If the Constitution is the supreme law which manifests the highest expression of popular sovereignty, then it follows – if we take this normative claim and its consequences seriously – that the people ought to have a direct and effective voice in the adoption of the Constitution, not only in a final referendum that ratifies or rejects it but also in shaping the text long before it reaches the referendum stage.

There are also practical arguments for a more participatory constitution building process. This is still a new and rapidly expanding field of study, with many unanswered questions, but a small body of evidence emerging from recent comparative scholarship seems to indicate that a successful constitutional outcome (i.e. a Constitution that provides a stable and legitimate legal-political basis for the consolidation of an effective democratic system) is more likely to occur from inclusive than from exclusive processes. This is because inclusive processes allow for disagreements to be expressed and for compromises to be reached at an early stage, such that polarisation is minimised. A broad swathe of the political spectrum and of the wider society can therefore feel that the constitution reflects their concerns and has not been imposed by others. Final approval by referendum may still be required as means of popular authorisation and legitimation, but this is no substitute for inclusive engagement in the earlier stages of the process.[a]

---

a   See: Wheatley, J. and Mendez, F., *Patterns of Constitutional Design: The Role of*

The contrast between the 1997 and 2014 referendums in Scotland is illustrative of the advantages of broad engagement and participation at the early stages. In 1997, the devolution scheme had been devised by a representative convention, including Labour, the Liberal Democrats, the Greens and other minor parties, churches, trade unions, the Scottish Federation of Small Businesses, the voluntary sector, local authorities, and other 'social partners'. The principle, and much of the detail, had already been agreed before the referendum, so the referendum confirmed and endorsed agreements that had been reached through an inclusive process of deliberation and negotiation. In 2014, in contrast, there was no attempt to build such agreement. There was a Yes/No vote, but no clear understanding, constitutionally, of what would occur in either eventuality. The result was not necessarily a ringing endorsement for the United Kingdom, but a lack of confidence in a future that – because of a lack of broad agreement – appeared uncertain.

Broad cross-party agreement also helps to ensure the longevity and success of the resulting constitution. Many historical constitutions have failed to create and maintain a democratic constitutional order precisely because they were not based on inclusive agreements, and so did not belong to the whole community. Even if motivated by well-intentioned zeal rather than a naked desire for power, such narrowly based, 'one-sided' constitutions necessarily exclude those citizens who do not belong to a dominant section or faction of society from full and equal participation in the state. These narrowly partisan constitutions, resting on an insufficiently wide base of agreement, are often perceived as illegitimate by opponents of the ruling party, and therefore easy to topple; they usually fail in the task of constitutionalising rather than personalising power and seldom outlive the particular persons or governments by which they were created.

The Arab Spring revolutions of 2011 provide contemporary examples of contrasting constitution building experiences, demonstrating how a good constitutional process aims to find common ground for democracy while bad processes seek to protect the power and privilege of dominant

---

Citizens and Elites in Constitution Making (Farnham: Ashgate Publishing, 2013). Although critical of public participation, the need for inter-elite co-operation also emphasised in Saati, A., *The Participation Myth: outcomes of participatory constitution building processes on democracy* (Umea, Sweden: University of Umea, 2015).

factions to the exclusion of others. Egypt is an example of a bad process. It was chaotic from the start. There was no attempt to achieve agreement on the parameters of a shared vision, nor agreement on the process itself. An election was held before making any attempt at reaching agreement on a shared vision or on the process itself. This left the winners of the election free to design a new Constitution (the short lived version of 2012–2013) without having to compromise with other parties. The text was submitted to a referendum and endorsed by a majority of votes cast – but only on a very low turnout because opponents, contesting the legitimacy of the vote, boycotted it. The lack of legitimacy resulting from this one-sided Constitution making process made it much easier for the Egyptian military to stage a coup in 2013 and to suspend the Constitution. This led to a second Constitution building process, which was entirely dominated by the interests of the military backed interim Government. Drafting was in the hands of an appointed Committee of Fifty who, although nominally inclusive of various interests and sections in Egyptian society, mostly belonged to the previous ruling establishment. Its work was conducted haphazardly and in secret, without heeding external advice, and the resulting Constitution (that of 2014) was also endorsed on a very low turnout. At no point was a consensus reached. First the Islamists, then the military-secular establishment, were able to impose authoritarian Constitutions that effectively solidified their own power.[a]

In Tunisia, in contrast, early agreement was reached on the general shape of the transition process. Having insisted on the use of Proportional Representation to select a Constituent Assembly, the *Ennahda* Party, although winning a plurality of votes, did not gain an overall majority of seats. This forced them to compromise with other parties, forming a three-party coalition with the center left. The Assembly ratified a 'little Constitution' to organise the transitional process. This included provisions

---

a It is worth noting that authoritarian Constitutions abound. These are not mere 'fig-leaves', but perform important functions in regulating authoritarian states – for example, by preventing inter-elite conflicts. Authoritarian constitutions are generally characterised by the concentration of power, the absence of checks and balances, and weak protections for civil liberties. The lesson is that simply having a Constitution is not sufficient. It must be a genuinely democratic one. See: Brown, N., *Constitutions in a Nonconstitutional world: Arab Basic Laws and the prospects for Accountable Government* (New York: State University of New York Press, 2001).

for the ratification of the final constitution, which would have to be approved by a two-thirds majority of the Assembly, or, if a two-thirds majority could not be achieved, by a referendum. This rule provided an incentive for negotiation, since seeking compromise to achieve a two-thirds majority would be a less risky strategy than insisting on a position and facing potential defeat in a referendum. Although the process was not without incident, and indeed nearly stalled during the summer of 2013, *Ennahda* showed willingness to compromise throughout. Civil society also had a much greater influence on the process than in Egypt, with a 'quartet' consisting of the Tunisian General Labor Union, the Employers' Union, The Tunisian Bar Association and the Human Rights League effectively interposing itself as a mediator between the government and opposition in order to establish a road map for dialogue. This, in turn, induced further compromise. The legitimacy of the final text was enhanced because it was approved by an overwhelming majority in the Constituent Assembly (200 for, 14 against, two abstentions).[5] Although the consolidation of democracy in Tunisia cannot be assured yet, both the text of the Constitution and the process by which it was adopted bode well for the future.

The circumstances of constitutional transition in Scotland – whether within or outwith the United Kingdom – are obviously very different from those in Egypt and Tunisia. We would not be transitioning from military dictatorship, but from an ill-functioning and oligarchic state to a better democracy, and from a centralised, hierarchical state to one in which the sovereignty and autonomy of the constituent nations are honoured. Yet the general principles are universal; a closed, exclusive, one-sided constitution building process is unlikely to produce a Constitution that reflects the common good (even in the basic sense of providing democratic means for the peaceful, orderly transfer, exercise and limitation of public power, protecting human rights, ensuring effective and accountable government, and preventing authoritarianism, incumbent manipulation and corruption).

As well as influencing the terms of the constitutional text, the nature of the process also does much to shape the landscape and tone of political debate that surrounds it. Inclusive processes can heal and reconcile a society, providing a basis for unity and progress; exclusive ones damage and divide, poisoning discourse with bitter distrust. Maturity, moderation and willingness to compromise during this crucial time of constitution building could pay large dividends later. On this point the contrasting experiences of authoritarian Zimbabwe and relatively democratic Botswana are of note. The experience of negotiation and compromise at the foundational moment of a nation's statehood, as in Botswana, promotes the values of 'tolerance toward diversity, along with trust and openness', providing a 'core for future democratic leadership', whilst a violent change characterised by violence and a breakdown in the rule of law, as in Zimbabwe, can cast a long shadow over the future democratic prospects of a country.[6]

ii Stages of the process

Having asserted the case for an inclusive constitution building process, the question of how millions of people can actually participate in constitution building in a meaningful way still remains. Obviously it is impossible for the whole nation to meet together and to write the Constitution with a single pen, so some sort of proxy mechanism, by means of public representation and consultation, must be adopted. In this regard there is no one right way to proceed. As long as certain principles of inclusion and participation are adhered to, the structure, institutional mechanism and timing of the process can be subject to many variations depending on the specific needs and circumstances of the country. However, it is important to remember that the chief difficulty of producing a good Constitution lies mainly not in the technical aspects of drafting – putting words on the page – but in building the consensus and agreement that gives those words meaning and authority; it is an inherently political process, with political decisions having to be made before, during and after actual drafting. It is also important to observe the main stages of the process in sequential order: in the same way that the building of a house begins with the foundations before attempting to erect the walls, the preconditions of a constitution must be in place and the formal mechanisms and processes agreed upon before questions of constitutional content are decided.

A prerequisite of successful constitution building is to ensure stable governance during the transition process. In the event of Scottish independence, it might be wise to start with an Interim Constitution that, while less ambitious than many would like, can at least provide a safe, stable and relatively neutral 'platform' on which to build an enduring Constitution. Matters on which there is broad common ground, such as the basic institutional structures of the state, can be embedded in the Interim Constitution from the outset, while the matters in dispute can be postponed until after a longer process of negotiation and engagement. However, in the context of a federal Constitution for the United Kingdom as a whole, an Interim Constitution is probably not necessary; life could continue under the present system of government until the new Constitution comes into effect.

An initial agreement should if possible be reached on how the new Constitution is to be made. That way, even if particular sections of society are dissatisfied with the content of the Constitution, they can at least accord it some respect and legitimacy because of the process by which it has been adopted. A multi-party round-table agreement may seek agreement, for example, on matters such as who needs to be brought to the table and how the participants are to be chosen. It might also be helpful to attempt to build an early consensus around the nature of the constitutional change to be undertaken and about the rules of constitutional decision making. What will be the terms of reference of the constitution drafting body? What timeline will they work to? What steps must be taken to adopt and ratify the new constitution? If agreements can be reached on these matters, on a consensual basis and at an early stage, the chances of the process being derailed will be reduced, while the legitimacy of the final text will be strengthened.

The next step is to establish, in accordance with those initial agreements, the formal institution by which the constitution will be prepared: the 'constitution-making body'. Again, many variations are possible, provided that there is a forum for effective deliberation between all politically relevant groups. In many cases, a directly elected Constituent Assembly is employed (France 1946; Brazil 1988; Tunisia 2011–2014) to draft the Constitution; in others, a smaller Convention or Commission, consisting of nominated members, may be used (Kenya 2010); some rely on a special committee of the interim legislature (Spain 1978; Poland 1997).[7]

The advantage of using a directly elected body is that (provided that the elections are free, fair and proportional), it has popular legitimacy and faithfully represents the political complexion of the country. However, only political parties will have much chance of fielding electable candidates, leaving potentially important non-partisan social and civic interests without direct representation. There is also a risk that a party-dominated body may find it hard to put short-term party advantage aside to focus on the longer-term goal of building democracy.[8] A nominated convention or commission[a] avoids the need for a special election, and so can be less politically divisive. It can also be structured in a way that represents those who may be less likely to win elections, but whose voices still need to be heard. As discussed in Chapter Four, the most reliable way to get a fair reflection of the composition of society is the use of random lot. In Ireland, a Convention consisting of 33 politicians and 66 members of the public selected by random lot was established to consider a series of amendments to the Constitution. Randomly selected Citizens' Assemblies have been used to consider options for electoral reform in British Columbia (2004) and Ontario (2006).[9] Whatever type of constitution making body is chosen, it must be broadly inclusive of the whole society, in all its political shades and demographic diversity.

Having established the constitution-making body, it is necessary to ensure that it is adequately organised and supported for the performance of its duties. It needs clear rules of procedure, a Convenor and a Secretariat. Depending on the precise format of the process, it might also need a Committee of Experts to give advice on constitutional options and their likely consequences.

Before getting down to drafting, the constitution making body may wish to engage in an initial consultation or discussion exercise in order to establish fundamental aims, values and principles. It is useful to consider the previous constitutional system, to think about what worked well and badly, who benefitted from it, and who was excluded from it. This will help to clarify the aims of the constitution-building process. In some cases, these questions might already have been settled at an earlier stage, for

---

a   The names do not always have the same meanings in different contexts, but in general a 'convention' is a larger and more representative body, whereas a 'commission' is a smaller and more expert body. These may be combined in various ways, and employed at different stages of the process: for example, a broad 'convention' may be gathered to discern principles and make major decisions, and its findings may then be presented to a select 'commission' for drafting.

example during the initial negotiations concerning the scope and structure of the process itself. Either way, it may be helpful to produce a pre-constitutional document such as a 'Statement of Principles', identifying common grounds and areas for negotiation and compromise. This will be a useful reference point to keep subsequent discussions on track and to prevent the overall vision and coherence of the Constitution being lost in special interest bargains.

Only then can the actual drafting take place. This is the point at which principles and compromises, promises and preferences, are woven together into a robust, workable text. If preliminary consultations have yielded consensus, this may chiefly be a technical task. If not, this is the opportunity for participants to share in a process of discernment where they seek to find common ground amongst the range of possible options.

A stylistic question to be addressed during the drafting stage is whether to draft the Constitution in 'plain English', rather than in the peculiar style, impenetrable to the uninitiated, used for the drafting of Acts of Parliament. In both South Africa (1996) and Kenya (2010), plain English copy-editors were brought in to help with the final language. The problem facing drafters is that plain English, when dealing with complex legal and constitutional subjects, is often only slightly more comprehensible than 'legal English'. If simplification is taken too far, tightness and precision may be lost. One cannot reiterate enough that Constitutions are not only legal documents: they are also political and social documents. Yet their function depends, to a greater or lesser extent, on interpretation by the courts. Drafting has to not only be clear to the average citizen, but also to those who are familiar with the various canons of legal interpretation; sometimes, a 'term of art' really is clearer and more precise than an attempt to state the same thing in plain English. There might be something to be said for a dual approach: a tight, detailed, legal text, and a gloss or summary for civic education purposes. The original 2002 SNP's text did this: it preceded the legal text with a short plain English summary outlining its content for the general reader.

Once the final draft has been approved by the constitution-making body, it must be formally adopted in a way that publically authorises and legitimates it. In a country that recognises the principle of the sovereignty of the people, this should take the form of a referendum. However, to prevent a narrow majority leading to the creation of one-sided constitution,[10] it may also be advisable to require approval by a super-majority of the constitution-making body before it is presented for a popular vote.

After the Constitution has been ratified and formally promulgated, it can come into effect as the new, supreme and fundamental law. When this happens, the legal order and the political order are changed. The new Constitution supersedes anything that has gone before. It is wrong, therefore, to think about conforming the Constitution to existing laws and practices. The Constitution is normatively superior; existing laws and practices must be brought into compliance with the Constitution, not the other way around.

Then begins the implementation phase, a crucial stage in the process that, if mishandled, can cause serious damage to the legitimacy and functionality of the new Constitution. Constitutionally mandated institutions must be created, the first elections under the new Constitution held, and new laws anticipated by the Constitution passed.

At each stage of the process, three different elements need to be brought to bear, albeit to varying extents: elites, experts and everyone. Elite support is crucial, although it might require some difficult compromises. The Icelandic process failed, in large part, because it sought to be so democratic as to exclude politicians from negotiations. The politicians responded by killing the process. The opinion-formers, the veto-players and those whose support will be vital in the implementation phase and beyond have to be brought onboard. There is also a legitimate role for expert involvement. Most people have not written a Constitution before, and few know their way around a constitutional text. In a country such as ours, which has no experience of living under a written Constitution, consideration should be given to the inclusion of experts who have knowledge of constitutional developments elsewhere in the world. This will help to ensure that good practice from elsewhere is incorporated, that elementary mistakes are avoided, and that we do not spend time 'reinventing the wheel'. Finally, and perhaps most importantly, 'everyone' must be involved. To ensure the legitimacy and success of the outcome, there should be ongoing public engagement, and the process should be characterised by its inclusivity, openness and opportunities for genuine public participation. The role of the people is most critical at the beginning and end of the process in determining aims and objectives and in adopting the constitutional text.

iii   Possible next steps

As the first edition of this book neared completion, current events included an attempt by the UK Government to exclude the Royal Family from Freedom of Information legislation, a chilling piece of 'emergency legislation' to permit the collection and retention of personal data on internet usage, the launch of HMS *Queen Elizabeth* (an aircraft carrier without aircraft), the benefit 'sanctioning' of a woman in Maryhill who was running a food-bank and had the audacity to speak out publicly against the ill treatment of the poor, and the alleged cover-up of a pedophile ring with links to the very highest levels of Government. As the second edition reaches completion, Scotland lies torn between the sweeping success of the SNP in the 2015 general election and the grim prospect of a Conservative majority government at Westminster, with all that means for withdrawal from the European Union, repeal of the Human Rights Act, the grossly anti-democratic Transatlantic Trade and Investment Partnership (which would lock countries into neo-liberal policies) and fracking (which could ruin the environment for many generations). These snapshots of woe are not unconnected incidents. They form a single, coherent narrative, telling of a systematically corrupt and increasingly oppressive country run for the private advantage of a privileged few, at the expense of ordinary people. The expenses scandal, the wars in Iraq and Afghanistan, the bank bailouts, the LIBOR rate-fixing scandal, the policies of austerity, the repression of protestors and the harassment of journalists all, likewise, point to the same fundamental cause: we live in an oligarchy, not a democracy.

This book has offered a democratic constitutional corrective for the oligarchic distortion of the state. In articulating the link between *folkric* and *folkweal*, it has shown that good policy fruit can only come from a good constitutional tree; if we want to have a state that serves the common good, in terms of its policy outcomes, then that state must rest on a democratic basis. A robust constitutional framework will keep the levers of control securely in our hands, enabling us to contest for the common good through open, deliberative institutions, and to protect ourselves from authoritarianism, manipulation and corruption. Such a Constitution – whether in an independent state or within a reformed UK – would be the crowning achievement of the Scottish renaissance, laying the foundations for freedom and justice for generations and perhaps centuries to come. Without such a Constitution, independence or greater autonomy would merely shift the locus of power without shifting its nature or basis.

In a book that hopes to have some longevity, it would be unwise to comment on the flashes and bangs of the moment. The political situation in Scotland and the rest of the UK is changing too fast. We do not know what the ultimate destination might be, and we do not know how or whether we will get there, but we do know that the UK cannot continue along its present course indefinitely. The No vote in the 2014 independence referendum was the start, and not the end, of our constitutional debate.

At the heart of a good Constitution lies the moral claim that the state is not a private association for the benefit of its rulers, but is a 'public thing': the commonweal is the association of all of us, devoted to the good in which each of us shares. As long as this moral claim continues to be made – that is, as long as the flame of freedom remains alive – the UK is bound to change. It must either cease to be, through the creation of an independent Scotland, or else it must thoroughly reinvent itself as a 'loosely United' Kingdom in which the almost-complete autonomy of Scotland is constitutionally recognised as part of a general democratisation. Until one of these stable end-states is reached, Scottish (and British) politics will remain in an uneasy limbo, and the effort that should be put into building up our country, improving the quality of life of our people, and addressing the economic, ecological, ethical and technological challenges of the future, will be squandered.

This moral claim holds true whatever our flag and borders might be. Independence, if it happens after a second referendum, provides an unparalleled opportunity to re-constitute a Scottish state on genuinely democratic lines, and thereby to ensure that the governance of Scotland is always in the hands of the people of Scotland. Aside from all the other arguments in favour of independence – that it will bring us not only control of our resources, but also a greater sense of psychological whole-ness, confidence and unity – it is worth noting that it will be much easier and less painful to make this change in the creation of a relatively small, new country, rather than trying to reform a large, old one. However, as discussed in the first chapter, independence alone is no guarantee of beneficial outcomes. The potential and promised benefits of independence will only be realised through a Scottish state that has strong constitutional guarantees in place. Likewise, the absence of independence, while it makes matters more complicated, is not – at least, not in principle – a barrier to transformation of the state from oligarchy to democracy, provided we can either negotiate a special position for Scotland (autonomy) or persuade the democratic elements in the other nations to join us in a radical change.

One possible approach is for the Scottish Government to build alliances with the Welsh and Northern Irish Assemblies, and to find allies in England both at Westminster and in the country, in order to pursue a British constitutional revolution on democratic and federal lines. The House of Commons Political and Constitutional Reform Committee has sadly been abolished, but the good work it did during the 2010–2015 Parliament shows that there are at least some prospective allies south of the border, who might be willing help to better connect, through federalism, the Scottish autonomy movement to the nascent democracy movements in other parts of these islands. If sufficient pressure could be placed on the UK Government, the next step in this case would be to provide, by an Act of the Westminster Parliament, for the election of a Constituent Assembly. This would have the authority to draft a Constitution for a federal and democratic UK, which would then be put to the people of the four nations for approval in a referendum. The resulting Constitution would not derive its authority from an Act of the Westminster Parliament, but directly from the peoples of the four nations. The chances of this happening, however, seem very slim, with a Conservative majority in power in Westminster. Although several senior Tory figures have made conciliatory moves in favour of federalism as a way to save the Union, I suspect these will be ignored, and that the generality of English Tories prefer to keep existing 'English' institutions and practices intact, and to avoid wholescale constitutional change, even if this means sooner or later losing Scotland.

Another possibility is for Scotland, despairing of the chance of change in England, to go ahead with a thorough reformation of the state while tarrying for none. The first step towards true Home Rule would be for the Scottish Government to commit itself to the creation of a Constitutional

Convention to find the common ground on which to build a new Constitution. A promise to establish such a Convention should be included in the SNP's manifesto for the Scottish Parliament elections. Scotland's Constitutional Convention could take many forms. As a minimum, like the Constitutional Convention of the 1990s of which it would be the successor, it should include all the major political parties, as well as the major representative institutions of civic Scotland. However, we can go further and do better than that: it could also, like its Irish counterpart, include randomly selected members of the general public, amounting to perhaps half or even two-thirds of the total, thereby giving it an exemplary democratic character.

This Constitutional Convention could formulate a relatively detailed declaration of principles that would serve as the baselines for any future constitutional settlement involving Scotland. Examples of such declarations of principles can be found in the Freedom Charter of the African National Congress (which was the moral and intellectual progenitor of the South African Constitution) and the Objectives Resolution of the Indian Constituent Assembly (which provided a general blueprint for the eventual Constitution of India). This declaration of principles might then form the basis of a draft Constitution for an autonomous Home Rule Scotland. This Constitution could be put to the people of Scotland in an advisory referendum or, if that route is closed, could be endorsed through an extensive public consultation process (the Scottish Parliament cannot, under current rules, make laws concerning constitutional arrangements or hold a binding referendum on a constitutional matter, but the Scotland Act can be stretched far enough to enable the Scottish Parliament to establish a Constitutional Convention with a remit to take evidence, consider options, make proposals, and put these to an advisory plebiscite). It would then be the responsibility of the UK Government to respond to that challenge in an appropriate way – knowing that a consensus of Scottish opinion lies behind it. This means that the people of Scotland would radically retake the constitutional agenda that was so firmly seized by the British establishment on the morning of 19 November 2014.

The year 2015 is the 800th anniversary of the signing of the Magna Carta, an event of great historical significance in England. The ruling establishment will attempt to use this anniversary as a way of showing that all is rosy in the garden, and has been for a very long time. Rather than smug congratulation, we should use this anniversary as an opportunity for deep introspection. Why is it that the UK is celebrating an 800-year-old royal charter, and not a decent democratic Constitution? What have we achieved since then, in the sphere of constitutional advancement? What guarantees does the citizen now have, against the abuse of power, corruption, and other forms of misrule? If we can cause people in England – and not only the poor oppressed commons, but also the stout-bellied middle classes – to think on these questions, and to reflect on the very inadequate answers that the establishment will give, then we should find ready allies. However, if the UK Government stalls, even after every entreaty for Scotland's constitutional demands to be met within the Union (either federally, or through full Home Rule), then independence will remain as the only option, and will, in the absence of fair dealing and reasonableness from the British Establishment, become increasingly attractive to a majority of the people of Scotland.

In summary, a Constitutional Convention for Scotland offers the best prospects for success, in or out of the Union. It would enable us to unify around certain democratic constitutional demands, to push – with the assistance of allies in the other home nations – for the realisation of those demands within the Union, and, if those demands are not met, to transform them into the basis on which an independent Scotland can be built. To work, however, the Constitutional Convention must not be smothered or controlled by the Government; its terms of reference must be wide, and its deliberations entirely free. It must neither rule in, nor rule out, independence, but must begin by finding out what sort of state Scots would like to live in, and then challenging the UK to become that state.

Every Constitution is imperfect. A Constitution is a human product, the offspring of noble intentions and base interests, of great scholarship and petty prejudices, of careful deliberation and difficult compromises. The Constitution of an independent Scotland, or a Constitution for a reformed UK, would be no different. The aim is not perfection, but a sound, workable, acceptable foundation for our civic and democratic life. If we can achieve that, we will have the institutions we need to realise the common good. We will be able to protect ourselves against the rich and powerful, to defend our rights, to assert common causes with our fellow-citizens and to guarantee all citizens a flourishing life.

Appendices

THE FOLLOWING FOUR appendices provide examples of some possible constitutional futures for Scotland.

Appendix A is a Constitution for an independent Scotland. This is based on the earlier *Model Constitution*. However, in order to illustrate some of the innovative proposals discussed in this book, this text goes beyond the 'moderate reformist' position of the *Model Constitution* and cautiously incorporates some more radical provisions. These include: (i) more extensive and prominent social and economic principles and a clearer mechanism for non-judicial enforcement of socio-economic rights; (ii) a recall mechanism enabling voters to dismiss their Members of Parliament; (iii) provision for the optional use of electoral quotas to promote the inclusion of marginalised sections of society in Parliament; (iv) Prime Ministerial term limits, limiting a Prime Minister to a maximum of two four-year terms; and (v) the replacement of the minority-veto referendum, which is dependent on the quality of the opposition, with an abrogative referendum. The most radical part of the Constitution is the inclusion of a system of participatory democracy designed to empower citizens through deliberative 'People's Assemblies'. These would enable panels of citizens, selected annually by lot, to discuss public affairs and to hold their elected representatives to account.

Appendix B is a new Treaty of Union, based loosely on sources such as the 'Dualism' of the Austro-Hungarian Empire (1867–1918) and inspired by Fletcher of Saltoun's idea of a 'non-incorporating Union'. It provides for a 'Union of the Crowns' in which foreign affairs, defence and such matters are dealt with through a shared executive body, while maintaining two separate Parliaments (there would be no 'UK Parliament').

Appendix C is a Home Rule Act that would establish a Constitution for an Autonomous Scotland. Formulated as an Act of the UK Parliament, it would nevertheless, cede and surrender Westminster's sovereignty over Scotland, such that the legislation enacted by the UK Parliament, in the domain of reserved matters, would be subject to the Scottish Constitution. A 'manner and form' provision would prevent amendment or repeal of the UK Act without the consent of the people of Scotland. A draft Constitution, which would be included as a Schedule to the Act, is not here presented; it could be very similar to the Constitution for an independent state, without provisions relating to reserved matters.

Appendix D, finally, is a Constitution for a Federal United Kingdom. I offer this in a very speculative way, simply to illustrate that a Federal Constitution is possible, should the political will exist. The text would provide for a rather loose, and slightly idiosyncratic, form of federalism, in that the Federal Assembly would be unicameral and the powers of the federal government narrowly limited. Yet this is my best projection, as things stand at the time of writing, of the sort of federal system that might give new life to the UK and might enable its nations to stand together on a basis of democracy, commonality and respect rather than begrudging tolerance and inertia.

As always, these texts do not pretend to either finality or perfection. They are presented simply as educational examples: as aids to the imagination and spurs for discussion.

A Constitution for an Independent Scotland

Part I – Foundations of the State

1 Sovereignty and Form of Government

Scotland is a free, sovereign and independent state; its form of government is a parliamentary democracy based upon the sovereignty of the people, social justice, solidarity and human rights.

2 Supremacy of the Constitution

This Constitution is the supreme and fundamental law of Scotland. All Acts of Parliament, treaties, regulations, and other laws, that are incompatible with this Constitution, are void to the extent of incompatibility.

3 Territory

The territory of Scotland comprises all the mainland and islands of Scotland, plus its territorial waters as recognised by international law.

4 Citizenship

  a Parliament shall enact laws to regulate the acquisition of Scottish citizenship by birth, marriage, or naturalisation, and to specify the manner in which citizenship may be lost or renounced.

  b Parliament shall specify the circumstances and conditions under which dual citizenship with other countries may be held.

  c Laws concerning the acquisition or renunciation of citizenship must not unfairly discriminate on the grounds of gender, ethnicity, religion, beliefs, disability, personal status or sexual orientation.

  d Adopted children shall for purposes of citizenship be treated as though they had been actually born to their adoptive parents.

5 Franchise

  a Subject to such further requirements as to residence as may be prescribed by law, all citizens of Scotland, who are at least 18 years old, shall be entitled to vote in all referendums and elections.

b Notwithstanding sub-Section (a), the right to vote may be subject to such reasonable restrictions as may be imposed by law with respect to those persons who are under guardianship due to severe mental incapacity, or who are serving a custodial sentence for a serious criminal offence.

c Parliament may by law extend voting rights to non-citizens lawfully resident in Scotland.

6 Capital City

The City of Edinburgh shall be the capital of Scotland; the seat of government may be moved to another place by a decision of the Government in the event of war, disaster or unrest.

7 Languages

The official languages of Scotland shall be English, Scots and Gaelic. Parliament shall be responsible for ensuring that adequate provision is made for the use of Scots and Gaelic, in addition to English, in parliamentary proceedings, local government, administration, public broadcasting and education.

8 Flag, Anthem, Emblem

a The national flag is the cross of St Andrew, blazoned: *azure, a saltire argent.*

b The national anthem shall be determined by Act of Parliament.

c The national emblem is the Thistle.

Part II – Fundamental Rights and Freedoms

9 General provisions

a The following provisions shall have effect for the purpose of guaranteeing the fundamental rights and freedoms of all Scottish citizens and all persons within the jurisdiction of Scottish Courts.

b The rights and freedoms guaranteed shall be enjoyed by all persons without discrimination on grounds such as sex, race, colour, religion, personal beliefs, abilities, status or sexuality.

c There shall be no limitation upon their exercise save such as is necessary to prevent or penalise acts by any person or group of persons calculated to infringe or destroy the rights and freedoms of other persons or groups, or forcibly to subvert the constitutional order which establishes and guarantees those rights and freedoms.

d Subject to the qualifications and limitations specified in this Constitution, no law may be passed which abrogates or derogates from guaranteed rights and freedoms.

e Every person shall be granted by a competent court a full and adequate and speedy remedy for any infringement whatsoever of his or her guaranteed rights and freedoms.

f None of the rights guaranteed in this Part of the Constitution shall be subjected to any restriction or limitation other than as expressly provided, nor shall any such restriction or limitation be applied for any purpose other than that expressly prescribed.

g The rights and freedoms guaranteed to persons under this Constitution or any law extend only to human beings; the extent to which such rights and freedoms may be extended to corporate bodies and other 'legal persons', on the grounds of public benefit, shall be determined by law.

10 Right to life

a Every person has the right to life. No person shall be condemned to death or executed.

b If any person's death occurs as a result of a lawful act of war, or of another person's acting in a manner which is permitted by law and which is no more than necessary to defend a person or persons from unlawful violence, or to effect a lawful arrest or to prevent the escape of a person lawfully detained, the action so taken shall not be rendered unlawful by the fact that death has result from it.

c This Section shall not prohibit voluntary euthanasia or the medical termination of pregnancy in accordance with the law.

11 Prohibition of torture

No person shall be subjected to torture, or to inhuman or degrading treatment or punishment.

12 Prohibition of slavery and forced labour

a No person shall be held in slavery or servitude, nor shall any person be required to perform forced or compulsory labour.

b For the purposes of this provision, 'forced or compulsory labour' shall not include:

i   any work, not of a hazardous or degrading nature, and not for the profit of any private person or corporation, required to be done in the ordinary course of detention imposed according to the provisions of Section 13, or during conditional release from such detention;

ii   any service of a military character or, in case of conscientious objectors, service exacted instead of military service;

iii   any service lawfully exacted in case of an emergency or calamity threatening the life or well-being of the community; or

iv   any work or service which forms part of normal civic obligations.

13 Personal liberty

a Every person has the right to personal liberty and security, and accordingly no person shall be deprived of liberty save in the following cases and in accordance with the procedures prescribed by the law of Scotland:

i   in the case of his or her lawful detention in accordance with the sentence passed by a competent Court upon his or her conviction of an offence;

ii   in the case of his or her lawful arrest or detention for non-compliance with the lawful order of a court;

iii   in the case of his or her lawful arrest or detention upon reasonable suspicion of having committed, or being engaged in the commission of, or being about to commit, a criminal offence under the law of Scotland;

iv   in the case of the detention of a person under the age of 16 years by lawful order for the purpose of his or her educational supervision or personal welfare;

v   in case of the lawful detention of a person who is of unsound mind and danger to themselves or others; or

vi   in the case of the lawful arrest of a person to prevent his or her unlawfully entering Scotland, or of a person against whom lawful action is being taken with a view to deportation or extradition.

b   Everyone who is arrested shall be informed promptly, in a language which he or she understands, of the reasons for his or her arrest and of any charge against him or her.

c   Everyone arrested or detained in accordance with the provisions of sub-section (a), paragraph (iii) of this Section shall be brought promptly before a judge or other officer authorised by law to exercise judicial power and shall be entitled to trial within a reasonable time or to release pending trial. Release may be conditioned by guarantees to appear for trial.

d   Everyone who is deprived of his or her liberty by arrest or detention shall be entitled to take proceedings by which the lawfulness of his or her detention shall be decided speedily by a court and his or her release ordered if the detention is not lawful.

e   Everyone who has been the victim of arrest or detention in contravention of the provisions of this Section shall have an enforceable right to compensation.

f   No person who has been committed for trial of any offence shall be detained in custody for more than 140 days from the date of such committal, except in so far as the High Court of Justiciary may grant lawful extensions.

14 Right to fair trial

a   Every person has the right to fair and impartial judicial proceedings to determine any question raised by process of law concerning his or her legal rights or obligations, or any criminal charge against him or her.

b   Every such question or charge shall be heard and determined by the competent court or tribunal established by law. Trials shall be conducted in public and judgment shall be pronounced publicly, except in so far as the law permits a court or tribunal to exclude members of the public from part of such proceedings or to prohibit publication of reports concerning part of such proceedings on all or any of the following grounds:

i   the protection of national security;

ii the prevention of disorder in court;

iii the protection of children or young people;

iv the protection of the personal privacy of both parties; or

v   in the interests of justice, in circumstances in which publicity would inevitably cause serious prejudice to the fair determination of an issue.

c   Every person charged with a criminal offence shall be presumed innocent until proved guilty according to law.

d   Every person charged with a criminal offence has the following rights:

   i   to be informed in detail, as soon as is possible in the circumstances of the case, and in a language which he or she understands, of the charge which is made against him or her;

   ii   to have adequate time and facilities for preparing a defence;

   iii to defend himself or herself in person or through a legal practitioner of his or her own choosing;

   iv   to such financial assistance as is necessary in the light of his or her means to secure adequate legal assistance if desired;

   v   to examine or have examined witnesses against him or her and to obtain the attendance and examination of witnesses on his or her behalf in the same conditions as witnesses against him or her;

   vi   to have all proceedings in court connected with the charge against him or her translated by a competent interpreter into the language which he or she best understands, if that language is not the language of the Court; and

   vii to be informed in a language which he or she understands of his or her rights under Sections 13 and 14, before the commencement of the trial.

e   Everyone convicted of a criminal offence by a tribunal shall have the right to have his conviction or sentence reviewed by a higher tribunal. The exercise of this right, including the grounds on which it may be exercised, shall be governed by law. This right may be subject to exceptions in regard to offences of a minor character, as prescribed by law, or in cases in which the person concerned was tried in the first instance by the highest tribunal or was convicted following an appeal against acquittal.

f   No one shall be liable to be tried or punished again in criminal proceedings for an offence for which he has already been finally acquitted or convicted in accordance with the laws of Scotland. Provided, that this provision shall not prevent the reopening of the case in accordance with the law and penal procedure of Scotland, if there is evidence of new or newly discovered facts, or if there has been a fundamental defect in the previous proceedings, which could affect the outcome of the case.

g The right to trial by jury, as such right existed under the law of Scotland at the time of the ratification of this Constitution shall not be suspended, restricted or abridged.

15 No punishment without law

No person shall be convicted of any criminal offence save in respect of an act or omission which, at the date of its commission, constituted a criminal offence under the law of Scotland or the law of nations, nor shall any penalty be imposed which is heavier than the maximum permitted under the law of Scotland at that date.

16 Compensation for wrongful conviction

When a person has by a final decision been convicted of a criminal offence and when subsequently his conviction has been reversed, or he or she has been pardoned, on the ground that a new or newly discovered fact shows conclusively that there has been a miscarriage of justice, the person who has suffered punishment as a result of such conviction shall be compensated according to the law, unless it is proved that the nondisclosure of the unknown fact in time is wholly or partly attributable to him or her.

17 Right to respect for private and family life

a Everyone has the right to respect for privacy in his or her personal affairs, family life, home, and correspondence.

b There shall be no interference with the exercise of this right except such as is in accordance with the law and is necessary in a democratic society in the interests of national security or public safety, for the prevention of disorder or crime, for the protection of health or morals, or for the protection of the rights and freedoms of others.

c Every person who suffers unlawful interference with his or her personal privacy shall be entitled to an adequate civil remedy.

d Provision shall be made by law for the safeguarding of personal data and information, and in particular to preserve the privacy and security of all communications and transactions conducted by electronic media.

18 Freedom of thought, conscience and religion

a Every person has the right to freedom of thought and of conscience and to the free confession and practice of religion. This right includes freedom to change his or her religion or belief and freedom (either alone or in community with others and in public or private) to manifest his or her religion or belief in worship, teaching, practice and observance. It also includes freedom not to believe or participate in any religion.

b Freedom to manifest one's religion or beliefs shall be subject only to such limitations as are prescribed by law and necessary in a democratic society in the interests of public safety, or for the protection of public order, health or morals.

c Nothing in this Section shall affect the existing status, freedom or liberties of the Church of Scotland, as recognized by the Church of Scotland Act 1921 and by the Articles Declaratory of the Constitution of the Church of Scotland in Matters Spiritual.

d In the exercise of any functions which it assumes in relation to education and to teaching, the state shall respect the right of parents to ensure such education and teaching in conformity with their own religious and philosophical convictions.

e Provision may be made by law for the public funding of denominational schools, provided that such provision does not discriminate in favour of or against any particular religion or denomination.

19 Freedom of expression

a Every person has the right to freedom of speech, writing and publication, and of the expression of opinion, including the right to impart and receive information and ideas freely to and from any other person or persons whatsoever.

b Provided, however, that the law may prohibit abuses of this right, to the extent necessary in a democratic society, in the interests of national security or public safety, for the prevention of disorder or crime, for the protection of health or morals, for the protection of the reputation or rights of others, for preventing the unlawful disclosure of personal or private information received in confidence, or for maintaining the authority and impartiality of the judiciary.

c The foregoing provisions shall not be interpreted as invalidating laws regulating the licensing of broadcast transmissions or cinemas, theatres and other like places of public resort.

20 Freedom of assembly and association

a Every person has the right to freedom of peaceful assembly and to freedom of association with others for all lawful purposes; this right shall include, but not be limited to, the freedom to freely form and to join political parties and trade unions.

b The right to freedom of assembly and of association shall be subject only to such restrictions as are prescribed by law and are necessary in a democratic society for the protection of national security, the prevention of crime or disorder, or the protection of the rights of others.

21 Freedom of movement

a Everyone lawfully within the territory of a Scotland shall, within that territory, have the right to liberty of movement and freedom to choose his residence, and shall have the freedom to leave the country at will.

b No restrictions shall be placed on the exercise of these rights other than such as are in accordance with law and are necessary in a democratic society in the interests of national security or public safety, for the prevention of crime or disorder, for the protection of public health, or for the protection of the rights and freedoms of others.

c Everyone in Scotland has the right of free access to hills, mountains, waterways and open countryside, except in cases in which unrestricted access is likely to cause substantial interference with agriculture, forestry or fishing, and subject to any provisions of the law which are necessary for the protection of national security or public safety, for the protection of public health, or for the protection of the physical environment.

22 No imprisonment for debt

No one shall be deprived of his or her liberty merely on the ground of inability to fulfil a contractual obligation.

23 No arbitrary expulsion

a No Scottish citizen shall be expelled, by means either of an individual or of a collective measure, from the territory of Scotland.

b No Scottish citizen shall be deprived of the right to enter Scotland.

c The collective expulsion of aliens is prohibited.

d A non-citizen lawfully resident in the territory of Scotland shall not be expelled therefrom except in pursuance of a decision reached in accordance with law and shall be allowed:

   i   to submit reasons against his or her expulsion;

   ii to have his or her case reviewed; and

   iii to be represented for these purposes before the competent authority or a person or persons designated by that authority.

24 Familial rights

a Men and women of marriageable age have the right to marry and to found a family in accordance with the laws governing the exercise of this right.

b Spouses shall enjoy equality of rights and responsibilities of a private law character between them, and in their relations with their children, as to marriage, during marriage and in the event of its dissolution. This shall not prevent the state from taking such measures as are necessary in the interests of children.

25 Property rights

a Every person has the right to hold private property, and to the peaceful enjoyment of his or her property.

b Parliament may, however, enact laws that control or restrict the use or acquisition of property in the general interest, in cases where Parliament determines that the needs of the community require to be given precedence over the rights of individuals.

c All laws which sanction measures of expropriation shall make provision for fair compensation.

d Nothing in this Part shall have the effect of invalidating any tax, duty or custom levied in accordance with the law, or the lawful collection of any service charge or administrative fee, or the lawful imposition of a criminal penalty of fine or forfeiture.

26 Freedom of Information

Every person shall have the right of access to governmental information. The right of access to official information can only be restricted by law to the extent necessary, in a democratic society, for the purpose of protecting personal privacy, national security or diplomatic confidentiality, or for ensuring the due process of judicial proceedings.

27 Restriction of Rights during State of Emergency

a   In times of war or other severe public emergency the Government may declare a State of Emergency. The State of Emergency shall lapse after seven days, unless during that time Parliament passes a resolution, by a two-thirds majority, authorising its extension for up to three months; such authorisation may be renewed at intervals of three months, so long as the emergency necessitating it continues, by means of a resolution of Parliament passed by a three-fourths majority of its members.

b   During a State of Emergency the Government shall have the authority to enact decrees, having the force of law; such decrees may suspend rights guaranteed by Sections 13(c) and 14(g) and may suspend or impose further restrictions on guaranteed rights according to Sections 17, 19, 20 and 21.

c   All decrees shall be subject to review and veto, on the grounds that they are unconstitutional, or unnecessarily burdensome or oppressive, by a majority decision of a Review Committee, which shall consist of all members of the Parliamentary Bureau and all Justices of the Supreme Court, under the joint convenorship of the Presiding Officer of Parliament and the Chief Justice of the Supreme Court.

Part III – Directive Principles

28 Status and Enforcement of this Part

a   The provisions of Sections 29 to 35 shall not be directly justiciable, but the directive principles contained therein are nevertheless fundamental to the governance of Scotland and:

i   it shall be the duty of Parliament and of the Government to ensure the progressive realisation of the directive principles through legislative and administrative action; and

    ii the courts shall have regard to the directive principles in the interpretation of this Constitution, Acts of Parliament, treaties, international agreements, and other laws.

b If in any proceedings a court determines that an Act of Parliament is repugnant to the directive principles, it shall issue a *Declaration of Incompatibility*, and shall report the matter to Parliament; but such Declaration shall not be binding on the parties and shall not affect the validity of the Act.

c A Minister, on presenting to Parliament any bill relating to social, economic or cultural affairs, or any treaty or international agreement concerning trade or commerce, must certify that in his or her judgment the bill, treaty or agreement is not inconsistent with the principles contained in this Part.

d Parliament shall establish a Monitoring Committee on Directive Principles, to be chaired by a member of the Opposition, to monitor compliance with this Part. The committee shall produce an annual report of its findings and recommendations, which shall be presented to Parliament and shall be subject to a plenary debate.

29 Workers' Rights

a Parliament shall be responsible for ensuring by legislation that:
    i   all persons have an adequate means of livelihood; and
    ii no-one is forced by economic necessity to engage in occupations unsuited to their age or strength; and
    iii every person has the right to conditions of work which are fair, healthy, and which respect the dignity of the person.

b In particular, Parliament shall ensure by means of appropriate legislation that every worker has the following rights, which may not be renounced by any contractual provision:
    i   safe and healthy conditions of work;
    ii an adequate minimum wage as determined by law;
    iii equal pay for equal work for both men and women;
    iv protection against arbitrary or unfair dismissal;
    v   maximum working hours, and sufficient entitlements to days of rest and holidays, to maintain health and to meet the obligations of family life;
    vi the right to bargain collectively and to enforce collective bargains

through strike action, except in the armed forces, police and essential public services; and

vii freedom from harassment, intimidation, humiliation or abuse in the workplace.

30 Social Security

Parliament shall be responsible for ensuring by legislation that every person who is unable to work by reason of physical or mental disability or infirmity, or by reason of family commitments, or because suitable employment is presently unavailable in their community, has a right to be provided with benefit payments or other social assistance as determined in accordance with the law.

31 Old-age Pensions

Parliament shall be responsible for ensuring by legislation that every person who has reached the age of retirement specified by law is entitled to a pension adequate for his or her dignity and well-being.

32 Public Healthcare

Parliament shall be responsible for ensuring by legislation that everyone has a right to adequate health care sufficient to secure well-being and human dignity. In particular, Parliament shall ensure that health services are properly regulated and maintained, and that a system of universal publicly funded health care, to the highest practicable standards of medical practice, is available to all.

33 Education

Parliament shall be responsible for ensuring by legislation that everyone has a right to a good education, and shall in particular ensure that:

i adequate provision is made for universal primary and secondary education; and

ii qualified students are entitled to publicly funded tuition and other means of financial support at institutions of higher learning, technical training and research.

34 Economic System

a Parliament may regulate trade and commerce for the common good, and in particular shall have a responsibility to enact laws protecting workers, consumers, local communities and the environment.

b Parliament shall take measures to ensure that:
   i the ownership and control of the material resources of the community are so distributed as best to serve the common good; and
   ii that the operation of the economic system does not result in the concentration of wealth and means of production to the common detriment.
c The Government, with the collaboration of professional associations, employers, trade unions and cooperative societies, may adopt a National Development Plan that coordinates state, private and cooperative business with a view to the most appropriate development of the national economy.
d Electricity supplies, water supplies, railways, other essential services and public infrastructure projects may be brought into public ownership and used for the common benefit of the citizens.

35 Environmental Stewardship

The state shall protect and nurture the natural environment and shall work towards a sustainable economy based on the good stewardship of natural resources and on respect for nature and for future generations.

Part IV – The Head of State

36 Succession

The office of Head of State shall be vested in Elizabeth Windsor, and shall be hereditary in her heirs and successors, according to the laws of succession, regency and exclusion enacted by Scotland's Parliament.

37 Coronation

a The Head of State shall be crowned in Scotland as 'His (or Her) Grace, King (or Queen) of Scots'.
b Before entering into the performance of his or her duties, the King (or Queen) of Scots shall take in the presence of Parliament the following oath or affirmation of office, which may be taken with or without religious invocation and is equally valid in either form:
   "*I... solemnly swear (or affirm) that I will faithfully execute the office and perform the duties of King (or Queen) of Scots, and that*

234

I will, to the best of my ability uphold, defend and obey the Constitution, laws and liberties of Scotland. (So help me God)."

39 Civil List and Royal Household

Parliament may make provision by law for the financial support of the Royal Family and the Royal Household in Scotland; the accounts thereof shall be presented annually to Parliament for scrutiny.

40 Powers and Functions

The Head of State shall possess only such powers and functions as are expressly vested in him or her by this Constitution, and shall, where so stated, exercise these powers and functions solely with the advice and consent of the responsible constitutional authorities, as follows:

i   representing the liberty, independence and integrity of Scotland, presiding over public ceremonies, and performing civic and ceremonial duties according to law;

ii   dissolving Parliament on the advice of the Presiding Officer in accordance with Section 47;

iii   granting or withholding assent to legislation, in accordance with Section 57;

iv   appointing the Prime Minister, in accordance with Section 64 and receiving the Prime Minister's resignation in accordance with Section 66.

v   appointing members of the judiciary in accordance with Section 75.

vi   granting pardons in accordance with the provisions of Section 79;

vii   appointing certain members of Independent Commissions in accordance with Sections 96 to 99;

viii   awarding civic honours in accordance with Section 103;

ix   serving as the ceremonial Commander-in-Chief of the Armed Forces, accrediting and receiving ambassadors, and performing other associated military and diplomatic duties, as directed by the Government; and

x   appointing officers of the Royal Household and Great Officers of State whose appointment is not otherwise provided for by this Constitution or by law.

41 Lord High Commissioner

a There shall be a Lord High Commissioner who shall act as the official representative of the Head of State in Scotland.

b Every reference to a power or function being vested in the Head of State under this Constitution or by law shall also be deemed a reference to that power or function being exercised in the name and on the authority of the Head of State by the Lord High Commissioner; provided, that nothing in this Constitution shall prevent the Head of State from exercising any power or performing any function in person, notwithstanding the fact that a Lord High Commissioner is appointed.

c Subject to any provisions prescribed by law, the Lord High Commissioner shall be appointed by the Head of State, on the joint nomination of the Prime Minister and the Leader of the Opposition.

d The Lord High Commissioner shall hold office for a term of five years, unless:

   i the Lord High Commissioner is removed by the Head of State, for stated cause, upon the joint request of the Prime Minister and the Leader of the Opposition; or

   ii the Lord High Commissioner submits his or her resignation to the Head of State.

e The office of Lord High Commissioner shall be incompatible with membership of Parliament and with all other public offices.

f The salary and allowances payable to the Lord High Commissioner shall be determined by law. The Palace of Holyrood House may be used by the Lord High Commissioner as an official residence during his or her term of office.

Part V – Parliament

42 Parliament

There shall be a Parliament of Scotland which shall be the supreme representative and deliberative assembly of Scotland and which may, subject to the provisions of this Constitution, make all laws for the peace, order and good government of Scotland.

43 Composition of Parliament

a Parliament shall consist of one chamber, the members of which shall be elected by secret ballot in accordance with a Mixed Member Proportional electoral system that ensures:

  i voters shall have two votes: one for a regional list and one for a constituency candidate;

  ii one half of the members shall be elected by plurality voting in single-member constituencies, and one half of the members shall be elected from regional lists;

  iii the total number of seats (including constituency and regional list seats) to be allocated to each party in a region shall be proportional to the share of the list votes received therein, calculated using the D'Hondt formula; and

  iv no artificial threshold for the distribution of regional list seats exceeding four per cent nationally shall be applied.

b The total number of members of Parliament shall be determined by law, but it shall not be fewer than 120 members, nor exceed 200 members.

44 Inclusive Representation

Subject to this Constitution, provision may be made by law for the promotion of gender balance in Parliament and for the adequate representation of minorities and members of marginalized social, economic or cultural groups, by means of reserved seats, candidate quotas, or by other means.

45 Constituency and Regional Boundaries

a Parliament shall review the boundaries of constituencies and regional districts after each decennial census and shall by law make such alternations to these boundaries, and to the allocation of seats between the regions, as shall be required in the interests of proportionality, provided that:

  i each constituency and region shall be a compact and contiguous geographical area;

  ii no region shall be so small, in terms of population, as to be entitled to elect fewer than seven list members, nor so large as to elect more than eleven list members; and iii any revision of boundaries shall have regard to the distribution and density of population, the means of communication, historical identities and community of interest, and existing local government boundaries.

b A bill for the alteration of electoral boundaries shall be introduced by a Minister on the basis of a proposal by the Electoral Commission, and the boundaries proposed by the Electoral Commission shall not be amended unless two-thirds of the members of Parliament consent to the amendment.

46 Eligibility and Disqualifications

a Subject to sub-sections (b) and (c) of this Section, every person eligible to vote in elections for the Scottish Parliament, who is at least 21 years of age, subject to such residency rules as may be prescribed by law, shall be eligible for election to Parliament.

b The following persons shall be disqualified from election to Parliament:
i the Lord High Commissioner;
ii members of the diplomatic corps;
iii civil servants (but excluding the staff of publicly funded schools and universities, employees of public corporations, and other public employees in non-administrative positions);
iv police officers, members of the prison service, and probation officers;
v members of the judiciary;
vi procurators-fiscal;
vii members of the armed forces (but excluding reservists not on active duty);
viii the Ombudsman, the Auditor-General, and members of any independent Commission established by this Constitution;
ix persons in Holy Orders; and
x members of the Royal Family.

c Parliament may further provide by law for the disqualification of persons who:
i have been convicted of a serious criminal offence involving bribery, corruption, or misconduct in office; or
ii are a party to (or a partner in a firm or a director or manager of a

company which is a party to) any contract with the Government for or on account of the public service, and who has not declared or divested such interest in the manner prescribed by law.

47 Term of Office and Dissolution

a Parliament shall, subject to the provisions of this Section, serve for a fixed term of four years and regular parliamentary general elections shall take place on the Thursday that falls most proximately to the fourth anniversary of the previous general election.

b Unless otherwise prescribed by this Constitution, the Head of State, on the advice of the Presiding Officer, shall dissolve Parliament at least 20 working days, but not more than 40 working days, before a general election is due to take place.

c A premature dissolution of Parliament shall be ordered by the Head of State only in the following circumstances:

  i if a two-thirds majority of the members of Parliament, by resolution, request a dissolution; or

  ii on the advice of the Presiding Officer, if a Prime Minister has not been elected within 30 days after the first meeting of Parliament following a general election, or within 30 days of the death, resignation or removal of the former incumbent Prime Minister.

d If Parliament is dissolved under the provisions of sub-section (c), a general election shall be held on a date specified by the Head of State, on the advice of the Presiding Officer, which must be no sooner than 20 working days, and no later than 30 working days, after the date of dissolution.

e Parliament shall have the power, in time of war or public emergency, to extend its term of office for a period not exceeding six months, by means of a resolution passed by a two-thirds majority of its members. This may be renewed for a further periods of three months, if conditions do not permit the peaceful conduct of a general election, by means of a resolution passed by a three-fourths majority.

48 Resignation and Removal

a A member of Parliament may resign from office, on grounds of illness or incapacity, or for compassionate reasons, by submitting a letter of resignation to the Presiding Officer.

b A member of Parliament shall be deemed to have been removed from office if:

   i he or she ceases to be qualified for membership of Parliament under this Constitution;

   ii he or she is recalled by the electors under the terms of Section 49.

c Further provision may be made by law for the removal of persons from Parliament who:

   i are serving a custodial sentence of not less than six months' duration for a criminal offence; or

   ii have been found to be in serious breach of Parliament's Code of Conduct and have been censured by a two-thirds majority vote of their peers.

d A person ceases to be a member of Parliament upon the dissolution of Parliament.

49 Recall

a Subject to the provisions of this Section the people shall have the right to remove members of Parliament by means of a recall vote.

b A recall vote shall be initiated by means of a petition to the Presiding Officer stating the grounds on which a member should, in the opinion of the petitioners, be recalled. This petition shall be valid only if signed by at least 10 per cent of the registered electors of the constituency or region represented by the member concerned.

c On receipt and validation of a recall petition, the Presiding Officer shall arrange with the Electoral Commission for a recall vote to be held in the said constituency or region, in which the voters shall be asked to vote for or against the recall of the named member. The recall vote which shall be held no sooner than 60 days, and no later than 90 days, after the date of the submission of the petition.

d If a majority of the votes cast in the recall vote are in favour of recall, and if these amount to at least 50 per cent of the total number of valid ballots cast in that constituency or region at the most recent general election, then the member shall be removed.

e If the member is not removed in accordance with the preceding sub-section, he or she shall retain office, and shall not be subject to another recall petition on the same grounds during the remainder of their term in office.

f A recall petition may not be submitted during the first year after a general election or during the last six months before a scheduled general election.

g The dissolution of Parliament has the effect of annulling recall petitions submitted on or before the date upon which Parliament is dissolved and of cancelling all recall votes scheduled to be held on or before that date.

h The death, resignation, or removal from Parliament for other lawful cause, of a member who is the subject of a recall petition has the effect of annulling the recall petition and cancelling the recall vote with respect to the member who has ceased to be a member of Parliament.

i Notwithstanding the provisions of this Section, a member of Parliament who holds office as Prime Minister, Deputy Prime Minister, Presiding Officer or Deputy Presiding Officer, shall not be subject to recall and the Presiding Officer may not accept any recall petition against such a member.

50 Vacancies

a Vacancies in Parliament arising from the death, resignation or removal of a member shall be filled within three months and unless a general election in due in that time, constituency vacancies shall be filled by a by election, regional vacancies by re-selection from the appropriate list.

b Parliament may act notwithstanding any vacancy in its membership, provided a quorum is present.

51 Presiding Officer and Deputy Presiding Officers

a Parliament shall elect from among its members a Presiding Officer and two Deputy Presiding Officers to convene its sessions and enforce its rules of procedure.

b These officers shall be elected as the first item of business after each general election, and whenever a vacancy occurs, by secret ballot and by an absolute majority.

c The Presiding Officer, and the Deputy Presiding Officers when in the chair, must perform their duties in a strictly non-partisan manner.

52 Sessions and Adjournments

a Subject to paragraph (b) of this Section, Parliament shall determine its own sessions and adjournments; provided, that:

  i it must assemble within seven days after each general election; and

  ii it must assemble each year for a regular session of at least 120 days.

b The Presiding Officer shall summon extraordinary sessions, whenever he/she deems it necessary, or if so demanded by the Government, or by one-third of the members of Parliament.

53 Parliamentary Bureau

a There shall be a Parliamentary Bureau, consisting of:

  i the Presiding Officer (as convenor); and

  ii one Member of Parliament nominated by each party or group having at least five members of Parliament.

b The members of the Bureau shall endeavor to reach agreement by consensus, but in the event of a matter being resolved by vote they shall cast bloc votes equal to the number of members they represent, and an absolute majority of the bloc votes cast shall be decisive.

c The Parliamentary Bureau shall, in addition to other functions vested in it by law or by the Standing Orders of Parliament, prepare Parliament's agenda and order of business.

d In the arrangement of parliamentary time, due precedence shall be given to the legislative proposals and other businesses initiated by the Government, but at least one-fourth of the parliamentary time shall be reserved for the opposition and private members' business.

54 Corporate Body

a There shall be a Parliamentary Corporate Body, consisting of:

  i the Presiding Officer (as convenor);

  ii the Deputy Presiding Officers; and

  iii four other members of Parliament elected by proportional representation at the commencement of each session, and whenever a vacancy arises.

b The Corporate Body shall, in accordance with the law and the Standing Orders of Parliament, manage Parliament's staff, buildings, facilities, security and budget.

55 Parliamentary Privileges and Procedures

a All members of Parliament shall enjoy:
  i Freedom of speech and debate in Parliament, subject only to Parliament's own rules of procedure (Standing Orders).
  ii Exemption from the law of defamation for anything spoken or written in the course of their duties.
  iii Freedom to vote in accordance with their consciences, free from imperative mandates, binding pledges or intimidation.
  iv Immunity from arrest and imprisonment during sessions of Parliament.
b Members shall be paid a moderate salary, and other incidental allowances, from the public treasury, as prescribed by law; but no law to increase their salary or allowance shall be enacted except by a two-thirds majority of the members of Parliament, and no such law shall come into effect until after a general election of members of Parliament shall have taken place.
c Subject to the provisions of this Constitution, Parliament shall adopt its own Standing Orders and regulate its own procedures.
d Parliament, its committees and commissions, shall be open to the public and press, unless a closed session is authorised, by a two-thirds majority vote, on the grounds of military secrecy or diplomatic security.

56 Legislative Process

a Except as provided in Section 58(a), bills may be proposed:
  i by a Minister on behalf of the Government;
  ii by the convenor of a committee on behalf of the committee;
  iii by any member of Parliament as a private member; or
  iv by means of a public petition signed by at least five per cent of the registered voters.
b The procedures for considering and voting on bills shall be determined by Parliament's Standing Orders, subject to the following conditions:

    i except in cases of urgency, as permitted by or in accordance with Standing Orders, all government bills shall be circulated for pre-legislative consultation prior to being voted upon in Parliament;

    ii each bill shall be referred to an appropriate committee for scrutiny before being finally voted upon, and the committee shall have the authority to conduct hearings and consultations on the bill to which representations may be made by or on behalf of all persons or groups interested in the subject matter of the bill;

    iii each bill shall be read and voted upon at least three times before being enacted, with opportunities for amendments to be proposed and debated by members before the final reading of the bill.

c Subject to any provisions of this Constitution specifying a qualified majority, a bill shall be deemed to have been passed if approved by a majority of members present and voting at a quorate sitting.

57 Assent to Legislation

a The Head of State, on the advice of the Presiding Officer, shall grant royal assent to, and thus enact as Acts of Parliament, all bills passed by Parliament in accordance with this Constitution.

b Provided, that if the Presiding Officer believes that the bill contains unconstitutional provisions, or has not been passed by the proper constitutional procedure, he or she shall not present such bill for royal assent, but shall instead refer it to the Supreme Court for an advisory ruling.

c The Supreme Court shall examine a bill referred to it under sub-Section (b) and shall issue its advisory ruling within a period of 30 days from the date of referral. If the Supreme Court rules that the bill contains unconstitutional provisions, or has not been passed by the proper constitutional procedure, the Presiding Officer shall advise the Head of State to withhold assent, and the bill shall be returned to Parliament for re-consideration; otherwise, the Presiding Officer shall advise the Head of State to grant assent and the Head of State shall without delay act in accordance with such advice.

d All laws made by Parliament shall be styled 'Acts of Parliament' and the words of enactment shall be "Be it enacted by the Parliament of Scotland."

58 Financial Provisions

a Except on the recommendation of the Government signified by a Minister, Parliament shall not:

i proceed upon any bill (including any amendment) which, in the opinion of the Presiding Officer, makes provision for imposing or increasing any tax, for imposing or increasing any charge on the Consolidated Fund or other funds of Scotland or for altering any such charge otherwise than by reducing it, or for compounding or remitting any debt due to Scotland;

ii proceed upon any motion (including any amendment) which would, in the opinion of the Presiding Officer, if the motion were carried, require the introduction of such a bill as is referred to in paragraph (i) of this sub-section to give effect to the motion; or

iii receive any petition which, in the opinion of the person presiding, requests that provision be made for any of the purposes aforesaid.

b No Act of Parliament for the levying of any form of general taxation whatsoever may remain in force for a period longer than eighteen months after the date on which such Act came into force.

c No public funds shall be expended for any purpose, save as authorised by or in accordance with an Act of Parliament.

d The Minister responsible for Finance shall submit the Government's budget to Parliament each year. If the budget for the coming financial year has not been passed by Parliament at least 30 days before the end of the current financial year, then the Minister responsible for Finance may request Parliament to approve an emergency budget. The emergency budget shall be deemed to have been passed by Parliament unless an absolute majority of the members vote against it; the rejection of an emergency budget shall be treated as a vote of no-confidence in the Government.

e There shall be a Consolidated Fund for Scotland, into which all public revenues which are not otherwise specifically allocated by law shall be paid.

f The salaries of the Lord High Commissioner, all members of the judiciary, of the ombudsman and the auditor general, and of all commissioners of independent commissions established under this Constitution, as well as the interest on the public debt of Scotland, shall be standing charges on the Consolidated Fund.

59 Regulatory Power

a For the purposes and to the extent specified in the Act of delegation, Parliament may delegate the authority to make administrative regulations, having the force of law, to the Government and other public authorities.

b Except as otherwise expressly provided by Act of Parliament or by Parliament's Standing Orders, all regulations shall be laid before Parliament for at least 30 days before they come into effect, and during this time a proposed regulation may be vetoed by a simple majority resolution of Parliament.

c Parliament may not delegate legislative authority concerning the levying of taxation, the creation of new criminal offences, the personal rights of citizens, the principles of civil or criminal law, or the administration of justice. No regulation shall ever amend, repeal, or suspend, an Act of Parliament.

60 Committees, Royal Commissions and Boards of Enquiry

a Parliament may, in accordance with its Standing Orders, appoint committees to inspect and oversee the government and to scrutinise legislation. Subject to any further requirements specified in Standing Orders, the membership of committees shall be assigned by proportional representation.

b Parliament may also appoint Royal Commissions and Boards of Enquiry, which may include expert advisors from outside of Parliament, in order to investigate and report on particular decisions or particular aspects of policy, legislation, or administration. Their composition, duration and terms of reference shall be specified by a parliamentary resolution.

c Parliamentary committees, Royal Commissions and Board of Enquiry shall enjoy a right of general access to official documents, files and other evidence, and the power to summon Ministers and other officials.

d Members of Parliament holding a ministerial office shall, by virtue of that office, be disqualified from membership of all select committees and from Parliament's Corporate Body. They may serve on Royal Commissions and Boards of Enquiry only where there is no conflict of interest.

61 Leader of the Opposition

a The elected leader of the largest parliamentary party or group which is not participating in or supporting the Government shall be designated by the Presiding Officer as Leader of the Opposition.

b In addition to any other rights accorded to the Leader of the Opposition by this Constitution, by Act of Parliament, or by Parliament's Standing Orders, the Leader of the Opposition has the right to be briefed, in confidence, by the Prime Minister on matters concerning foreign affairs, defence and security, and to be consulted by the Prime Minister on strategic military and diplomatic decisions.

Part VI – The Government

62 Executive Authority

a Executive authority is vested in the Government. Save as otherwise provided in this Constitution, that authority may be exercised directly by Ministers or through officers subordinate to Ministers.

b All prerogatives, powers, rights and duties vested in the Crown or in Scottish Ministers according to the law of Scotland immediately prior to the coming into effect of this Constitution shall be transferred to the Government, except for such prerogatives, powers, rights and duties as are abolished, or transferred to other authorities, by this Constitution or by any Act of Parliament.

c Nothing in this Section shall preclude persons or authorities other than the Government from exercising such functions as may be conferred upon them by any law.

63 Composition of the Government

a The Government shall consist of:
   i   the Prime Minister;
   ii the Deputy Prime Minister; and
   iii such Ministers, including any Junior Ministers and Ministers-without-Portfolio, as may be appointed to office by the Prime Minister in accordance with this Constitution and the law.

b The total number of persons holding office as members of the Government shall not at any time exceed one-sixth of the total membership of Parliament.

64 Election of the Prime Minister

a The Prime Minister shall be elected by Parliament, from amongst the members thereof, by a simple majority vote. Subject to the provisions of this Constitution, Parliament may provide by Standing Orders for the election of the Prime Minister. The Prime Minister-elect shall be formally appointed to office by the Head of State upon the formal advice and with the counter-signature of the Presiding Officer.

b Provided, that no person may be elected as Prime Minister more than twice.

c The election of a Prime Minister shall take place within 30 days after:
   i   the first meeting of Parliament following a general election; and
   ii the death, resignation or removal of the former incumbent Prime Minister.

d If a Prime Minister has not been elected during the period specified in the preceding sub-section then the Presiding Officer may advise the Head of State to dissolve Parliament under Section 47(c)(ii).

65 Appointment of Ministers

a The Deputy Prime Minister and the other Ministers, including any Junior Ministers or Ministers-without-Portfolio, shall be appointed and dismissed by the Prime Minister.

b Ministers shall be appointed from amongst the members of Parliament, provided that:

    i a Minister who was a member of Parliament at the time of his or her appointment to ministerial office, and who ceases to be a member of Parliament by reason of the dissolution of Parliament, shall not on such grounds be disqualified from continuing as a Minister for a period not exceeding three months; and

    ii Ministers continuing in office under the terms paragraph (i) of this sub-Section shall have the right to sit and to speak in Parliament, but not to vote therein.

66 Responsibility and Removal

a The Government shall be collectively responsible to Parliament for the general policy, conduct and administration of the Government and each member of the Government shall be individually responsible to Parliament for the performance of his or her duties and for his or her own conduct.

b If Parliament, by an absolute majority vote, passes a vote of no-confidence:

    i in the Prime Minister, the Prime Minister shall cease to hold office;

    ii in any other Minister, including the Deputy Prime Minister and any Junior Minister or Minister-without-Portfolio, that Minister shall cease to hold office.

c The Prime Minister shall also cease to hold office:

    i when the members of Parliament meet to elect a Prime Minister following a general election in accordance with the provisions of Section 64;

    ii if he or she ceases to be a member of Parliament for any reason other than a dissolution of Parliament;

    iii if he or she is elected as Presiding Officer or as a Deputy Presiding Officer; or

    iv if he or she resigns such office by writing under his or her hand addressed to the Head of State.

d A Minister other than the Prime Minister, including the Deputy Prime Minister and any Junior Minister or Minister-without-Portfolio, shall cease to hold office:

    i upon the election of a person to the office of Prime Minister;

    ii if he or she ceases to be a member of Parliament for any reason other than a dissolution of Parliament;

    iii if he or she is elected as Presiding Officer or as a Deputy Presiding Officer;

    iv if he or she resigns such office by writing under his or her hand addressed to the Prime Minister; or

    v if he or she is dismissed from office by the Prime Minister.

67 Performance of Government Functions

a The Prime Minister shall:

    i summon regular meetings of the Government, and as far as it is practicable to do so, attend and preside over such meetings; and

    ii be responsible for the general direction of the Government and for ensuring the co-ordination of Government policy and the implementation of Government decisions.

b Prime Minister, may, by directions in writing, assign to any Minister responsibility for the conduct (subject to the provisions of this Constitution and any other law) of any business of the Government, including responsibility for the administration of any department of the Government.

c All ministerial orders, regulations, instructions, writs, and other documents, issued by or on the authority of the Government, shall be signed by the Minister who is responsible for their execution.

d Whenever the Prime Minister is unable, by reason of illness or absence, to perform the functions conferred on him by this Constitution, those functions shall be performed by the Deputy Prime Minister; provided, that if the Deputy Prime Minister is unable to perform these functions, the Head of State, acting in so far as it is practicable on the advice of the Government, shall authorise in writing some other Minister to perform those functions, and that Minister may perform those functions until his or her authority is revoked by the Head of State.

68 Caretaker Governments

a Upon the removal of the Prime Minister by a vote of no-confidence, or upon the resignation of the Prime Minister, and also upon the dissolution of Parliament, the members of the Government, including the Prime Minister, shall continue to perform their functions in caretaker capacity until a Prime Minister is elected and a new Government formed in accordance with this Constitution.

b When serving in a caretaker capacity, the Government should attend only to matters of routine administration and matters of urgency. This sub-section shall not be justiciable in any court, nor shall any governmental act be rendered invalid solely on the grounds that it was ordered or authorised by a Government acting in a caretaker capacity.

69 Civil Service

The administrative corps, subordinate to the Government, shall be organised by law as a permanent, professional and non-partisan civil service, which shall be based upon merit and shall be regulated by the Public Service Commission according to law.

70 Special Advisors

a The Prime Minister may appoint a number of Special Advisors, not exceeding 12, to advise and assist the Prime Minister in the preparation and delivery of policies.

b Special Advisors shall serve at the pleasure of the Prime Minister. They shall not be members of the permanent civil service, nor members of Parliament, but are subject to the Code of Conduct for public servants.

71 Armed Forces

a High command of the Armed Forces, subject to the Constitution and laws, shall be vested in the Government.

b The Armed Forces shall be responsible, in accordance with the law, for:

i protecting Scotland from enemy attack in time of war or threat of invasion;

ii contributing to international peacekeeping and security forces in accordance with international law;

iii contributing to collective defence in accordance with treaty commitments;

iv ensuring the protection of essential infrastructure and the safety of civilian populations in event of a natural disaster, epidemic, attack, or other calamity, and providing assistance to fire and rescue services, ambulance services, and other civilian emergency services, when required and authorised according to law;

    v the defence of Scotland's territorial waters and coasts, fishery protection, the protection of off-shore assets, air-sea rescue, meteorological services, and the prevention of smuggling, illegal trafficking by sea, and piracy; and

    vi associated duties specified by law.

c No declaration of war may be made, nor deployment of troops undertaken, except with the prior consent of a two-thirds majority of Parliament; provided, that if Scotland is under actual or imminent enemy attack the Government shall at once undertake all necessary defensive action and shall report its actions to Parliament at the earliest practicable opportunity.

d The recruitment, pay, discipline and organisation of the Armed Forces shall be regulated by law.

72 International Relations

a No treaty or international agreement of any kind shall come into effect unless it is ratified by Parliament (either by a majority resolution or, to the extent that it concerns domestic laws, by enabling legislation).

b Treaties delegating legislative, administrative, judicial, military or fiscal powers to any union, alliance, confederation, or international organisation, shall be binding only if ratified by a two-thirds majority of Parliament.

Part VII – Judiciary

73 Judicial Authority

a The judicial authority shall be vested in:

    i the Supreme Court;

    ii the Court of Session;

    iii the High Court of Justiciary;

    iv Sheriff Courts; and

    v such other Courts and Tribunals as may be established by Acts of Parliament.

b Subject to the provisions of this Constitution, the organisation, powers, structure, jurisdiction, privileges, and procedures of the various Courts shall continue as heretofore, until altered or amended by Act of Parliament.

74 Establishment of Supreme Court

a There shall be a Supreme Court of Scotland, which shall consist of a Chief Justice and at least six, but not more than eight, other Justices, as prescribed by Act of Parliament.

b In addition to any additional jurisdiction vested in it by law, the Supreme Court shall have final appellate jurisdiction over all cases:
  i concerning the validity of Acts of Parliament, treaties, and other laws, under the terms of this Constitution; and
  ii concerning the interpretation of this Constitution.

c Reference of a bill to the Supreme Court for an advisory ruling in accordance with Section 57 shall not prevent the subsequent judicial review of the constitutionality of the Act resulting from that bill.

75 Appointment of Judges

a The Chief Justice and Associate Justices of the Supreme Court, members of the Court of Session and the High Court of Justiciary, Sheriffs, and all other members of the judiciary, with the exception of Justices of the Peace, shall be appointed by the Head of State, acting on the advice of the Judicial Appointments Commission.

b To be appointed to any judicial office it is necessary to be citizen of Scotland, at least 30 years of age, and to meet such standards of good character, conduct, and legal training and experience as may be specified by Act of Parliament.

c In the appointment of judges, the Judicial Appointments Commission shall give due consideration to the need for the bench to reflect the diversity of Scotland's society, and, in particular, to ensure that women as well as men, ethnic and religious minorities, and people from all socio-economic backgrounds, are adequately represented on the bench.

d The appointment of Justices of the Peace shall be regulated by law.

76 Judicial Tenure

a   Members of the judiciary shall enjoy security of tenure during good behaviour. They may only be removed on the grounds of misconduct, neglect of duty, or incapacity, by means of a motion of censure passed by a two-thirds majority vote of Parliament, on the advice of the Judicial Appointments Commission.

b   The Judicial Appointments Commission shall have the authority to suspend a judge, on full pay, for a period of up to three months, pending the outcome of Parliament's decision in his/her case.

77 Judicial Independence

a   Judicial office shall be incompatible with all other public offices and with membership of any political party. Additional incompatibilities maybe prescribed by Act of Parliament.

b   The salaries and privileges of members of the judiciary shall be determined by Act of Parliament, and shall not be diminished during their tenure. A bill amending the salaries or privileges of members of the judiciary shall be introduced only by the Minister of Justice after having consulted the Judicial Appointments Commission.

c   Members of the judiciary may not be transferred against their will. Transfer to a higher or lower court shall be deemed a new appointment and shall be subject to the ordinary appointment process.

d   The Chief Justice and Associate Justices of the Supreme Court shall retire at the age of 70 years of age, and the judges of other courts at 65 years of age. Early retirement may be granted by the Judicial Appointments Commission on the grounds of illness or infirmity, or for personal or compassionate reasons.

78 Lord Advocate and Procurators Fiscal

a   The Lord Advocate and Procurators-Fiscal shall be appointed by the Government. They shall be appointed on merit, and on a non-partisan basis, after consultation with the Judicial Appointments Commission and with the Public Service Commission.

b   The office of Lord Advocate or Procurator-Fiscal is incompatible with membership of Parliament and of the Government, with all other public offices, and with membership of any political party.

c In the performance of his or her duties in relation to public prosecutions, the Lord Advocate shall act independently of the advice or instruction of any other person or authority.

d The Lord Advocate shall hold office for renewable terms of four years and may only be removed before the expiry of his or her term on the grounds of misconduct, neglect of duty, or incapacity, by means of a motion of censure passed by a two-thirds majority vote of Parliament. The terms of office of Procurators-Fiscal, and the circumstances and means in which they may be removed from office, shall be determined by Act of Parliament.

79 Pardons

a The right of pardon, and of remitting punishments, shall be vested in the Head of State, and exercisable upon the advice of the Minister of Justice.

b An independent advisory board may be established by law to make recommendations to the Minister of Justice in the exercise of this power.

Part VIII – Local Government

80 District and City Councils

a For the purposes of local government and administration, Scotland shall be divided by law into Districts and Cities.

b Each District and City shall be governed according to law by a Council, consisting of a number of councillors to be determined by or in accordance with the law, who shall be directly elected by the local enfranchised citizens, by secret ballot and proportional representation, as prescribed by law.

c District and City Councils shall have such legislative, administrative and fiscal powers as may be devolved to them by law, in accordance with the principle of subsidiarity, in relation to:

i economic development;

ii housing, land use and planning;

iii infrastructure;

iv transport;

    v   the upkeep of streets, roads and public spaces;

    vi public health;

    vii the control and recycling of waste;

    viii education and training;

    ix environmental protection;

    x   libraries, museums, the arts and culture;

    xi poor relief and social services;

    xii public safety;

    xiii parks, garden and allotments;

    xiv recreational facilities; and

    xv any other matter of local concern.

d Each District and City Council shall elect from amongst its members a Lord Provost, Provost, or Convenor, to preside over the Council and to act as its ceremonial head and a Council Leader to set priorities, co-ordinate policy and direct the local administration. Provided, however, that provision may be made by law for the direct election of an 'Executive Provost' to combine these functions.

81 Community and Burgh Councils

a Districts and Cities may be further sub-divided into Communities and Burghs according to law.

b The powers and organisation of the Community and Burgh Councils shall be determined by law.

c City and District Councils shall transfer a proportion of their annual discretionary expenditure to the Community and Burgh Councils, to be managed by them and to be spent on local improvements and services, subject to such rules may be prescribed by the District or City Council according to law.

Part IX – Referendums

82 Constitutional Referendums

a A binding referendum shall be held, in accordance with the provisions of Section 106, to ratify bills to amend the Constitution that have been passed by Parliament prior to submission for royal assent.

b The referendum shall be held on a date determined by the Government, which must be within six months, but no sooner than three months, from the date of the approval of the amendment bill by Parliament.

c If a majority of the votes cast in the referendum are in favour of the amendment, the amendment bill shall be deemed to have been approved by the people and shall be presented for royal assent.

d If a majority of the votes cast in the referendum are against the amendment bill, the amendment bill shall be deemed to have been rejected by the people and shall not be presented for royal assent.

83 Abrogative Referendums

a The people, by means of a petition to the Presiding Officer of Parliament signed by at least 5 per cent of registered electors, may demand a referendum on the repeal of any law enacted during the period of four years prior to the submission of the petition, other than a law concerning public finances or an amendment to the Constitution, or a law that has been the subject of a consultative referendum.

b The referendum shall be held on a date determined by the Government, which must be within six months, but no sooner than four months, from the date of the submission of the petition. Provided, that no referendum shall be held if Parliament, within three months after the date of the petition:

  i repeals the law which is the subject of the petition; or

  ii passes a resolution, by a three-fifths majority vote, stating that a referendum would not be in the public interest.

c If a majority of the votes cast in the referendum are in favour of repealing the law in question, and if the votes in favour of repeal amount to at least one-third of those eligible to vote, the law shall be deemed to have been repealed with immediate effect.

d If a majority of the votes cast are not in favour of repealing the law in question, or if the votes in favour of repeal amount to less than one-third of those eligible to vote, the law shall remain in effect and may not be the subject of a second petition for an abrogative referendum under this Section.

84 Consultative Referendums

a Parliament may, by means of a resolution supported by a majority of its members, authorise the holding of a consultative referendum on any proposed bill or treaty, or any matter of general policy.

  b A consultative referendum shall not be held on the following subjects:

    i   money bills;

    ii the appointment or removal of any particular person;

    iii any question that is to be determined by the courts;

    iv any bill or general policy that, if enacted or adopted, would be in violation of the fundamental rights and liberties of citizens, or otherwise contrary to the Constitution.

  c No consultative referendum shall take place unless:

    i   the Electoral Commission has certified that the question to be put is clear, fair and balanced; and

    ii the Supreme Court has certified that the referendum is not inconsistent with the provisions of sub-section (b) of this Section.

  d Consultative referendums are advisory only, and are of no legal effect.

85 Local Referendums

District, City, Community and Burgh Councils may, by means of a resolution supported by a majority of the councillors, hold a local consultative referendum on any matter within their competence.

Part X – People's Assemblies

86 People's Assemblies

  a The People's Assemblies are institutions of deliberative and participatory democracy.

  b There shall be a People's Assembly in and for each of the regional districts designated for the election of regional list members of Parliament.

87 Selection of People's Assembly Members

  a Each People's Assembly shall consist of 200 members.

  b The members of the People's Assemblies shall be selected annually by random lot from amongst the enfranchised citizens who are resident and registered to vote in each region.

  c The following persons, however, shall be ineligible for selection:

    i   those who hold, or who have within the last ten years held, ministerial office;

ii those who hold, or who have within the last five years held, an office that would disqualify them from membership of Parliament;

iii those who hold, or have within the last five years held, office as a member of Parliament or of a City or District Council; and

iv those who are exempted, excused or disqualified from jury service in accordance with the law.

d Lots shall be drawn by the Electoral Commission on behalf of the Parliamentary Corporate Body. Lots shall be drawn each year on or before the first Monday in December, to hold office during the year following. Those selected to serve as People's Assembly members shall be notified forthwith.

e Provision shall be made by the Parliamentary Corporate Body, in accordance with any provisions specified by law, for those who are unable to serve as members of the People's Assembly, because of illness or incapacity, or for personal or compassionate reasons, to refuse or defer service. Further lots shall be drawn, in lieu of those who refuse or defer, until 200 people have been selected.

f A People's Assembly may act notwithstanding any vacancy in its membership, provided there is a quorum of not less than one hundred members present.

88 Organisation of People's Assemblies

a Each People's Assembly shall have a Steering Committee, the duties of which shall be:

i to determine the People's Assembly's agenda and order of business;

ii to prepare resolutions for discussion by the People's Assembly;

iii to correspond with other public authorities on behalf of the People's Assembly.

b Each Steering Committee shall consist of 24 members, who shall be chosen by lot from amongst those who volunteer for service at the first meeting of each People's Assembly following the annual selection of members; and any vacancies arising in a Steering Committee shall be filled by the drawing of lots at the next meeting of the People's Assembly.

c A member of a Steering Committee:

i may be removed from office by a vote of censure passed by a majority vote of the People's Assembly; and

    ii may resign from the Steering Committee by submitting a letter of resignation to the People's Assembly;

  d Each People's Assembly shall elect a Convenor, whose duties, subject to the standing orders of the People's Assembly, shall include presiding over the meetings of the People's Assembly, keeping order, calling upon members to speak, and putting questions to a vote.

  e Subject to this Constitution and to any general rules lawfully prescribed by the Parliamentary Corporate Body, each People's Assembly may adopt its own standing orders and regulate its own procedures; the members of each People's Assembly shall have the right to free speech subject only to such reasonable limits as may be prescribed by such standing orders in the interests of good order.

89 Timing and Location of People's Assembly Meetings

  a Except if prevented by *force majeure*, each People's Assembly shall meet at least once during each month; and, subject to any general rules prescribed by the Parliamentary Corporate Body, the days and places of meeting shall be specified by the Steering Committee of each People's Assembly.

  b Members of People's Assemblies have a duty to attend promptly, soberly and diligently.

  c No employer may deny an employee time off to attend People's Assemblies. This shall not be deducted from the employee's wages or holiday entitlement.

90 Logistical and Administrative Support to People's Assemblies

  a The Parliamentary Corporate Body shall be responsible on behalf of Parliament for providing logistical and administrative support to the People's Assemblies in accordance with this Constitution and the law.

  b The Parliamentary Corporate Body shall make provision according to law for:

    i the reimbursement of travel costs for members attending the People's Assembly;

    ii the payment of a *per-diem* to members of the People's Assembly in attendance, which shall be equal to one and a half-times the median daily wage; and

    iii defraying the administrative costs of the People's Assemblies.

    iv making a town hall or other convenient place of meeting available for each People's Assembly; and

    v facilitating attendance at People's Assembly meetings, through the provision of light refreshments, crèche facilities, access for the disabled, transport, and by other lawful means.

c A Clerk shall be appointed to each People's Assembly by the Parliamentary Corporate Body. The Clerk shall have legal training and shall not be a member of the People's Assembly. In addition to any other powers or duties vested in or entrusted to the Clerk by the Parliamentary Corporate Body, the Clerk shall advise the People's Assembly on matters of law and procedure and maintain its records.

91 Functions of People's Assemblies

Each People's Assembly shall have the authority to:

    i debate and consider any matter of public concern;

    ii pass declaratory resolutions on any matter of public concern;

    iii submit petitions to Parliament or any committee thereof;

    iv submit petitions to the Government or any department thereof;

    iv pose oral or written questions to members of Parliament representing the region or constituencies in the region, concerning their conduct and voting record; and

    v scrutinise legislative bills and submit reports, recommendations, or proposed amendments to bills to Parliament, or any committee thereof, for consideration.

92 Duty of Members of Parliament to attend People's Assemblies

Members of Parliament (both constituency members whose constituencies lie within the region and the regional list members) shall have a duty to make every reasonable effort to attend the meetings of the People's Assembly in their region in order to answer questions and to give an account of their conduct in Parliament.

Part XI – Independent Regulatory and Oversight Bodies

93 Ombudsman

a There shall be an Ombudsman, whose duty it shall be to examine and investigate all complaints of maladministration, injustice, neglect of duty, incompetence, delay, or mistake, alleged to have been committed by, or to have been caused by the negligence or mistake of, Ministers, civil servants, local Councils, public utilities, or other public authorities.

b The Ombudsman:

i may initiate enquires at the request of a member of Parliament, or in response to a complaint lodged by a citizen, or at his or her own initiative;

ii shall have full powers of administrative investigation, including access to all records and correspondence, and the right to summon witnesses and hear evidence on oath;

iii may refer cases of suspected criminal activity to the police or to the Crown Office;

iv may advise authorities to take disciplinary action or remedial action;

v shall have such additional powers and duties as may be vested in the office of Ombudsman by law; and

vi shall submit an annual report of his or her activities to Parliament.

c The Ombudsman shall be nominated by the Presiding Officer on the advice of the Parliamentary Bureau, and shall be appointed by a two-thirds majority vote of Parliament, on a nonpartisan basis.

d The office of Ombudsman shall be incompatible with all other public offices and with membership of any political party. Additional incompatibilities maybe prescribed by Act of Parliament.

e The Ombudsman shall serve for renewable terms of six years, and may only be removed for misconduct, incapacity, or other due cause, by a two-thirds majority of Parliament.

f The Ombudsman shall have the same privileges, salary, and pension, as judge of the Court of Session.

g The Ombudsman shall be independent of any other person or authority in the exercise of his or her duties.

94 Auditor-General

a There shall be an Auditor-General, whose duty it shall be:

i to conduct a thorough audit of the public accounts, to ensure that all public monies are properly accounted for, and are expended only in accordance with the law; and

ii to make recommendations to Parliament for improving the economy of public spending, and for eliminating waste and corruption.

b The Auditor-General:

i shall have full powers of financial investigation, including access to all records and correspondence, and the right to summon witnesses and hear evidence on oath;

ii may advise authorities to take disciplinary action or remedial action; and

iii shall have such additional powers and duties as may be vested in the office of Auditor-General by law.

c The Auditor-General shall be nominated by the Presiding Officer on the advice of the Parliamentary Bureau, and shall be appointed by a two-thirds majority vote of Parliament, on a nonpartisan basis.

d The office of Auditor-General shall be incompatible with all other public offices and with membership of any political party. Additional incompatibilities maybe prescribed by Act of Parliament.

e The Auditor-General shall serve for renewable terms of six years, and may only be removed for misconduct, incapacity, or other due cause, by a two-thirds majority of Parliament.

f The Auditor-General shall have the same privileges, salary, and pension, as judge of the Court of Session.

g The Ombudsman shall be independent of any other person or authority in the exercise of his or her duties.

95 Information Commissioner

a There shall be an Information Commissioner, who shall be responsible in accordance with this Constitution and the law for promoting transparency in government and for ensuring compliance with the freedom of information provisions of Section 26; and, without prejudice to any additional powers or duties vested in the Open Government Commission by law, all powers and duties vested in the Scottish Information Commissioner at the coming into effect of this Constitution shall be vested in the Open Government Commission until and unless otherwise provided by Act of Parliament.

b The Information Commissioner shall be nominated by the Presiding Officer on the advice of the Parliamentary Bureau, and shall be appointed by a two-thirds majority vote of Parliament, on a nonpartisan basis.

c The office of Information Commissioner shall be incompatible with all other public offices and with membership of any political party. Additional incompatibilities maybe prescribed by Act of Parliament.

d The Information Commissioner shall serve for renewable terms of six years, and may only be removed for misconduct, incapacity, or other due cause, by a two-thirds majority of Parliament.

e The Information Commissioner shall have the same privileges, salary, and pension, as judge of the Court of Session.

f The Information Commissioner shall be independent of any other person or authority in the exercise of his or her duties.

96 Judicial Appointments Commission

a There shall be a Judicial Appointments Commission, which shall be responsible in accordance with this Constitution and the law, for advising on judicial appointments; and, without prejudice to any additional powers or duties vested in the Judicial Appointments Commission by law, all powers and duties vested in the Judicial Appointments Board for Scotland at the coming into effect of this Constitution shall be vested in the Judicial Appointments Commission until and unless otherwise provided by Act of Parliament.

b The Judicial Appointments Commission shall consist of seven members:

    i the Minister responsible for Justice, as Convenor;

    ii the Lord Advocate;

    iii three members shall be elected from amongst the higher judiciary, or professors of law, by the existing members of the Supreme Court and the Senators of the College of Justice; and

    iv two members shall be appointed by the Head of State on the nomination of the professional associations representing the legal profession.

97 Electoral Commission

a There shall be Electoral Commission, which shall be responsible, in accordance with this Constitution and the law, for:

    i   ensuring the free and fair conduct of all elections and referendums;

    ii proposing changes to the boundaries of constituencies and electoral regions;

    iii overseeing registration of voters;

    iv enforcing the laws on campaign spending and on donations to political parties and campaigns;

    v registering political parties and auditing their accounts according to law; and

    vi making recommendations to Parliament concerning the impartial administration of elections and referendums.

b The Electoral Commission shall consist of seven members:

    i   Three executive members, including the Convenor, shall be appointed by the Head of State, on the joint nomination of the Prime Minister and the Leader of the Opposition, on merit, according to their qualifications and experience, of which at least one shall be a serving or former judge with experience of electoral law; and

    ii Four non-executive members shall be elected by Parliament, by secret ballot and on a nonpartisan basis, by single transferable vote, to represent the public interest.

98 Public Service Commission

a There shall be a Public Service Commission, which shall be responsible, in accordance with this Constitution and the law, for:

    i   maintaining the impartiality of the civil service;

    ii supervising the recruitment, selection, training, promotion, pay, and discipline of public officials; and

    iii making recommendations to the Government for senior civil service appointments and appointments to public bodies.

b The Public Service shall consist of seven members:

    i   Three executive members, including the Convenor, shall be appointed by the Head of State, on the joint nomination of the Prime Minister and the Leader of the Opposition, on merit, according to their qualifications and experience, or which at least one shall be or have been a senior civil servant of at least ten years' standing and at least one shall be nominated in consultation with trade unions of civil servants; and

    ii Four non-executive members shall be elected by Parliament, by secret ballot and on a nonpartisan basis, by single transferable vote, to represent the public interest.

99 Broadcasting Commission

a There shall be an independent, non-partisan Broadcasting Commission, which shall be responsible, in accordance with the Constitution and the law, for the regulation of public broadcasting services.

b The Broadcasting Commission shall consist of seven members:

    i Three executive members, including the Convenor, shall be appointed by the Head of State, on the joint nomination of the Prime Minister and the Leader of the Opposition, on merit, according to their qualifications and experience; and

    ii Four non-executive members shall be elected by Parliament, by secret ballot and on a nonpartisan basis, by single transferable vote, to represent the public interest.

100 Tenure and Independence of Commissions

a A member of the Judicial Appointments Commission, Electoral Commission, Public Service Commission, or Broadcasting Commission, with the exception of an ex-officio member of the Judicial Appointments Commission, shall serve for non-renewable terms of six years and may only be removed for misconduct, incapacity, or other due cause, by a two-thirds majority of Parliament.

b Membership of the Judicial Appointments Commission, Electoral Commission, Public Service Commission, or Broadcasting Commission, shall be incompatible with all other public offices and with membership of any political party. Additional incompatibilities maybe prescribed by Act of Parliament.

c The salaries and allowances of members of the Judicial Appointments Commission, Electoral Commission, Public Service Commission, or Broadcasting Commission shall be determined by law; but no law to diminish their salary or allowances, or to increase their salary or allowances above the rate of inflation, shall be enacted except by a two-thirds majority of the members of Parliament.

Part XII – Integrity in Public Life

101 Principles of Public Life and Codes of Conduct

a The administration of the state and the conduct of public life shall be guided by the principles of Selflessness, Integrity, Objectivity, Accountability, Openness, Honesty and Leadership, as set out in the First Report of the Committee on Standards in Public Life (Nolan Report) 1995.

b In order to give effect to these principles:

   i Parliament shall adopt a Code of Conduct for members of Parliament, members of the Government, members of Local Councils, and all others in elective office;

   ii the Public Service Commission shall adopt a Code of Conduct for civil servants, police officers, and all others in public employment, including the management of public enterprises; and

   iii the Judicial Appointments Commission shall adopt a Code of Conduct for members of the judiciary.

c Parliament may provide by law for the effective enforcement of these Codes of Conduct.

102 Conflicts of Interest

a There shall be for Parliament and for each local Council a public Register of Members' Interests, in which all private and business interests of members, including any gifts, donations or contracts, must be recorded. No member of Parliament or Councillor may vote on any matter in which he or she has a conflicting private or business interest.

b No person who has been a member of the Government or of a parliamentary committee may, for a period of ten years thereafter, be employed by, or act as a consultant or advisor to, any company with which he or she had dealings in an official capacity.

103 Civic Honours

a The Head of State may, subject to this Constitution and the law, confer civic honours on citizens who have greatly contributed to public life and national culture.

b The grades and titles of honours, and the circumstances under which they may be awarded, shall be established by law.

c Honours shall not be hereditary, nor accompanied by any legal privileges.

d No person who has during the preceding five years, directly or through an intermediary, given any donation or made any loan to any political party, candidate, or election or referendum campaign, or who has within the preceding five years has held any elective public office, shall be eligible for any honour.

e Parliament shall establish an all-party committee to advise the Head of State on the award of honours, and no honour shall be awarded unless authorised by a resolution of that committee.

104 Oath of Office

All members of Parliament, members of the Government, civil servants, police, military and diplomatic officers, local Councillors, members of the judiciary, the Auditor-General, Ombudsman, and members of independent commissions, shall take the following oath or affirmation of office, which may be taken with or without religious invocation and is equally valid in either form:

"I, being elected / appointed to the office of [name of office], do hereby solemnity swear / affirm that I will defend and uphold the Constitution of Scotland, and that I will perform my duties with honesty and integrity, to the best of my ability, in accordance with the Constitution and the law (so help me God)."

Part XIII – Adoption and Amendment of the Constitution

105 Adoption

This Constitution shall be adopted by the people of Scotland on being approved by a majority of the votes cast in a referendum. Within ten days after the referendum, the Constitution shall be formally proclaimed by the Presiding Officer, and shall come into effect immediately upon such proclamation.

106 Amendment Process

a This Constitution may be amended only in accordance with the provisions of this Section.

b   A bill to amend this Constitution must specify in its Short Title that it is a bill to amend the Constitution.

c   A period of at least 90 days shall elapse between the publication of a bill to amend the Constitution and the final vote on such bill.

d   A bill to amend the Constitution shall be deemed to have been passed by Parliament only if a three-fifths majority of the total membership of Parliament vote in favour of the bill on its final reading.

e   Subject to the provisions of sub-section (f) a bill to amend the Constitution shall not be presented for royal assent unless it has been approved by a majority of votes cast in a national referendum held under the terms of Section 82.

f   A bill to amend the Constitution may be submitted for royal assent without having been put to the people in a referendum if it is passed on its final reading by a three-fourths majority of the total membership of Parliament; provided, that this sub-section shall not apply to any bill that contains any provision amending, either directly or consequentially, any of the following Sections:

   i   Sections 1 to 5 inclusive;
   ii   Sections 9 to 27 inclusive;
   iii Sections 36, 40 and 41;
   iv   Sections 42 to 49 inclusive;
   v   Sections 62 to 67 inclusive;
   v   Sections 74 to 77 inclusive;
   vi   Sections 82 to 85 inclusive;
   vii Sections 86 to 92 inclusive; or
   vii this Section.

g   A bill to amend the Constitution that is presented for royal assent in accordance with this Section shall receive royal assent within three working days and an official consolidated text of the amended Constitution shall then be promulgated in the official gazette.

h   Constitutional amendment bills are subject to judicial review under Sections 57 or 74 only on procedural grounds.

i   No amendment may be made during a state of emergency or during enemy occupation of the country.

'A New Treaty of Union'

An agreement between the Government of Scotland and the
Government of the United Kingdom concerning the Establishment
of New Articles of Union

1 **The United Kingdom**

   1 There shall continue to be a United Kingdom of Great Britain and
   Northern Ireland (the 'United Kingdom').

   2 The United Kingdom is a democratic confederal Union consisting
   of two equal states:

   a England, Wales and Northern Ireland; and

   b Scotland.

   3 Each state regains its sovereignty, freedom, and autonomy, and
   every power, jurisdiction and right, which is not by these Articles
   delegated to the institutions of the United Kingdom.

   4 The United Kingdom under these Articles continues as a sovereign
   state in accordance with international law; it maintains all its existing
   treaty rights and obligations in accordance with international law.

2 **Status of the Articles of Union**

These Articles of Union shall be the supreme law of the United Kingdom;
any Act of Parliament, treaty or other law that is inconsistent with these
Articles shall, to the extent of inconsistency, be void.

3 **European Convention on Human Rights**

   1 Every person in the United Kingdom or subject to the jurisdiction
   thereof has the rights and freedoms set out in the Convention for
   the Protection of Human Rights and Fundamental Freedoms, agreed
   by the Council of Europe on 4 November 1950, and the protocols
   thereto to which the United Kingdom has acceded or shall hereafter
   accede ('the Convention').

   2 No law may be enacted by the Council of the United Kingdom or
   by either Parliament that is incompatible with the rights and

freedoms set out in the Convention, and the public authorities of the United Kingdom and of the states must, in carrying out their functions, respect and comply with those rights and freedoms.

4 Head of State

1 Her Majesty and Her heirs and successors shall continue to be Head of State of the United Kingdom.

2 The powers, duties, functions, privileges and responsibilities of the Head of State in relation to the United Kingdom shall be determined by these Articles, and the powers, duties, functions, privileges and responsibilities of the Head of State in each state shall be determined by the Constitution and laws of that state.

3 Any change to the laws of succession, regency and exclusion must be approved by both Parliaments (the Parliament of England, Wales and Northern Ireland, and the Parliament of Scotland).

5 Separation of the Parliaments

1 The Union of Parliaments is dissolved. There shall be no Parliament for the United Kingdom.

2 Upon the coming into effect of these Articles:

a the members of the House of Commons elected from Scottish constituencies and Scottish peers shall cease to hold office as such; and

b the members of the House of Commons elected from constituencies in England, Wales and Northern Ireland and peers other than Scottish peers shall sit, according to the law and custom of Parliament, as the Parliament of England, Wales and Northern Ireland.

3 The Parliament of England, Wales and Northern Ireland shall have no sovereignty or legislative authority over Scotland.

4 The Scottish Parliament shall have no sovereignty or legislative authority over England, Wales and Northern Ireland.

6 Council of the United Kingdom and Secretariat

1 The United Kingdom shall be governed by a 'Council of the United Kingdom' consisting of:

a the Prime Minister of England, Wales and Northern Ireland (or some other senior member of the Government of England, Wales and Northern Ireland designed by the Prime Minister thereof), as President of the Council of the United Kingdom;

b The Prime Minister of Scotland (or some other senior member of the Government of Scotland designed by the Prime Minister thereof), as Vice-President of the Council of the United Kingdom;

c Four United Kingdom Secretaries of State:
   i   a Secretary of State for Foreign affairs;
   ii a Secretary of State for Defence;
   iii a Secretary of State for Finance;
   iv a Secretary of State for Home Affairs.

2 The United Kingdom Secretaries of State shall be appointed and removed by Her Majesty, in Her capacity as Head of State of the United Kingdom, on the joint advice of the President of the Council of the United Kingdom and the Vice-President of the Council of the United Kingdom.

3 There shall be a Secretary-General of the United Kingdom, who shall be appointed by Her Majesty, in Her capacity as Head of State of the United Kingdom, on the advice of the Council of the United Kingdom.

4 The Secretary-General of the United Kingdom shall keep the records and archives of the Council of the United Kingdom, prepare its business and correspondence, and perform such other duties as may be lawfully entrusted to him or her by the Council of the United Kingdom.

5 The staff of the secretariat shall be seconded from the civil services of the two states in accordance with such regulations as the Council of the United Kingdom shall adopt.

7 Defence and Foreign Policy

1 The United Kingdom shall maintain a common defence and foreign policy.

2 The Council of the United Kingdom, acting through the Secretary of State for Foreign Affairs, shall be responsible for:
   a foreign affairs generally;

b relations with the European Union, NATO and the United Nations;

c diplomatic and consular services;

d the negotiation of treaties on behalf of the United Kingdom, provided that:

    i no matter especially concerning either state should be agreed without the consent of the Prime Minister of that state (or other designated Minister of that state), who shall have the right to be present in such discussions; and

    ii treaties and international agreements of the United Kingdom shall apply only if adopted into law or ratified by both Parliaments, or, in so far as they concern only one state, by the Parliament of that state.

3 The Council of the United Kingdom, through the United Kingdom Secretary of State for Defence, shall be responsible for defence policy, and shall direct and command of the Armed Forces of the United Kingdom, of which Her Majesty shall be titular Commander-in-Chief.

4 The raising, recruitment, organisation, discipline, pay and administration of the Armed Forces shall be determined by laws enacted by the two Parliaments.

5 The regulation of territorial and civil defence troops, and of coastal and fisheries protection forces, shall be the responsibility of each State under its own laws.

8 Finance

1 The United Kingdom shall maintain a common treasury and a common currency.

2 The United Kingdom Secretary of State for Finance shall be responsible, in accordance with the regulations enacted by the Council of the United Kingdom, for the management of the common treasury and for preparation of the budget and estimates of the Council of the United Kingdom, which shall be adopted by a majority vote thereof.

3 Each State shall be responsible for paying to the common treasury of the United Kingdom such sums as are authorized by the Council

of the United Kingdom, based on distribution of burdens between the States according to their populations.

4   The United Kingdom Secretary of State for Finance shall also be responsible, subject to such regulations as the Council of the United Kingdom may enact, for matters concerning the common currency, money supply and the regulation of the Bank of England.

9   Home Affairs

1   There shall be freedom of movement within the United Kingdom, and the citizens of either State may live, work, vote, and hold office in their own State and in the other State.

2   The Council of the United Kingdom may enact uniform laws throughout the United Kingdom with respect to citizenship and naturalisation, immigration, extradition, asylum, passports and border security. The United Kingdom Secretary of State for Home Affairs shall be responsible for the enforcement and administration of these laws.

10 Co-operation

The Council of the United Kingdom may make proposals for co-operation on the following matters of mutual interest, subject to approval by means of parallel legislation passed by the two Parliaments:

a   railways, roads and other forms of communication between the states;

b   driver and vehicle licensing;

c   postal, telephonic and internet services;

d   harmonisation of tax rates;

e   economic co-operation;

f   scientific research;

g   meteorological, oceanographic, coastguard and navigational services; and

h   the joint funding of infrastructure projects.

11 Supreme Court

1   In addition to any other jurisdiction conferred upon it by the constitution or laws of either state or by the Council of the United Kingdom, the Supreme Court of the United Kingdom shall have appellate jurisdiction over all questions concerning the interpreta-

tion of these Articles or the validity of any law or treaty under the terms of these Articles.

2 No alteration to the appointment, composition or tenure of the Supreme Court of the United Kingdom, or the privileges and immunities of the judges thereof, shall be made except by means of parallel legislation adopted by both Parliaments.

12 Internal Government of the States

1 The internal government of 'England, Wales and Northern Ireland', subject to these Articles, shall until otherwise provided for by law be based on the existing statutes and other laws and conventions in effect.

2 The internal government of Scotland, subject to these Articles, shall be conducted according to the Scottish Constitution, which shall be adopted by the people of Scotland in accordance with such provisions as the Scottish Parliament shall prescribe.

3 Nothing in this Charter shall affect:
   i the continuing existence or powers of devolved institutions in Wales or Northern Ireland; or
   ii the Good Friday (Belfast) Agreement, 1998.

13 Secession

1 Either state may leave the United Kingdom by a decision of the people of the state, by means of a majority of the votes cast in a referendum held in accordance with the constitution and laws of that state.

2 If either state secedes, the United Kingdom shall thereupon be dissolved, and England, Wales and Northern Ireland, and Scotland, shall both be equal successor states.

14 Adoption and Amendment

1 These Articles shall be adopted by parallel legislation passed by the United Kingdom Parliament and the Scottish Parliament and shall come into effect after having been approved by a majority of the votes cast in parallel referendums held in England, Wales and Northern Ireland and in Scotland.

2 Any changes to these Articles shall be made only on the proposal

of the Council of the United Kingdom, with the approval of both Parliaments, and subject to ratification by the people of both states in parallel referendums, to be held in accordance with the constitution and laws of each state.

A Home Rule and Full Fiscal Autonomy Settlement for Scotland

Scotland (*Home Rule and Full Fiscal Autonomy*) Act

An Act to provide for the Home Rule and full fiscal autonomy of Scotland within the United Kingdom, to give effect to the sovereignty of the people of Scotland, and for connected purposes.

Be it enacted by the Queen's most Excellent Majesty, by and with the advice and consent of the Lords Spiritual and Temporal, and Commons, in this present Parliament assembled, and by the authority of the same, as follows:

1 Short Title and Application

1. This Act may be cited as the Scotland (Home Rule and Full Fiscal Autonomy) Act, 2015.
2. This Act shall be in force in Scotland and, unless the context otherwise requires, shall apply to Scotland only.

2 Home Rule

1. From the commencement of this Act Scotland is to be an autono‐mous and internally self-governing jurisdiction within the United Kingdom.
2. Subject to this Act and to the Scottish Constitution set out in Schedule One, the Scottish Parliament shall have the authority to make all laws for the peace, order and good government of Scotland.
3. The Parliament of the United Kingdom shall not have the authority to legislate for Scotland, except in the manner and to the extent permitted by Schedule Two.

3 Sovereignty

1. In Scotland, the people have the sovereign right to self-determination and to choose freely the form in which their institutions are to be constituted and how they are governed.

2 All State power and authority in Scotland accordingly derives from, and is subject to, the sovereign will of the people, and those exercising State power and authority are accountable for it to the people.

3 Scotland, in the free exercise of its sovereign rights, hereby expresses its determination to remain within the United Kingdom and to be governed as an autonomous jurisdiction of the United Kingdom subject to the following provisions:

a while a substantial section of the people in Scotland have a legitimate wish for independence, the present wish of a majority of the people of Scotland, freely expressed in the referendum held on 18 September 2014, is to maintain the Union;

b accordingly, Scotland's status as part of the United Kingdom reflects and relies upon that wish, and it would be wrong to make any change in the status of Scotland save with the consent of a majority of its people;

c it is for the people of Scotland alone to exercise their right of self-determination to bring about an independent state, if that is their wish, accepting that this right must be achieved and exercised with and subject to the agreement and consent of a majority of the people of Scotland in a referendum held in accordance with the Constitution and laws of Scotland; and

d if in the future, the people of Scotland exercise their right of self-determination on the basis set out in this sub-Section to bring about an independent Scotland, it will be a binding obligation on both Governments to introduce and support in their respective Parliaments legislation and other measures to give effect to that wish.

4 Representation of Scotland in UK Parliament

1 With effect from the commencement of this Act, members of the House of Commons representing constituencies in Scotland shall not:

a sit, speak or vote in the House of Commons except in relation to matters concerning Scotland and specified in Section Two;

b participate in any vote of confidence or no-confidence in the House of Commons, or in any vote on the dissolution of Parliament;

   c be eligible for any ministerial office in the UK Government;

   d serve as Speaker or as a Deputy Speaker of the House of Commons; or

   e be a member of any committee of the House of Commons, except as a member of a committee concerning a matter specified in Schedule Two.

2 Scotland shall continue to be represented in the House of Commons by elected members in proportion to Scotland's share of the population of the United Kingdom.

3 Nothing in this Act or in the Scottish Constitution shall prevent any person from being appointed to the House of Lords solely on the grounds that such person was born in, or is ordinarily resident in, Scotland.

5 Scottish Constitution

The Constitution set out in the Schedule One (herein referred to as 'the Scottish Constitution') shall from the commencement of this Act be adopted and recognised as the supreme constitutional law of Scotland.

6 External affairs and defence

1 Subject to the provisions of this Act, the external affairs and defence of Scotland, as part of the United Kingdom, shall continue to be the responsibility of the Government of the United Kingdom.

2 In so far as it is practicable to do so:

   a the United Kingdom's responsibilities for external affairs and defence shall be discharged after consultation with the Scottish Government; and

   b provision shall be made for Ministers of the Scottish Government to be consulted with regard to foreign policy decisions and relations with the European Union and other international organisations, on matters affecting Scottish interests.

3 No treaty or other international agreement entered into by the United Kingdom shall affect the borders of Scotland, its maritime claims, its domestic law, or its financial status, unless such treaty or agreement is adopted into domestic law by an Act of the Scottish Parliament.

4 Nothing in this Act or in the Scottish Constitution shall affect the

United Kingdom's continued obligations under international law or its membership of any inter-governmental or supranational organisation.

5 Scotland may engage in external relations for the purposes of promoting cultural, economic, academic, sporting and humanitarian exchange.

7 British nationality and citizenship

1 Nothing in this Act or in the Scottish Constitution shall affect the status of any person as a British citizen.

2 There shall be a common citizenship for the United Kingdom without any distinction between persons born or resident in Scotland and persons born or resident in other parts of the United Kingdom.

3 Persons born or resident in Scotland shall have full rights of residence in all other parts of the United Kingdom and persons born or resident in other parts of the United Kingdom shall have full rights of residence in Scotland.

8 Common Travel Area

Nothing in this Act shall affect:

a the continued existence of the Common Travel Area; or

b the continued responsibility of the UK Government for the security of the external border of the United Kingdom.

9 Common Currency

Until and unless otherwise determined by an Act of the Parliament of the United Kingdom:

a Scotland shall continue to use the pound sterling as its currency;

b the Bank of England shall be the lender of last resort for Scotland; and

c provision shall be made by order-in-council for:

   i the management of a common currency area between Scotland and the other parts of the United Kingdom; and

   ii the representation of the Scottish Government on the Board of Governors and the Monetary Policy Committee of the Bank of England.

10 Fiscal Autonomy

1 All taxes, charges, customs and duties arising from the residents of Scotland or from economic activity in Scotland, including revenues from off-shore resources, shall be:

   a levied solely or in accordance with Acts of the Scottish Parliament; and

   b payable to the Scottish exchequer.

2 Scotland shall defray the costs incurred by the United Kingdom on behalf of Scotland in the following manner:

   a the Scottish Government shall pay the Government of the United Kingdom for the full cost of United Kingdom services provided solely in and for Scotland;

   b the Scottish Government shall pay the Government of the United Kingdom a share of the cost of services provided for the United Kingdom as a whole in proportion to Scotland's share of the overall population of the United Kingdom at the most recent census; and

   c the Scottish Government shall pay the Government of the United Kingdom a share of the cost of servicing the national debt of the United Kingdom, in proportion to Scotland's share of the overall gross domestic product of the United Kingdom.

3 Payments due in accordance with this Section shall be a charge on Scotland's Consolidated Fund.

11 Entrenchment

A bill for an Act of the United Kingdom Parliament that would amend or repeal this Act, whether expressly or otherwise:

   a shall not be introduced to either House of the United Kingdom Parliament, unless such bill has previously been approved by a majority vote of the Scottish Parliament; and

   b shall not be presented for Royal Assent, unless approved by the people of Scotland in a referendum to be held in accordance with the Constitution and laws of Scotland.

12 Commencement

This Act shall come into force on a date to be appointed by the Secretary of State for Scotland, being within 90 days of the passing of this Act.

Schedule 1: Scottish Constitution

[For reasons of space, I have not reproduced a Constitution in full here. Something like the <u>Model Constitution</u> would be suitable, with only such minor amendments as are necessary for a non-independent state, such as the removal of provisions related to citizenship and the armed forces.]

Schedule 2: United Kingdom Legislation Applicable to Scotland

1 The United Kingdom Parliament shall have the exclusive authority to legislate for Scotland, as part of the United Kingdom, with respect to the following matters:
   a the succession to the office of the Head of State;
   b the appointment of a regent or council of state;
   c royal titles;
   d the civil list;
   e the regulation of the Royal Household;
   f defence, including regulation of the armed forces and security services;
   g currency, coinage, legal tender, the Bank of England and monetary policy;
   h passports, citizenship, naturalisation and immigration;
   i extradition and asylum;
   j foreign relations, and diplomatic and consular services;
   h the representation of Scotland in the House of Commons.

2 The United Kingdom Parliament shall have authority to legislate for Scotland with respect to the following matters, concurrent with the right of the Scottish Parliament to legislate in respect of such matters; and in the event of any incompatibility between Acts of the United Kingdom Parliament and Acts of the Scottish Parliament with respect to these matters, the latter shall prevail:
   a railways between Scotland and the rest of the United Kingdom;
   b air traffic control, airports, ports and UK border security;
   c quarantine and the prevention and containment of epidemics;
   d disaster relief, response to emergencies, and civil defence; and
   e meteorological, oceanographic, coastguard and navigational services.
   f driver and vehicle licensing;

g postal services and telecommunications services; and

h funding and promotion of scientific research, without prejudice
to the ability of the Scottish Parliament to make additional provision for the funding of such research.

3 Acts of the United Kingdom Parliament shall have effect in Scotland
only in so far as they are not incompatible with the Scottish
Constitutions or with the rights and freedoms guaranteed thereby.

A Constitution for a Federal United Kingdom

Part 1: Foundational Principles

1 **The Federation**

   1 The United Kingdom of Great Britain and Northern Ireland ("United Kingdom") is a federation of States founded on the principles of democracy and the values of liberty, equality and solidarity.

   2 The capital and seat of government of the United Kingdom shall be the City of York.

   3 Until otherwise provided for by an Act of the Federal Assembly, the flag and anthem of the United Kingdom shall be the same as those in common use prior to the coming into effect of this Constitution.

2 **The States**

   1 The United Kingdom consists of four States –

     a England;

     b Scotland;

     c Wales; and

     d Northern Ireland.

   2 The boundaries of the States shall be those recognised immediately prior to the coming into effect of this Constitution, and shall not be amended except by an Act of the Federal Assembly.

   3 No bill for amending the boundaries of any state shall be presented for Royal Assent unless the boundary amendments proposed in the bill have been endorsed by-

     a the State Parliament of each of the states affected by the change; and

     b a majority of the voters in each affected area, by means of a referendum.

   4 Each State regains its sovereignty, freedom and autonomy, and every

power, jurisdiction and right, which is not expressly delegated to the Federal institutions of the United Kingdom by this Constitution.

5 The capital and seat of government of each State shall be as follows –
a England, Westminster;
b Scotland, Edinburgh;
c Wales, Cardiff;
d Northern Ireland, Belfast.

6 Each State shall adopt its own flag and anthem by an Act of the State Parliament.

3 Sovereignty

1 The people of each State have the sovereign right to self-determination and to determine the form of Government best suited to their needs.

2 All public power and authority accordingly derives from, and is subject to, the sovereign will of the peoples, and those exercising public power and authority are accountable for it to the peoples.

3 The sovereign will of the peoples is expressed in the Constitution and, in accordance with the constitution and laws made under it, through the people's elected representatives, at referendums and by other means provided by law.

4 Hierarchy of Laws

1 This Constitution is the supreme law of the Federation. Any Act of the Federal Assembly, Act of a State Parliament, treaty, order-in-council, regulation, or other law, which is repugnant to this Constitution shall, to the extent of the repugnancy, be void.

2 Each State shall be a distinct legal jurisdiction with its own law and its own courts, but the Welsh jurisdiction shall not be established until an Act of the National Assembly for Wales so provides, and until such time as such an Act comes into effect England and Wales shall continue to form a common legal jurisdiction.

3 The courts in each jurisdiction shall apply, in order of hierarchy –
a this Constitution;
b treaties entered into by the United Kingdom and duly ratified;
c Acts of the Federal Assembly and Acts of the State Parliament, in their respective areas of legislative competence, giving priority

to Acts of the State Parliaments in areas of concurrent competence;

d   regulations, orders-in-council and other subordinate legislation.

5   **Electoral Franchise**

1   Subject to the provisions of this Article, a person shall be qualified to be registered as a voter for referendums and for the election of the Federal Assembly and State Parliaments, and for the election of local authorities, and shall not be qualified to be so registered unless:

a   he or she is a citizen of the United Kingdom;

b   he or she is lawfully resident in the United Kingdom and has been domiciled in the constituency or other electoral district of the election for a continuous period of ninety days immediately prior to the date of registration.

2   A person who has not been resident as required by sub-paragraph (b) of paragraph (1), by reason of service in the public service or as a member of the Armed Forces of the United Kingdom, shall not be disqualified from registering to vote on account of such absence.

3   A person shall not be qualified to be registered as a voter under this Article if –

a   he or she has not attained sixteen years of age;

b   he or she is under legal guardianship on grounds of mental incapacity in accordance with the law.

6   **Languages**

1   The official language of the United Kingdom is English.

2   Each State Parliament may make provision for –

a   the official status of any languages, in addition to English, in that State;

b   the promotion of the use of any languages, in addition to English, in public education, administration, and broadcasting, in that State.

Part 2: Institutions of the Federation

7   **Head of State**

1   Her Majesty and her heirs and successors according to law shall continue to be Head of State of the United Kingdom.

2 In relation to this Federation, Her Majesty in right of the United Kingdom shall have only such powers, duties, functions, privileges and responsibilities as are vested in the Head of State by or in accordance with this Constitution.

3 The Federal Assembly may by law provide for –
   a the succession to the throne;
   b regencies during the minority or incapacity of the Head of State;
   c excluding particular persons from the succession on grounds of incapacity;
   d the regulation of the Royal Household;
   e the Civil List; and
   f the style and title of the Head of State.

4 In the performance of duties and the exercise of powers in relation to the United Kingdom, the Head of State shall only act in accordance with the advice of the Executive Council, except where it is expressly provided in this Constitution or in an Act of the Federal Assembly that the Head of State is to act with the advice of any other official or institution, or at her discretion.

8 Federal Assembly

1 There shall be a Federal Assembly of the United Kingdom, which shall, subject to this Constitution, be the legislative, representative and deliberative assembly of the Federation.

2 The Federal Assembly shall consist of 120 members, or such greater number of members, not exceeding 200, as may be determined by an Act of the Federal Assembly. The distribution of the seats amongst the States shall be determined by Act of the Federal Assembly according to the following method:[1]
   a one half of the seats shall be divided equally amongst the four States; and
   b one half of the seats shall be divided amongst the four States in proportion to their share of the population of the United Kingdom at the most recent census.

3 Members of the Federal Assembly shall be directly elected by the registered electors of each State, by secret ballot, in accordance with the Party List system of proportional representation. Provision may be made by law for:

    i   promoting the inclusion of under-represented sections of society by means of quotas;

    ii enabling voters to exercise a personal choice of candidates through preferential voting to determine the ranking order of candidates on the list of their choice; and

    iii the recall of members by means of a public recall vote.

4   Scotland, Wales and Northern Ireland shall each form one electoral region for the election of members. England shall be divided into at least six but not more than ten electoral regions by an Act of the English Parliament, on the proposal of an independent Boundaries Commission to be established by law – and, until so provided for, the electoral regions used in the most recent European Parliament election shall be used for the election of the Federal Assembly.

5   Vacancies arising in the Federal Assembly from the death, resignation, removal or recall of any member shall be filled by means of a writ from the President of the Assembly addressed to the person who at the previous election of Assembly members was the next-ranking unelected candidate from the State, region and party concerned who is still willing and qualified to serve.

6   The Federal Assembly shall not proceed to business unless at least one-half of its members, including at least one-third of the members from each of three-fourths of the States, are present.

7   The qualifications and disqualifications for serving as a member of the Federal Assembly in and for a State shall be the same as those for the Parliament of the State that they represent.

8   Subject to the provisions of paragraph (9) of this Article, the members of the Federal Assembly shall be elected for a term of four years, and a general election of members of the Federal Assembly shall take place every fourth year on a date to be prescribed by the Executive Council, provided such day is no earlier than 30 days before, and no later than 30 days after, the fourth anniversary of the previous general election. An election to the Federal Assembly shall also take place, on a date to be prescribed by the Executive Council, within 60 days of the premature dissolution of Parliament.

9   The Federal Assembly may be prematurely dissolved by the Head of State only if:

   a a resolution calling for a dissolution is passed by a two-thirds majority of the Federal Assembly; or

   b the Federal Assembly has failed to elect a Prime Minister within 30 days of a general election, or within 30 days of the office of Prime Minister becoming vacant.

10 The Federal Assembly shall adopt its own Standing Orders, shall elect its own Presiding Officer, and shall appoint its own Clerks and other staff. The Standing Orders shall provide for:

   a the establishment of committees for the scrutiny of legislation and for the investigation of the policy and conduct of the Executive Council;

   b the election of committee chairs by the Federal Assembly such that chairs are proportionately distributed amongst the parties represented in the Assembly;

   c the recognition of a Leader of the Opposition, being the person who is the leader of the largest party or group in the Federal Assembly that is in opposition to the Executive Council; and

   d the allocation of at least one-fourth of parliament time in the Federal Assembly to opposition and private members' business.

11 The Federal Assembly shall be summoned and prorogued by the Executive Council, but it shall meet at least once each year for an ordinary session of at least 90 days' duration, and it shall be summoned whenever requested by one-third of its members for the discussion of urgent business.

12 The Federal Assembly shall have exclusive the legislative power throughout the United Kingdom in relation to the following matters only –

   a defence, including regulation of the armed forces and security services;

   b foreign relations, the ratification of treaties, and diplomatic and consular services;

   c security of the United Kingdom border;

   d passports, citizenship, naturalisation and immigration;

   e extradition and asylum;

   f currency, coinage, legal tender;

   g the Bank of England and monetary policy;

h the borrowing of money on the public credit of the Federation;

i the maintenance of an internal common market within the United Kingdom;

j relations of the United Kingdom with the Channel Islands and the Isle of Mann, and with British overseas territories;

k the acquisition of property on just terms from any State or person for any purpose in respect of which the Federal Assembly has pow er to make laws;

l matters necessary for the execution of any power vested by this Constitution in the Federal Assembly or Executive Council, or in any department or officer of thereof;

m the regulation of the public service of the Federation; and

n other matters declared by this Constitution to be within the exclusive power of the Federal Assembly.

13 The Federal Assembly shall have concurrent legislative power with the legislatures of the States in relation to the following matters only, but in the event of any conflict arising between Federal and state legislation in relation to these matters, state legislation shall prevail –

a railways, truck roads and other forms of transport between the states;

b driver and vehicle licensing;

c postal, telephonic and internet services;

d harmonisation of rates of sales, income and corporation taxes;

e scientific research;

f broadcasting;

g weights and measures;

h copyrights, patents of inventions and designs, and trademarks;

i air traffic control, airports and ports;

j quarantine and the prevention and containment of epidemics;

k disaster relief, response to emergencies, and civil defence;

l meteorological, oceanographic, coastguard and navigational services;

m fishing and fishery protection;

n environmental protection; and

o prevention of terrorism and serious and organised crime.

14 Subject to the provisions of this Constitution, the Federal Assembly shall pass bills by a majority of the members present and voting at a quorate meeting. Every bill shall be subjected to three readings, as laid down in the Standing Orders of the Federal Assembly, and if passed on its third reading shall be presented by the Presiding Officer to the Head of State for royal assent.

15 Every bill, unless declared to be urgent by a two-thirds majority of the members of the Federal Assembly, shall be circulated to the State Parliaments for a period of at least 30 days before the final reading of the bill in the Federal Assembly. During that period the Parliament of any State may, by a simple majority vote, make an address to the Federal Assembly stating its objection to the bill or proposing any amendments to the bill. If such an address is received, the Federal Assembly shall consider it, and any proposed amendments, in plenary session before finally voting on the bill.

16 When a bill is presented for royal assent the Head of State shall within 30 days of the date of presentation either –

a grant assent to the bill and thereby enact it as an Act of the Federal Assembly; or

b if so requested by the Presiding Officer of the Federal Assembly, or by the Government of any State, suspend the granting of assent to the bill, pending the referral of the bill to the Supreme Court for an advisory ruling on its constitutionality.

17 If a bill is referred to the Supreme Court in accordance with sub-paragraph (b) of the preceding paragraph, the Supreme Court shall within 90 days of the date of referral issue an advisory ruling on the constitutional validity of the bill. If the Supreme Court advises that the bill is, in whole or in part, repugnant to this Constitution, the Head of State shall refuse assent to the bill, and shall return the bill to the Federal Assembly for reconsideration within a further period of ten days; otherwise, the Head of State shall grant assent to the bill and enact it as an Act of the Federal Assembly without delay. If a bill that has been returned to the Federal Assembly for reconsideration is passed again, during the same session, with or without amendment, by a two-thirds majority of the members of the Federal Assembly, royal assent shall not be refused a second time;

but this shall not prohibit the Supreme Court from subsequently ruling on the constitutionality of the law during legal proceedings.

9 Executive Council

1 The executive powers of the Federal Government shall be exercised by an Executive Council consisting of five United Kingdom Ministers –

   a a Prime Minister, who shall preside over the Executive Council, co-ordinate the work of the other Ministers, and act as spokes-person of the Executive Council;

   b a Minister of Defence;

   c a Minister of Foreign Affairs;

   d a Minister of Finance; and

   e a Minister of Co-operation and Home affairs.

2 The Prime Minister shall be appointed by the Head of State on the advice of the Presiding Officer of the Federal Assembly, from amongst the members of the Federal Assembly, following an election held as prescribed in paragraph 3. The other Ministers shall be appointed by the Head of State, from amongst the members of the Federal Assembly, upon the advice of the Prime Minister.

3 The Prime Minister of the United Kingdom shall be elected by the members of the Federal Assembly by open ballot. In order to be elected, a candidate must receive an absolute majority of votes cast. If no candidate receives an absolute majority of votes cast, a run-off election between the two highest polling candidates shall be held, and the candidate who wins the greatest number of votes in the run-off shall be elected. The election of a Prime Minister shall be the first item of business of the Federal Assembly after it has elected its Presiding Officer following a general election, and shall also take place within 30 days whenever a vacancy in the office of Prime Minister occurs.

4 If the Federal Assembly, by an absolute majority of its members, passes a vote of no-confidence or censure against the Prime Minister, the Executive Council shall resign, and the Federal Assembly shall proceed to elect a new Prime Minister. If the Federal Assembly, by an absolute majority of its members, passes a vote of no-confidence

or censure against a Minister other than the Prime Minister, that Minister shall resign, and the Prime Minister shall nominate a replacement.

5 A person who has resigned, or who is required to resign, under the preceding paragraph, shall continue in office until the appointment of their successor, but shall serve in a 'caretaker' capacity and shall undertake only routine administrative actions or such emergency actions as may not, in the judgment of the Executive Council, be delayed until the appointment of their successor. This paragraph shall not, however, be justiciable, and shall not affect the legal validity of any action performed in a caretaker capacity.

6 One member of the Executive Council shall, in addition to the responsibilities of their portfolio, be designated by the Prime Minister as Deputy Prime Minister. The Deputy Prime Minister shall preside over the Executive Council during the absence or incapacity of the Prime Minister, and shall assist the Prime Minister in the co-ordination of the Executive Council's work.

10 Council of the States

1 There shall be a Council of the States for the discussion of matters of common interest or concern amongst the Governments of the States.

2 The Council of the States shall consist of –
   a the Prime Minister of the United Kingdom;
   b the United Kingdom Minister for Co-operation and Home Affairs; and
   c the First Minister of each State.

3 In event of the absence or incapacity of the Prime Minister or of a First Minister, they may be represented in the Council of States by their respective deputies.

4 The Prime Minister of the United Kingdom shall summon regular meetings of the Council of States at least four times each year, but any First Minister may, on written application to the Prime Minister, demand a meeting of the Council of States to be held within 30 days.

5 The Chief Ministers of the Channel Islands and the Isle of Mann may participate in sessions of the Council of the States in a non-voting capacity.

11 Foreign Relations

1 The Executive Council, acting through the United Kingdom Minister for Foreign Affairs, and subject to this Constitution and to Acts of the Federal Assembly, shall be responsible for –

   a conducting relations with foreign states and international organisations; and

   b administering diplomatic and consular services.

3 The Executive Council, acting through the United Kingdom Minister for Foreign Affairs shall negotiate treaties on behalf of the United Kingdom, provided that –

   a no matter especially concerning a State should be agreed without the consent of the Government of that State; the State Government shall have the right to be consulted and to be present through an official delegation in such discussions; and

   b no treaty or international agreement shall be of any effect unless it is ratified by means of a resolution of the Federal Assembly, or, to the extent that it affects domestic law, by enabling legislation enacted by the Federal Assembly.

   c the approval of a two-thirds majority of the members of the Federal Assembly, including a majority of members from each of the States, shall be required for –

     i the ratification of any treaty or agreement by which the United Kingdom becomes a member of any international organisation to which legislative, fiscal, judicial or military powers are delegated;

     ii the ratification of any treaty or agreement concerning a substantial change in the terms of membership of any such international organisation; or

     iii the withdrawal of the United Kingdom from any such international organisation.

12 Defence

1 The Executive Council, through the United Kingdom Minister for Defence, shall be responsible for defence policy, and shall direct and command of the Armed Forces of the United Kingdom.

2 The Head of State shall be titular Commander-in-Chief of the

Armed Forces, but shall act in that capacity only on the advice and with the consent of the Executive Council.

3 The raising, recruitment, organisation, discipline, pay and administration of the Armed Forces shall be determined by laws enacted by the Federal Assembly.

4 Nothing in this Article shall prevent any state from maintaining its own fisheries and coastal protection forces, and its own civil defence forces, provided such forces are of a non-military nature.

5 No war may be declared, nor any force deployed abroad on active military service, except as authorised by a resolution of the Federal Assembly approved by an absolute majority vote.

13 Finance and Currency

1 The United Kingdom Minister for Finance shall be responsible for the management of the treasury of the United Kingdom subject to the laws enacted by the Federal Assembly.

2 The United Kingdom Minister for Finance shall be responsible for preparation of the annual budget and estimates of the Executive Council, which shall be adopted by a majority vote of the Federal Assembly.

3 The Federal Assembly shall have the authority to levy charges upon the states for the defrayment of the costs of the Federation, provided that each State shall contribute to the Federation in accordance with its share of the Gross National Product of the Federation.

4 Each State shall be responsible for paying to the Federation such sums, provided by its own revenues, as are required by Acts of the Federal Assembly in accordance with this Article.

5 If any State refuses or fails to pay its contribution, within the time period prescribed by Acts of the Federal Assembly, the Executive Council may, after having given 28 days' notice to the State concerned, requisition the required monies directly from the treasury of the State.

6 The United Kingdom Minister for Finance shall also be responsible, subject to such laws as the Federal Assembly may enact, for the administration of matters concerning the common currency, money supply and the regulation of the Bank of England.

7 There shall be a Consolidated Fund for the United Kingdom. Except as expressly provided by an Act of the Federal Assembly, all monies received by the Federation shall be paid into the Consolidated Fund.

8 The interest on the public debt of the United Kingdom shall be a standing charge on the Consolidated Fund.

15 Co-operation and Home Affairs

1 The United Kingdom Minister for Co-operation and Home Affairs, in accordance with Acts of the Federal Assembly, shall ensure –

 a the service and execution throughout the Federation of the civil and criminal process and the judgments of the courts of the States;

 b recognition throughout the Federation of the laws, the public Acts and records, and the judicial proceedings of the States;

 c the operation of the common market throughout the States.

2 The United Kingdom Minister for Co-operation and Home Affairs, after consultation with the Council of States, may enter into agreements with States, on behalf of the Executive Council, whereby a State authorises and requires the Federation, or any agency or department thereof, to deliver or to provide for the delivery of a public service in and for that State, in relation to any matters enumerated in paragraph 13 of Article 8. Such agreements (known as 'Shared Service Agreements') shall be valid if approved by the Federal Assembly and by the Parliament of the State to which it applies. They may be entered into for a period not exceeding 25 years, but may be renewed.

16 Supreme Court of the United Kingdom

1 There shall be one Supreme Court in and for the Federation, to be known as the Supreme Court of the United Kingdom.

2 The Supreme Court of the United Kingdom, in addition to any other powers and duties vested in or entrusted to it by this Constitution, or, subject to this Constitution by Acts of the Federal Assembly, shall have final appellate jurisdiction over all questions concerning –

 a the validity of any law or treaty under the terms of this Constitution;

 b the rights of citizens under this Constitution; or

c   the interpretation of this Constitution.

3   The Supreme Court of the United Kingdom shall consist of twelve justices, who shall be appointed by the Head of State acting on the advice of a Judicial Appointments Commission, which shall consist of the following members –

a   the United Kingdom Minister responsible for Co-operation and Home Affairs;

b   two judicial representatives from each legal jurisdiction nominated by the higher judiciary thereof;

c   two legal representatives from each legal jurisdiction (of which one shall be a barrister or advocate, and one a solicitor) nominated by their professional bodies;

d   two lay representatives from each State, not being members of the judiciary or the legal profession, and not being members of any Parliament, elected by the State Parliaments, by secret ballot, for terms of four years.

4   Subject to this Constitution and to any further provisions prescribed by Acts of the Federal Assembly, the United Kingdom Minister responsible for Co-operation and Home Affairs may issue regulations concerning the organisation, composition and functions of the Judicial Appointments Commission.

5   The Federal Assembly may by law prescribe the legal qualifications and other criteria necessary to be appointed as a member of the Supreme Court of the United Kingdom.

6   In making nominations, the Judicial Appointments Committee shall, in addition to any such qualifications and criteria required by law, have regard to the following characteristics –

a   legal training and experience;

b   qualities of character, integrity and neutrality;

c   personal skills, including communication, management and leadership skills;

d   the need for the Court to be representative of society in terms of race, gender, regional or state identities, class, and diversity of religious and cultural values;

7   If at any time it appears to the Prime Minister of the United Kingdom or to the First Minister of any State that a question of law

has arisen, or is likely to arise, which is of such a nature and of such public importance that it is expedient to obtain the opinion of the Supreme Court upon it, he or she may refer the question to the Supreme Court for consideration and the Supreme Court may, after such hearing as it thinks fit, report its opinion thereon.

8 Subject to the provisions of paragraphs 9 and 10 of this Article, members of the Supreme Court of the United Kingdom shall until retirement at the age of 70 years; provided, that those first appointed to a judicial office before 31 March 1995 shall retire at the age of 75 years.

9 Early retirement may be granted according to law on the grounds of illness or incapacity.

10 A member of the Supreme Court may be removed, on the grounds of misconduct, neglect of duty, or incapacity by means of a resolution of the Federal Assembly passed by a two-thirds majority vote. The Federal Assembly shall not vote on any such resolution unless the matter has been investigated by the Judicial Appointments Commission and the Judicial Appointments Commission has recommended to the Federal Assembly that the person should be removed.

11 Members of the Supreme Court shall be independent in the performance of their duties.

12 A members of the Supreme Court shall not:
   a hold any popularly elected public office;
   b be a member of any political party; or
   c undertake business or commercial activities, or other paid employment, that may reasonably be thought to compromise their independence, impartiality, or integrity.

Part 3: Institutions of the States

17 State Parliaments

1 Each State shall have a State Parliament, which shall be the legislative, representative and deliberative assembly of the people of that State.

2 Until otherwise provided in accordance with Article 22, the State Parliament for England shall be composed of two Houses –

a a House of Commons, consisting of all members elected from constituencies in England, according to the laws regulating such elections at the time of the coming into effect of this Constitution; and

b a House of Lords, initially composed according to paragraph 2 of Article 52.

3 The State Parliament for Scotland shall be the Scottish Parliament, as established by the Scotland Acts 1998 and 2012.

4 The State Parliament for Wales shall be the National Assembly for Wales, as established by the Government of Wales Acts 1998 and 2006.

5 The State Parliament for Northern Ireland shall be the Northern Ireland Assembly, as established by the Northern Ireland Act 1998.

6 Each State Parliament shall have the right to elect its own Presiding Officer, to adopt its own Standing Orders, and such other rights and privileges as may be determined by Acts of the State Parliaments enacted in accordance with this Constitution.

18 Powers of State Parliaments

1 Subject to the provisions of this Constitution, each State Parliament shall have authority to enact, amend and repeal all laws for the peace, order and good government of the State.

2 A State Parliament shall make no law concerning a matter which is declared by this Constitution to be an exclusive competence of the Federation.

3 A State Parliament shall make no law –

a that would restrict the franchise for State and local elections from that guaranteed by this Constitution;

b that would abolish the State Parliament, or infringe the basic principles of parliamentary democracy;

c that would extend the duration of a State Parliament beyond five years;

d that would exceed the powers of the State Parliament under this Constitution;

e that would infringe the fundamental rights of citizens under this Constitution;

f   that would be in breach of the United Kingdom's commitments and obligations under international law; or

g   that would otherwise be repugnant to this Constitution.

19 State Governments

1   Each State shall have a Government, which shall possess executive power in and for the State.

2   Each State Government shall consist of –

a   a First Minister, who shall be the chief executive of the State; and

b   a Deputy First Minister, who shall deputise for the First Minister as needed; and

c   such Ministers as may be appointed to administer the several ministries of the State, subject to any laws in effect in that State limiting the number of Ministers.

3   Each State Government shall be –

a   nominated by the State Parliament (or, in the case of a State with a bicameral Parliament, by the lower House) from amongst the members of the Parliament;

b   formally appointed by the Head of State, according to the laws of each State; and

c   responsible to the State Parliament (or, in a State with a bicameral Parliament, to the lower House thereof), which may remove the Government, or any State Minister, by means of a vote of no-confidence passed by an absolute majority of its members.

4   Subject to the provisions of this Constitution, each State Parliament may, by Act of the State Parliament, provide for the functions, organization and structure of the State Government.

5   Subject to the provisions of this Constitution, the powers, duties, functions, privileges and responsibilities of Her Majesty in each state shall be determined by the laws of that State.

20 State Judiciaries

1   The superior judges in each State shall be appointed on the advice of an independent and non-partisan appointing authority, as follows –

a   subject to the provisions of this Constitution, and until otherwise provided for by an Act establishing a separate jurisdiction for

Wales, judges of Courts in England and Wales shall be appointed by the Head of State on the advice of the Judicial Appointments Commission in accordance with the Constitutional Reform Act 2005.

b subject to the provisions of this Constitution, the judges of the Courts of Scotland shall be appointed by the Head of State on the advice of the Judicial Appointments Board for Scotland in accordance with the Judiciary and Courts (Scotland) Act 2008.

c Subject to the provisions of this Constitution, the judges of the Courts of Northern Ireland shall be appointed by the Head of State on the advice of the Northern Ireland Judicial Appointments Commission in accordance with the Justice (Northern Ireland) Acts 2002 and 2004.

2 Subject to the provisions of paragraphs 3 and 4, members of the superior courts in each State shall continue in office for life, but shall retire on reaching the retirement age prescribed by law.

3 Early retirement may be granted according to law on the grounds of illness or infirmity.

4 A member of the superior courts of any State may be removed, on the grounds of misconduct, neglect of duty, or incapacity by means of a resolution of the State Parliament passed by a two-thirds majority vote, but only after investigation by the judicial appointment body of the State.

5 Members of the State judiciaries shall be independent in the performance of their duties.

6 Members of the State judiciaries shall not:
   a hold any popularly elected public office;
   b be members of any political party; or
   c undertake business or commercial activities, or other paid employment, that may reasonably be thought to compromise their independence, impartiality, or integrity.

21 Independent Scrutiny and Oversight Institutions

1 There shall be in each State –
   a an authority for making or advising on public appointments;
   b a public services ombudsman or commissioner for administra-

tion, to whom complaints of maladministration may be made; and

c an auditor-general, who shall be responsible for the scrutiny of public finances.

2 These institutions shall be established on an independent and non-partisan basis by Acts of the State Parliaments, to be enacted in accordance with the procedure specified in Article 22.

22 Changes to State Institutions

1 Subject to the provisions of this Constitution, each State Parliament shall have the authority to enact laws amending or reforming the internal constitution or institutions of the State.

2 A law concerning the internal constitution or institutions of a State shall not be valid unless –

a it is approved, on its final reading, by at least three-fifths of the members of the State Parliament (or of the lower House thereof, if there are two Houses); and

b before being presented for royal assent or otherwise enacted, it is referred to the people in a State-wide referendum and is approved by a simple majority of the votes cast in that referendum.

3 For the purposes of this Article, a 'law amending or reforming internal constitution or institutions of a State' shall include laws concerning –

a the composition of the State Parliament or the method of electing its members;

b the rights, privileges, immunities of members of the State Parliament;

c the terms of office of the State Parliament, and the mode and manner by which the State Parliament may be dissolved;

d the establishment or abolition of a second chamber of the State Parliament, or concerning the powers and functions of a second chamber;

e the mode of selecting and removing the members of the State Government;

f the process for passing bills and enacting Acts of the State Parliament;

> g the status and composition of the superior courts in each jurisdiction;
>
> h the mode of appointing and removing judges, and their privileges and immunities;
>
> i the mode of appointing and removing the Law Officers of the State, and their privileges and immunities;
>
> j the mode of appointing and removing the members of independent scrutiny and oversight institutions of the State, and their privileges and immunities;
>
> k the basic laws governing the holding of referendums in the State; and
>
> l any alteration to the established status of a national religion or church.

4 Each State may, in accordance with the procedure prescribed by paragraph 2 of this Article –

> a adopt a declaratory statement of Directive Principles of State Policy in regard of social, economic and cultural rights; or
>
> b adopt a justiciable charter of social, economic and cultural rights.

23 Local Government in the States

1 For the purposes of local self-government, the territory of each State shall be divided and subdivided into such cities, regions, counties, burghs, communities, and other local authority areas as may from time to time be determined by Acts of the State Parliament.

2 Subject to this Article, the State Parliaments shall by law determine the duties, powers, responsibilities, organisation, composition and functioning of local authorities.

3 Until otherwise determined by Acts of the State Parliaments, the existing local authorities in each State shall continue in being with their existing powers and duties.

4 Each local authority shall be administered by a directly elected Council consisting of Councillors who are directly elected by the enfranchised citizens resident in the locality, at intervals of not greater than four years, by secret ballot.

5 Nothing in this Article shall prohibit the establishment of other

directly elected local offices, including but not limited to directly elected Mayors, School Boards and Police Commissioners, according to the law in each State.

Part 4: *Fundamental Rights and Liberties*

24 Right to Life

1 Everyone's right to life shall be protected by law.
2 Deprivation of life shall not be regarded as inflicted in contravention of this Article when it results from the use of force which is no more than absolutely necessary:
  i in defence of any person from unlawful violence;
  ii in order to effect a lawful arrest or to prevent the escape of a person lawfully detained;
  iii in action lawfully taken for the purpose of quelling a riot or insurrection; or
  iv in a lawful act of war.
3 The death penalty is prohibited. No one shall be condemned to death or executed.

25 Prohibition of Torture

All forms of torture and of cruel, degrading and dehumanizing punishment are prohibited.

26 Prohibition of Slavery

1 No one shall be held in slavery or servitude.
2 No one shall be required to perform forced or compulsory labour. For the purpose of this Article the term 'forced or compulsory labour' shall not include:
  i any work, not of a cruel, degrading or dehumanizing nature, required to be done in the ordinary course of detention imposed according to the provisions of Article 27 of this Constitution or during conditional release from such detention;
  ii any lawfully imposed service of a military character or, in case of conscientious objectors, service exacted instead of compulsory military service;

    iii any service exacted in case of an emergency or calamity threatening the life or wellbeing of the community;

    iv any work or service which forms part of normal civic obligations.

27 Right to Liberty and Security

1 Every person has the right to personal liberty and security, and accordingly no person shall be deprived of liberty save in the following cases and in accordance with the procedures prescribed by law –

    i   in the case of his or her lawful detention in accordance with the sentence passed by a competent Court upon his or her conviction of an offence;

    ii   in the case of his or her lawful arrest or detention for non-compliance with the lawful order of a court;

    iii in the case of his or her lawful arrest or detention upon reasonable suspicion of having committed, or being engaged in the commission of, or being about to commit, a criminal offence under the law;

    iv in the case of detention of a person under the age of 16 years by lawful order for the purpose of his or her educational supervision or personal welfare;

    v   in case of the lawful detention of a person who is of unsound mind and danger to themselves or others;

    vi in the case of the lawful arrest of a person to prevent his or her unlawfully entering the United Kingdom, or of a person against whom lawful action is being taken with a view to deportation or extradition.

2 Every person who is arrested or detained shall be informed, as soon as is possible in the circumstances of the case, in a language which he or she understands, of the reason for his or her arrest or detention and of any charge which is to be laid against him or her; he or she shall be entitled to inform a member of his or her family of his or her whereabouts and of the stated reason for his or her detention, and shall be entitled as soon as possible to consult a legal practitioner.

3 Every person who is arrested or detained in accordance with sub-paragraph (iii) of the first paragraph of this Article shall, wherever

it is practicable to do so, be brought before a competent court not later than the first lawful day after being taken into custody, such day not being a public or local holiday: failing which, he or she shall be brought before a competent court as soon as is possible thereafter.

4 Every person who has been deprived of liberty by arrest or detention has the right to petition a competent court of law, and shall be liberated by order of the court as soon as is practicable in the circumstances of the case unless such deprivation of liberty is proven to be lawful; if a person so deprived of liberty is for any reason unable to take proceedings on his or her own behalf any other person who can show good cause for so doing may petition the court in his or her name to test the lawfulness of any such detention.

28 Right to Fair Trial

1 Every such question or charge shall be heard and determined by the competent court or tribunal established by law. Trials shall be conducted in public and judgment shall be pronounced publicly, except in so far as the law permits a court or tribunal to exclude members of the public from part of such proceedings or to prohibit publication of reports concerning part of such proceedings on all or any of the following grounds:

i   the protection of national security;

ii   the prevention of disorder in court;

iii   the protection of children or young people, or other vulnerable persons;

iv   the protection of the personal privacy of both parties; or

v   in the interests of justice, in circumstances in which publicity would inevitably cause serious prejudice to the fair determination of an issue.

3 Every person charged with a criminal offence shall be presumed innocent until proven guilty according to law.

4 Every person charged with a criminal offence has the following rights:

i   to be informed in detail, as soon as is possible in the circumstances of the case, and in a language which he or she understands, of the charge which is made against him or her;

ii   to have adequate time and facilities for preparing a defence;

iii to defend himself or herself in person or through a legal practitioner of his or her own choosing;

iv to such financial assistance as is necessary in the light of his or her means to secure adequate legal assistance if desired;

v   to examine or have examined witnesses against him or her and to obtain the attendance and examination of witnesses on his or her behalf in the same conditions as witnesses against him or her;

vi to have all proceedings in court connected with the charge against him or her translated by a competent interpreter into the language which he or she best understands, if that language is not the language of the Court; and

vii to be informed in a language which he or she understands of his or her rights under Articles 27, 28 and 29 of this Constitution.

5 Everyone convicted of a criminal offence by a tribunal shall have the right to have his or her conviction or sentence reviewed by a higher tribunal. The exercise of this right, including the grounds on which it may be exercised, shall be governed by law, and may be subject to exceptions in regard to offences of a minor character, as prescribed by law, or in cases in which the person concerned was tried in the first instance by the highest tribunal.

6 No one shall be liable to be tried or punished again in criminal proceedings for an offence for which he has already been finally acquitted or convicted in accordance with the law. Provided, that this shall not prevent the reopening of a case, in accordance with the law, if there is evidence of new or newly discovered facts, or if there has been a fundamental defect in the previous proceedings, which could affect the outcome of the case.

29 No Punishment without Law

No one shall be held guilty of any criminal offence on account of any act or omission which did not constitute a criminal offence under national or international law at the time when it was committed, nor shall a heavier penalty be imposed than the one that was applicable at the time the criminal offence was committed.

30 Right to Respect for Private and Family Life

1 Everyone has the right to respect for his or her private and family life, home and correspondence.

2 There shall be no interference by a public authority with the exercise of this right except such as is in accordance with the law and is necessary in a democratic society in the interests of national security, public safety or the economic wellbeing of the country, for the prevention of disorder or crime, for the protection of health or morals, or for the protection of the rights and freedoms of others.

3 No person's communications, whether electronic or otherwise, may be monitored or intercepted except on the authority of a judicial warrant issued according to law.

31 Freedom of Thought, Conscience and Religion

1 All citizens shall enjoy freedom of thought, conscience and religion. This right includes freedom to change his or her religion or belief and freedom, either alone or in community with others and in public or private, to manifest his or her religion or belief in worship, teaching, practice and observance.

2 Freedom to manifest one's religion or beliefs shall be subject only to such limitations as are prescribed by law and are necessary in a democratic society in the interests of public safety, for the protection of public order, health or morals, or for the protection of the rights and freedoms of others.

3 In the exercise of any functions which it assumes in relation to education and to teaching, the State shall respect the right of parents to ensure such education and teaching in conformity with their own religious and philosophical convictions.

4 Nevertheless, and without detriment to the equal rights and status of those of other religions, or no religion, it is recognised that Christianity has a valued place in Britain's culture, society and national heritage, and nothing in this Article shall be construed as rendering unconstitutional:

i in England, the established position of the Church of England;

    ii in Scotland, the existing status, freedom or liberties of the Church of Scotland, as recognized by the Church of Scotland Act 1921 and by the Articles Declaratory of the Constitution of the Church of Scotland in Matters Spiritual; or

    ii in any State, any provision made by law for the public funding of denominational schools, provided that such provision is awarded on a non-discriminatory basis.

32 Freedom of Expression

1 Everyone has the right to freedom of expression. This right shall include freedom to hold opinions and to receive and impart information and ideas without interference by public authority and regardless of frontiers.

2 The exercise of these freedoms, since it carries with it duties and responsibilities, may be subject to such formalities, conditions, restrictions or penalties as are prescribed by law and are necessary in a democratic society, in the interests of national security, territorial integrity or public safety, for the prevention of disorder or crime, for the protection of health or morals, for the protection of the reputation or rights of others, for preventing the disclosure of information received in confidence, or for maintaining the authority and impartiality of the judiciary.

3 This Article shall not prevent the States from requiring the licensing of broadcasting, television or cinema enterprises according to law, provided that this the authorities shall not, in the exercise of this regulatory power, discriminate on grounds of political or other belief.

33 Freedom of Assembly and Association

1 Everyone has the right to freedom of peaceful assembly and to freedom of association with others, including:

    i   the right to form and to join trade unions for the protection of his or her interests;

    ii the right to form and to join political parties and campaigning organisation; and

    iii the right to take part in peaceful demonstrations and manifestations.

2 No restrictions shall be placed on the exercise of these rights other than such as are prescribed by law and are necessary in a democratic

society in the interests of national security or public safety, for the prevention of disorder or crime, for the protection of health or morals or for the protection of the rights and freedoms of others.

3 This Article shall not prevent the imposition of lawful restrictions on the exercise of these rights by members of the armed forces, of the police, of civil servants, or of members of the judiciary.

4 No one shall be required to join a political party, trade union, or campaigning organisation.

34 Right to Marry

1 Men and women of marriageable age have the right to marry and to found a family, according to the laws governing the exercise of this right.

2 Spouses shall enjoy equality of rights and responsibilities of a private law character between them, and in their relations with their children, as to marriage, during marriage and in the event of its dissolution. This shall not prevent the States from taking such measures as are necessary in the interests of children.

35 Protection of Property

1 Every natural or legal person is entitled to the peaceful enjoyment of his or her possessions. No one shall be deprived of his possessions except in the public interest and subject to the conditions provided for by law.

2 The preceding provisions shall not, however, in any way impair the right of the States to enforce such laws as it deems necessary to control the use of property in accordance with the general interest or to secure the payment of taxes or other contributions or penalties.

36 Freedom of Movement

1 Everyone lawfully within the territory of the United Kingdom shall, within that territory, have the right to liberty of movement and freedom to choose his or her residence. Everyone shall be free to leave the country.

2 No restrictions shall be placed on the exercise of the rights expressed in the first paragraph of this Article other than such as are in accordance with law and are necessary in a democratic society in

the interests of national security or public safety, for the maintenance of public order, for the prevention of crime, for the protection of health or morals, or for the protection of the rights and freedoms of others.

3 The rights set forth in the first paragraph may also be subject, in particular areas, to restrictions imposed in accordance with law and justified by the public interest in a democratic society.

4 No citizen of the United Kingdom shall be expelled, by means either of an individual or of a collective measure, from the territory of the United Kingdom, nor deprived of the right to enter that territory.

37 Procedural safeguards relating to expulsion of aliens

1 A non-citizen lawfully resident in the territory of the United Kingdom shall not be expelled therefrom except in pursuance of a decision reached in accordance with law and shall be allowed:

  i to submit reasons against his or her expulsion,

  ii to have his or her case reviewed, and

  iii to be represented for these purposes before the competent authority or a person or persons designated by that authority.

2 A non-citizen may be expelled before the exercise of his or her rights under paragraph 1 of this Article, when such expulsion is necessary in the interests of public order or national security.

38 Compensation for Wrongful Conviction

When a person has by a final decision been convicted of a criminal offence and when subsequently his conviction has been reversed, or he has been pardoned, on the ground that a new or newly discovered fact shows conclusively that there has been a miscarriage of justice, the person who has suffered punishment as a result of such conviction shall be compensated according to law, unless it is proved that the nondisclosure of the unknown fact in time is primarily attributable to him or her.

39 Freedom of Information

1 There shall be freedom of information, including a general right of public access, on request, to all official records and documents and a general obligation on the public authorities to act in a way that is transparent.

2 This right may be limited by law to the extent necessary in a democratic society for the protection of national security and public order, for the prevention and detection of crime, for the maintenance of personal privacy, and for ensuring the integrity of judicial proceedings.

40 Limitation on the use of Restrictions on Rights

1 The restrictions permitted under this Part to the said rights and freedoms shall not be applied for any purpose other than those for which they have been prescribed.

2 Any act aimed at the destruction of any of the rights and freedoms set forth in this Chapter, or at their limitation to a greater extent than is provided for in the Chapter, is prohibited.

41 Right to an Effective Remedy

Everyone whose rights and freedoms as set forth in this Part are violated shall have an effective remedy before the courts, notwithstanding that the violation has been committed by persons acting in an official capacity.

42 Prohibition of Discrimination

1 The enjoyment of the rights and freedoms set forth in this Part shall be secured without discrimination on any ground such as sex, race, colour, language, religion, political or other opinion, national or social origin, association with a national minority, property, birth or other status.

2 Non-citizens lawfully domiciled in the United Kingdom shall enjoy the same rights, freedoms and protections as citizens, except that restrictions on the political activities of non-citizens may be imposed by law.

43 States of Emergency

1 If the Prime Minister of the United Kingdom is satisfied that a grave emergency exists whereby the peace, security and safety of the United Kingsom, or any State thereof, is threatened by war, invasion, disaster, unrest, epidemic, or other cause, he or she may, by means of a public proclamation, declare that a state of emergency exists in the United Kingdom or any part thereof.

2 Before making a declaration under paragraph 1, the Prime Minister shall, so far as it is practicable to do so, consult with the Council of the States.

3   A declaration of emergency lapses at midnight on the seventh day after the publication of the declaration, unless within that time the Federal Assembly approves the declaration by means of a resolution passed by a two-thirds majority of its members.

4   A declaration of emergency that has been approved by a resolution of the Federal Assembly in accordance with paragraph (3) remains in force, subject to the provisions of paragraph (5), for three months from the date of the resolution, or for such shorter period as the resolution may prescribe.

5   The Prime Minister shall revoke a declaration of emergency –
    a   if so requested by a simple majority of the members of the Federal Assembly;
    b   by his or her own decision, according to his or her personal judgment and discretion, he or she is convinced that there is no longer the need or justification for a state of emergency to be in effect.

6   A provision of this Article that a declaration of emergency lapses or ceases to be in force at a particular time does not prevent the making of a further such declaration whether before or after that time. Provided, that a declaration of emergency shall not be renewed without the prior consent the Federal Assembly, by means of a resolution passed by a two-thirds majority.

7   During the period during which a declaration of emergency is in force, the Executive Council, or any Minister or officer of the Federation to whom such authority may be delegated by the Prime Minister, may make such orders as are reasonably required for securing public safety, maintaining public order or safeguarding the interests or maintaining the welfare of the Federation.

8   An order made under paragraph (7) shall have the force of law, but shall not be valid or binding if it exceeds the reasonable restrictions which may be placed on fundamental rights and freedoms in accordance with the provisions of this Part.

9   An order made under paragraph (7) of this Article –
    a   shall cease to have effect immediately upon the lapse of the state of emergency; and

b may at any time before the lapse of the state of emergency be revoked by –

    i the authority which issued the order; or

    ii a resolution of the Federal Assembly.

10 No elections shall be held during a State of Emergency. Any election that is due to be held during a State of Emergency shall be postponed and shall take place within three months of the end of the State of Emergency.

Part 5: Political Integrity

42 Electoral Commission

1 There shall be an Electoral Commission consisting of 15 members, who shall be appointed by the Head of State in the following manner –

    a two shall be appointed on the advice of the Prime Minister of the United Kingdom;

    b two shall be appointed on the advice of the Presiding Officer of the Federal Assembly, given after having consulted the leaders of the opposition parties in the Federal Assembly;

    c one shall be appointed on the advice of the First Minister of each State;

    d one shall be appointed on the advice of the Speaker or Presiding Officer of each State Parliament, given after having consulted the leaders of the opposition parties in the State Parliament; and

    e three shall be appointed on the advice of the aforementioned members of the Electoral Commission, of which –

        i two shall be public officers, qualified and experienced in the conduct of elections; and

        ii one shall be a former judge who is learned in electoral law.

2 Subject to the provisions of paragraph (5) of this Article, members of the Electoral Commission shall hold office for a period of five years from the date of their appointment.

3 A person shall be disqualified for appointment as a member of the Electoral Commission if he or she is –

    a a member of the Federal Assembly or of a State Parliament;

   b a candidate at any election to the Federal Assembly or a State Parliament; or

   c the spouse of any person disqualified under the preceding two sub-paragraphs.

4 A person shall not, while he or she holds or is acting in the office of a member of the Electoral Commission or within a period of five years commencing with the date on which he or she last held or acted in that office, be eligible for appointment to or to act in any public office, or to be a candidate for any election.

5 The office of a member of the Electoral Commission shall become vacant –

   a if he or she becomes disqualified for appointment under paragraph (3) of this Article;

   b if he or she tenders his or her resignation to Her Majesty;

   c if the Federal Assembly, by a two-thirds majority vote, passes a resolution praying for his or her removal, on the grounds of misconduct, neglect of duty, or incapacity.

6 The member of the Electoral Commission appointed under sub-paragraph (e)(ii) of paragraph 1 of this Article shall serve as Convenor of the Electoral Commission; during the absence or incapacity of the Convenor, the Electoral Commission shall designate a Deputy.

7 If there is any vacancy in the membership of the Electoral Commission, the Head of State shall appoint a person to fill the vacancy, according to paragraph (1) of this Article. Provided, that until such member of the Commission is appointed, the Electoral Commission may perform its functions notwithstanding any vacancy in its membership.

8 The Electoral Commission shall be responsible, in accordance with this Constitution and such laws as may be enacted by the Federal Assembly and the laws of each State, for the direction and supervision of the registration of voters, the registration of political parties, ensuring the free and fair conduct of elections and referendums, and all matters connected therewith.

9 The Electoral Commission may make recommendations to the Federal Assembly and to the Parliaments of the States with respect to the reform and improvement of the laws concerning –

    a the registration of voters;
    b the registration of political parties;
    c the suppression of corrupt practices;
    d the disclosure of political donations; and
    e the financing of parties, referendums and election campaigns.
  10 In the exercise of its functions the Electoral Commission shall act
     impartially and shall not be subject to the direction or control of any
     other person or authority.

43 Principles of Public Life

  1 This Article applies to:
    a the Prime Minister and United Kingdom Ministers;
    b the First Ministers and Ministers of the States;
    c members of the Federal Assembly;
    d members of the Parliaments of the States;
    e members of the Electoral Commission;
    f scrutiny and integrity officials whose offices are established under
       Article 21;
    e all judges and persons exercising judicial authority;
    f all members of the Judicial Appointments Commission and of
       judicial appointments bodies in each state;
    g local councillors and any other local officials, whether elected
       or otherwise;
    h police officers; and
    i all other public officials of the Federation or of the States.
  2 The persons to whom this Article applies shall adhere to the
     following principles:
    a they should uphold the law and act in accordance with the law
       and the public trust placed in them;
    b they have a duty to act solely in terms of the public interest, and
       must not act in order to gain financial or other material benefit
       for themselves, family or friends;
    c they must not place themselves under any financial or other
       obligation to any individual or organisation that might reasonably
       be thought to influence them in the performance of their duties;
    d they must make decisions solely on merit when carrying out
       public business;

e   they are accountable for their decisions and actions to the public, and they have a duty to consider issues on their merits, taking account of the views of others;

f   they must ensure that resources are used prudently and in accordance with the law;

g   they have a duty to be as open as possible about decisions and actions they take, giving reasons for their decisions and restricting information only when the wider public interest clearly demands;

h   they have a duty to act honestly, and must declare any private interests relating to their public duties and take steps to resolve any conflicts arising in a way that protects the public interest.

i   they should exhibit these principles in their own behaviour, actively promoting and robustly supporting these principles and being willing to challenge poor behaviour wherever it occurs.

3   To give effect to these and other relevant principles of good conduct:

a   the Federal Assembly shall adopt Codes of Conduct for –
i   members of the Federal Assembly;
ii   members of the Executive Council;
iii other public officers of the Federation.

b   each State Parliament shall adopt Codes of Conduct for –
i   members of the State Parliament;
ii   members of the State Government;
iii other public officers of the State; and
iv   local government councillors and officials in the State.

c   the Judicial Appointments Commission specified in paragraph 3 of Article 16 shall adopt a Code of Conduct for the Supreme Court and the bodies specified in paragraph 1 of Article 20 shall adopt Codes of Conduct for members of the State Courts.

4   The Federal Assembly, in relation to Codes of Conduct adopted under para. (a) of paragraph 3, and the State Parliaments, in relation to Codes of Conduct adopted under para. (b) of paragraph 3, shall have the authority to enforce observance of these Codes of Conduct by means of legislation.

44 Payment of members of the Federal Assembly and State Parliaments

1   No increase to the salaries, benefits and allowances payable to

members of the Federal Assembly or the members of any State Parliament shall be adopted except with the approval of a two-thirds majority vote of the Federal Assembly, or State Parliament, as the case may be.

2   Any increase to the salaries, benefits and allowances payable to members of the Federal Assembly or the members of any State Parliament shall be applied only to those members who are first elected to the Federal Assembly, or the State Parliament, as the case may be, after the increase has been applied.

45 Conflicts of Interest

1   In the Federal Assembly and in each State Parliament there shall be a register of interests, which shall be published and made available for public inspection, in which shall be recorded the private, financial, business and other interests (including gifts and benefits in kind) of all members.

2   A member of the Federal Assembly or of a State Parliament who has a private, financial, business or other interest, in any matter being considered by that Assembly or Parliament must –
   a   declare that interest before taking part in any parliamentary proceedings, including committee proceedings, relating to that matter; and
   b   abstain from voting on that matter.

3   A member of the Federal Assembly or of a State Parliament may not advocate or initiate any cause or matter on behalf of any person, organisation, or corporation, in consideration of any payment or benefit in kind.

46 Civic Honours

1   The Head of State may award –
   a   United Kingdom honours, in recognition of outstanding public service to the United Kingdom; and
   b   State honours, in recognition of outstanding public service to the State, or distinguished contributions to the culture or community thereof.

2   Honours shall be awarded on the advice of an independent and non-partisan nominating committee, to be established –

    a by an Act of the Federal Assembly, in relation to United Kingdom honours; and

    b by an Act of the State Parliament, in relation to State honours;

3 The grades of honours and the grounds on which they may be awarded shall be determined –

    a by Acts of the Federal Assembly, in relation to United Kingdom honours; and

    b by Acts of the State Parliament, in relation to State honours.

4 Honours granted shall not be hereditary and shall not entitle the bearer to any special privileges.

5 Unless otherwise provided by law, honours shall not be accompanied by any financial reward.

47 Conduct of Referendums

1 Subject to the provisions of this Constitution, referendums may be conducted –

    a across the United Kingdom, by a decision of the Federal Assembly; and

    b in any State, by a decision of the State Parliament or according to State law.

2 A referendum shall not be conducted unless –

    a the Electoral Commission has certified that the question to be put in the referendum is clearly worded, unambiguous, fair and balanced.

    b the Supreme Court has certified that the subject matter of the referendum is –

        i within the competence of the authority proposing to conduct it; and

        ii not repugnant to this Constitution, or the rights guaranteed thereby.

3 Referendums shall be binding if held –

    a on the alteration of State boundaries, under paragraph 2 of Article 2;

    b on the reform of the constitution or institutions of a State, under Article 22;

    c on amendments to this Constitution, under Article 49; or

d on the secession of any State under Article 50.

4 Referendums on any matter not specified in paragraph 3 of this Article shall be advisory.

48 Oaths of Office and Allegiance

1 The Head of State shall be required to take the following oath of office upon coronation:

'I [full name], being [King/Queen] of the United Kingdom, solemnly swear/affirm that I will faithfully and conscientiously perform my duties as Head of State in accordance with the Constitution and the laws, and that I will uphold, defend and obey the same. (So help me God).'

2 Every member of the Federal Assembly and of a State Parliament taking their seat shall be required to take the following oath of allegiance:

'I [full name] do swear that will be faithful and bear true allegiance to the people of [name of State], according to the Constitution of the United Kingdom and the laws. (So help me God).'

3 Every member of the Executive Council or of a State Government, on appointment, shall be required to take the following oath of office:

'I [full name] solemnly swear/affirm that I will faithfully and conscientiously perform my duties as [name of office] in accordance with the Constitution and the laws. (So help me God).'

4 Every person appointed to a judicial office shall, on appointment, be required to take the oath of office specified in paragraph (3) of this Article and the following oath of integrity:

'I will do right to all manner of people after the laws and usages of this State and of the United Kingdom, without fear or favour, affection or ill-will. (So help me God).'

5 Every person appointed to any other diplomatic, civil, military or other public office under this Constitution, shall be required to take, in addition to the oath specified in paragraph (2) of this Article, such oath of office, if any, as may be required by law.

6 Oaths under this Article may also be taken in the form of a solemn affirmation without religious invocation.

Part 6: *Constitutional Amendments and Secession*

49 Amendments to the Constitution

1 Subject to the provisions of this Article, the Federal Assembly may by law amend any provision of this Constitution by way of repeal, addition, amendment, or otherwise.

2 A bill to amend this Constitution must state its intention to do so in its title.

3 A bill to amend this Constitution shall not be deemed to have been passed by the Federal Assembly unless it has been approved, on its final reading, by at least two-thirds of the members of the Federal Assembly.

4 A bill to amend this Constitution shall not be presented for royal assent unless it has been referred to the people of each State in a referendum and has been approved by a majority of votes cast in the referendum in each State; provided, that if an amendment applies only to one State, or to any particular States, it may be presented for royal assent if approved by a majority of votes cast in the State or States to which it applies, notwithstanding that it is not approved in any other States.

5 No amendment to this Constitution shall be made during a State of Emergency, nor during any time when the United Kingdom, or any part thereof, is under enemy occupation.

50 Secession

1 Subject to the provisions of this Article, a State may secede from the United Kingdom.

2 A State shall not secede unless –

   a a proposal for a referendum on secession is approved by an absolute majority of the members of the State Parliament; and

   b at the referendum, a majority of the votes cast are in favour of secession.

3 A referendum under paragraph 2 shall not be proposed or conducted during a period of 20 years following the most recent referendum on the question of secession in that State.

4 If a State votes for secession in accordance with this Article, the Government of that State and the Executive Council of the United

Kingdom shall negotiate the terms of the secession and shall prepare a Secession Agreement to be approved by the Federal Assembly and the State Parliament.

5 So long as at least two States remain in the United Kingdom, this Constitution shall remain in effect between them, subject to such consequential amendments as may necessarily arise from the reduction in the number of States.

6 In accordance with the Good Friday Agreement, a decision by Northern Ireland to seek secession from the United Kingdom may be combined, in such manner as the State Parliament of Northern Ireland may prescribe, with a decision to seek incorporation into or union with Ireland.

51 Adoption, Proclamation and commencement of the Constitution

1 This Constitution shall be adopted by the peoples of the United Kingdom on being approved by a majority of the votes cast in a referendum in England, Scotland, Wales and Northern Ireland.

2 The Constitution shall, within ten days after the certification of the result of the referendum, be formally proclaimed by Her Majesty, who shall thereupon take the oath prescribed for the Head of State by paragraph 1 of Article 48.

3 The Constitution shall come into effect immediately upon such proclamation.

52 Transitional Provisions

1 The United Kingdom Parliament is hereby abolished, but the House of Commons of the United Kingdom elected in May 2015, after the withdrawal of members elected from Scottish, Welsh and Northern Irish Constituencies, shall remain in being as the House of Commons of England until provision is otherwise made in accordance with this Constitution.

2 Until provision is otherwise made in accordance with this Constitution, the House of Lords of England shall consist of all existing life peers and lords spiritual whose normal place of residence is in England. The future creation of peerages shall be regulated by an Act of the Parliament of England, passed in accordance with the provisions of Article 22 of this Constitution.

3 The persons holding office as Prime Minister of the United Kingdom, Secretary of State for Foreign Affairs, Secretary of State for Defence, Chancellor of the Exchequer, and Secretary of State for Justice immediately prior to the coming into effect of this Constitution shall form a temporary Executive Council under this Constitution pending the first elections thereto.

4 The first elections to the Federal Assembly shall take place on a date to be prescribed by the temporary Executive Council, such date being no later than three months after the coming into effect of this Constitution; and the temporary Executive Council shall have the authority to adopt regulations, consistent with this Constitution, for the conduct of those first elections.

5 The person holding office as Secretary of State for Home Affairs immediately prior to the coming into effect of this Constitution shall become the acting First Minister of England under this Constitution pending the first election to that office by the House of Commons of England.

6 The persons holding any other office in the Government of the United Kingdom immediately prior to the coming into effect of this Constitution shall, except as otherwise directed by the acting First Minister of England, continue as Ministers in the State Government of England under this Constitution, until removed or replaced in accordance with this Constitution and the laws.

7 All powers, rights and prerogatives vested in the Crown in right of the United Kingdom shall, upon the coming into effect of this Constitution, be transferred to the Crown in right of England, except to the extent that such powers, rights and prerogatives are by or in accordance with this Constitution –

   a assigned to the Federation or to the Head of State or Executive Council thereof;

   b assigned to the Crown in right of Scotland, Wales or Northern Ireland; or

   c abolished.

8 There shall be a separate civil service for each State and for the Federation. Transitional provision shall be made by the Executive Council for the transfer of all persons who immediately before the

coming into effect of this Constitution held a public office in the United Kingdom or any part thereof, or were employed within the civil service or public sector in the United Kingdom or any part thereof, to continue as an official or employee either of the State in which they serve or of the Federation, depending upon the department and nature of their employment, and subject to and in accordance with the applicable laws regulating such office or employment.

9 With the exception of any rule of law inconsistent with this Constitution, every rule of law in force in the United Kingdom or in any part thereof at the date at which this Constitution comes into effect shall remain in force until such time, if any, as it is repealed or amended by Act of the Federal Assembly, Act of a State Parliament, or other competent legislative act.

Endnotes

Introduction

1   Bulmer, W.E., *A Model Constitution for Scotland: Making Democracy Work in an Independent State* (Edinburgh: Luath Press, 2011).
2   Viroili, M., Republicanism (Hill & Wang, 2001)

Chapter One

1   Elliot Bulmer, 'A Scottish constitution to serve the common weal'. *The Herald*, 13 July 2013.
2   Paine, T., *The Rights of Man* (London: Penguin Classics, 1984).
3   Hassan, G., (2014) 'A Scotland Beyond Yes and No: My journey to Yes', National Collective, 2014. [nationalcollective.com/2014/06/26/gerry-hassan-a-scotland-beyond-yes-and-no-my-journey-to-yes/, accessed 12 July 2014]
4   Danson, M. & Trebeck, K., *No More Excuses: How a Common Weal approach can end poverty* (The Reid Foundation, 2013) p.4
5   Carter, L. & Kahya, D., 'What energy interests do the House of Lords' economic affairs committee have?', Greenpeace Energydesk News, 8 May 2014 [www.greenpeace.org.uk/newsdesk/energy/news/who-are, accessed 28 July 2014].
6   Peralta, E., 'Guardian Editor: UK Government Destroyed Hard Drives with NSA Leaks', The Two Way: Breaking News from National Public Radio [www.npr.org/blogs/thetwo-way/2013/08/19/213605067/guardian-editor-u-k-govt-destroyed-hard-drives-with-nsa-leaks, accessed 28 July 2014]
7   Economist Intelligence Unit, Democracy Index, 2012.
8   *Ibid.*
9   Vajpeyi, A. *Righteous Republic: The Political Foundations of Modern India* (Cambridge, Massachusetts: Harvard University Press, 2012). p. 1
10 *Ibid.*, p. 2
11 Keating, M., 'Reforging the Union: Devolution and Constitutional Change in the United Kingdom', Publius (28/1, 1998). pp. 217–234; Kellas, J.G., The Scottish Political System (4th ed.) (Cambridge: Cambridge University Press, 1989).
12 Hassan, G., *Caledonian Dreaming* (Edinburgh: Luath Press, 2014).
13 Bellamy, R., *Political Constitutionalism: A Republican Defence of the Constitutionality of Democracy* (Cambridge: Cambridge University Press, 2007); Tomkins, A., *Our Republican Constitution* (Oxford: Hart Publishing, 2005).
14 Cairney, P., 'How can the Scottish Parliament be Improved as a Legislature', Scottish Parliamentary Review, (1/1, 2013).
15 Gerring, J. & Thacker, S.C., *A Centripetal Theory of Democratic Governance* (Cambridge: Cambridge University Press, 2008).
16 Lijphart, W. E., 'The Future of Democracy: Reasons for Pessimism, but also some Optimism', Scandinavian Political Studies (23/3, 2000) pp. 265–272.
17 Negretto, G., *Making Constitutions: Presidents, Parties and Institutional Choice in Latin America* (Cambridge: Cambridge University Press, 2013) pp. 3–4.

18 The Scottish Government, Scotland's Future (White Paper on Independence, November 2013).
19 Report of the Smith Commission for further devolution of powers to the Scottish Parliament, 27 November 2014.
20 Report of the Smith Commission for further devolution of powers to the Scottish Parliament, 27 November 2014.
21 Anderson, G., *Federalism: An Introduction* (Oxford: Oxford University Press, 2008). p. 4.
22 'A New Magna Carta?' (Second Report of the Political and Constitutional Reform Select Committee), House of Commons, 3 July 2014. [www.publications.parliament.uk/pa/cm201415/cmselect/cmpolcon/463/ 46302.htm, accessed 28 July 2014].
23 Taylor, A. J. P., *The Habsburg Monarchy 1809–1918: A History of the Austrian Empire and Austria-Hungary* (London: Penguin, 1990).

Chapter Two

1   Bulmer, W. E., *A Model Constitution for Scotland: Making Democracy Work in an Independent State* (Edinburgh: Luath Press, 2011). p. 29.
2   *Ibid*, pp. 27–28.
3   Constitution of Massachusetts, 1780: Article VII.
4   Aristotle, *The Politics* (Sinclair, T. A., trans., Saunders, T., ed.) (London: Penguin Classics, 1981).
5   Honohan, I., *Civic Republicanism* (Abingdon: Routledge, 2002). pp. 15–42.
6   Manin, B., *The Principles of Representative Government* (Cambridge: Cambridge University Press, 2002); see also McCormick, J.P. Machiavellian Democracy (Cambridge: Cambridge University Press, 2011).
7   Myers, A. R., *Parliaments and Estates in Europe to 1789* (Boston, Massachusetts: Houghton Mifflin, 1975).
8   Calvin, J., *Institutes of the Christian Religion* (Book IV, Chapter 20), hosted by the Centre for Reformed Theology and Apologetics, [www.reformed.org/master/index.html?mainframe=/books/institutes/, accessed 28 July 2014]
9   Viroli, M., *Republicanism* (Hill & Wang, 2001). p. 3.
10 *Ibid*. p.3
11 Miller, D. (2003) 'Political Philosophy: A very short introduction', Oxford University Press. p. 1.
12 *Ibid.*, p. 2–3.
13 *Ibid.*, p. 2–3.
14 *Ibid.*, p. 2–3.
15 *Ibid.*, p. 2–3.
16 *Ibid.*, p. 2–3.
17 *Ibid.*, p. 2–3.
18 *Ibid.*, p. 2–3.
19 Waley, D., (1988) 'The Italian City Republics' (3rd Edition), Longman. p. 37.
20 *Ibid.*, p. 38.
21 Viroli, M., op. cit. p.27.
22 Velasquez, M., Andre, C., Shanks, T. & Meyer, M. J., 'The Common Good',

Markkula Centre for Applied Ethics, Santa Clara University [www.scu.edu/ethics/practicing/decision/commongood.html, accessed 12 May 2014]

23   Coote, A., 'Basic Human Needs: What are they really?', New Economics Foundation, 2014 [www.neweconomics.org/blog/entry/basic-human-needs-what-are-they-really, accessed 20 July 2014].

24   Bulmer, W. E., 'Not just King Eck's Realm', *The Scotsman*, 22 December 2011.

25   1 Cor. 12:14–20

26   Mr Lees-Smith MP (Labour, Keighley), Hansard: House of Commons Debates, 13 May 1940, vol 360, cc1501–25.

27   Viroli, M., The Liberty of Servants: Berlusconi's Italy (Shugaar, A., trans.) (Princeton, New Jersey: Princeton University Press, 2011).

Chapter Three

1   Lerner, H. *Making Constitutions in Deeply Divided Societies* (Cambridge: Cambridge University Press, 2011).

2   'Lord Patten's BBC Trust role approved by MPs', BBC News, 12 March 2011 [www.bbc.co.uk/news/uk-12719136, accessed 29 July 2014]

3   Moss, V., 'David Cameron accused of plot to pack public bodies with Conservative supporters', *The Mirror*, 1 February 2014 [www.mirror.co.uk/news/uk-news/david-cameron-accused-plot-pack-3103499#.Uu7F1Cjlfww, accessed 28 July 2014].

4   International IDEA, What is a Constitution? (Constitution Building Primers series) (Stockholm: International Institute for Democracy and Electoral Assistance, 2014).

5   Tierney, S., 'Constituting Scotland: A Retreat from Politics', Scottish Constitutional Futures Forum, 3 April 2014. [www.scottishconstitutional futures.org/OpinionandAnalysis/ViewBlogPost/tabid/1767/articleType/ArticleView/articleId/3319/Stephen-Tierney-Constituting-Scotland-a-Retreat-from-Politics.asp, accessed 7 July 2014)].

6   Poli, F., 'Alex Salmond to replace the Queen on new Scottish pound coin', *The Telegraph*, 1 April 2014.

7   International IDEA, op. cit. p.8.

8   Aristotle, op. cit.

9   Campbell, P., *French Elections and Electoral Systems since 1789* (New York: Faber & Faber, 1958).

10   'The Fair Elections Act: Kill this Bill', *The Globe* and *Mail* (editorial), 23 March 2014.

11   Swift MacNeill, J.G., 'Thoughts on the Constitution of the Irish Free State', Journal of Comparative Legislation and International Law, (5/3, 1923). pp. 52–62.

12   Gallagher, M., 'The Constitution and the Judiciary', in Coakley, J. & Gallagher, M. (eds.), Politics in the Republic of Ireland (4th ed.), Chapter 3, pp. 72–102. (Abingdon: Routledge 2007). p. 74.

13   Elkins, Z., Ginsburg, T. & Melton, J., *The Endurance of National Constitutions* (Cambridge: Cambridge University Press, 2009).

14   O'Toole, F., *Enough is Enough: How to Build a New Republic* (London: Faber & Faber, 2010).

15 Toth, G. A., Constitution for a Divided Nation: On Hungary's 2011
    Fundamental Law (Budapest: Central European University Press, 2012).
16 Bonime-Blanc, A., 'Constitution Making and Democratisation: The Spanish
    Paradigm', in Miller, L. E. ed. Framing the state in times of transition: Case
    Studies in Constitution-Making (Washington DC: United States Institute for
    Peace Press, 2010). pp. 417–434.
17 Aristotle, op. cit.
18 Prebble, J., The Lion in the North: One Thousand Years of Scotland's History
    (London: Penguin Books, 1981).
19 The Scottish Covenant (Trustees of the National Library of Scotland)
    [www.scran.ac.uk/database/record.php?usi=000-000-135-967-C, accessed
    29 July 2014]
20 Dudley-Edwards, O., (ed.) A Claim of Right for Scotland (Edinburgh:
    Polygon, 1989).
21 Reid, A., and Davies, M., A Modest Proposal for the Agreement of the People
    (Edinburgh: Luath Press, 2014).
22 Re The Initiative and Referendum Act [[1919] A. C. 935]

Chapter Four

1   Manin, B., op. cit.
2   Database and Search Engine for Direct Democracy (www.sudd.ch)
    [www.sudd.ch/list.php?lang=en&area=schweiz&topic=&first=&last=&sense
    =desc, accessed 25 May 2014].
3   International IDEA Direct Democracy (Constitution Building Primers series)
    (Stockholm: International Institute for Democracy and Electoral Assistance,
    2014).
4   The Scottish Parliament, Official Report, 26 January 2012. [www.scottish.
    parliament.uk/parliamentarybusiness/28862.aspx? r=7560, accessed 29 July
    2014].
5   Constitution of Spain, Arts. 166–169.
6   Constitution of Latvia, Arts, 76 & 77.
7   Bulmer, W. E., A Model Constitution for Scotland, Making Democracy Work
    in an Independent State (Edinburgh: Luath Press). pp. 71–73.
8   Constitution of Italy, Art, 75.
9   Constitution of Latvia, Arts, 78–79; also see Arts. 72–74.
10 Constitution of New South Wales, Sect. 5B.
11 Constitution of Denmark, Art. 42.
12 Constitution of Slovenia, Art. 90.
13 Bulmer, W.E., 'Constrained Majoritarianism: Westminster constitutionalism in
    Malta', Commonwealth & Comparative Politics (52/2, 2014); Coakley, J. &
    Gallagher, M. (eds.), Politics in the Republic of Ireland (4th ed.), (Abingdon:
    Routledge: 2007).
14 Kenny, M., and Mackay, F., 'Election 2011: The Gender Balance', Holyrood
    Magazine, 13 May 2011. [www.holyrood.com/2011/05/finding-a-balance/,
    accessed 29 July 2014].
15 Differential Impact of Electoral Systems on Female Political Representation

(Directorate-General for Research, European Parliament, 1997) [www.europarl.europa.eu/workingpapers/femm/w10/4_en.htm, accessed 5 June 2014].

16   Hassan, G., *Caledonian Dreaming* (Edinburgh: Luath Press, 2014).

17   Hope, C. 'Cabinet is worth around 70 million', *The Telegraph*, 27 May 2012.

18   Gilens, M., and Page, B., (2014) 'Testing Theories of American Politics: Elites, Interest Groups and Average Citizens', Perspectives on Politics (forthcoming, 2014). www.princeton.edu/.../Gilens%20and%20Page%202014- Testing%20 Theories%203-7-14.pdf

19   Lijphart, A., *Patterns of Democracy*, Yale University Press. pp. 287–288.

20   Assinder, N., 'Public Far to the Left of Labour Party Finds Poll', International Business Times, 5 November 2013. [www.ibtimes.co.uk/left-wing-price-controls-nationalisation-yougov-poll-519684, accessed 29 July 2014].

21   Wilks-Heeg, S., 'How Democratic is the UK? The 2012 Audit', Political Insight (3/2, 2012). pp. 8–11.

22   The Scottish Government, op. cit.

23   Manin, op. cit.; McCormick, op. cit.

24   Dowlen, O., *The Political Potential of Sortition: A Study of the Random Selection of Citizens for Public Office*, (Exeter: Imprint Academic, 2008); McCormick, op. cit; Viroli, M., *Machiavelli* (Oxford: Oxford University Press, 1998).

25   The Economist Intelligence Unit, Democracy Index 2014.

26   Hay, D., *Europe in the Fourteenth and Fifteenth Centuries*, 2nd Edition. (London: Longman, 1989) pp. 124–126.

27   Manin, op. cit.; Gilens & Page, op. cit.

28   (Bill, J., and Springborg, R., *Politics in the Middle East*, (London: Longman, 1999). p. 291

29   Constitution of India, 1950 (as amended to 2014): Article 330. (See also Delimitation Act 2000, Sections 8 and 9).

30   Instrument of Government, Sweden: Chapter 2, Art. 22.

31   Instrument of Government, Sweden: Chapter 8, Arts. 20-22.

32   Instrument of Government, Sweden: Chapter 13, Art. 1.

33   Constitution of Estonia, Art. 104.

34   Constitution of Estonia, Art. 110.

35   Rommetvedt, H., Rise of the Norwegian Parliament: Studies in Norwegian Parliamentary Government pp. 41–44. (London: Frank Case, 2003).

36   Manin, op. cit.

37   Strom, K., Mueller, W. & Bergman, T., *Delegation and Accountability in Parliamentary Democracies* (Oxford: Oxford University Press, 2006).

38   Pettit, P., *On the People's Terms: A Republican Theory and Model of Democracy* (Cambridge: Cambridge University Press, 2012.) pp. 195–207.

39   Bort, E., McAlpine, R., and Morgan, G., The Silent Crisis: Failure and Revival in Local Democracy in Scotland (Biggar: Reid Foundation, 2012).

40   Riddoch, op. cit.

41   Shafi, J. 'Missing Inaction', Bella Caledonia, 17 April 2014 [http://bella caledonia.org.uk/2014/04/17/missing-inaction/, accessed 29 July 2014]

42   Valmorbida, A., Workshop on Local Democracy, 4–6 November 2014,
     International Institute for Democracy and Electoral Assistance, Stockholm.
43   Valmorbida, A., 'Citizens' Participation at Local Level' (Peter Lang, 2014)
44   Basic Law of the Federal Republic of Germany, Art. 21.
45   Constitution of Poland, 1997, Articles 11 & 13.

Chapter Five

1   Blaug, R., 'Direct Accountability at the End' in White, S. and Leighton, D.,
     Building a Citizen Society: the Emerging Politics of Republican Democracy
     (London: Lawrence & Wishart, 2008). pp. 101–111.
2   Manin, op. cit.
3   Greenidge, A. H. J., *Roman Public Life* (London: MacMillan, 1901).
4   Constitution of the Commonwealth of Pennsylvania, 1776 (section 47).
5   Madison, J., 'The Federalist No. 48: These Departments Should Not Be So Far
     Separated as to Have No Constitutional Control Over Each Other' (1788)
     www.constitution.org/fed/federa48.htm accessed 8 May 2015.
6   Sheldon, A., 'Trust: How we lost it and how to get it back' (BiteBack, 2009).
7   Commons Second Reading: Recall of MPs Bill. [www.parliament.uk/business/
     news/2014/october/commons-second-reading-recall-of-mps-bill/ accessed 10
     November 2014]
8   Waley, op. cit.
9   Machiavelli, N., *The Prince* (Bull, G. trans.) (London: Penguin Classics, 2003).
     pp. 40–44.
10   Hart, G., *Restoration of the Republic: The Jeffersonian Ideal in Twenty-First
     Century America* (Oxford: Oxford University Press, 2004). pp. 204–217.
11   Robertson, J., (ed) *Andrew Fletcher: Political Works* (Cambridge: Cambridge
     University Press, 1997). p. 139.
12   Hume, D., 'Idea of a Perfect Commonwealth', in Claeys, G. (ed.) Utopias of
     the British Enlightenment, (Cambridge: Cambridge University Press, 1994).
     pp. 55–70
13   Hodgson, W., 'Commonwealth of Reason', in Clayes op. cit. pp. 199–248.
14   Bulmer, W. E., Proposed Constitutional Platform Act (Constitutional
     Commission, 2013). [www.constitutionalcommission.org/production/byre/
     images/assets/file/Resources%20Folder/A%20MODEL%20
     CONSTITUTION %20FOR%20SCOTLAND.pdf, accessed 17 May 2014]

Chapter Six

1   Ginsburg, T., Foti, N., and Rockmore, D., 'We the Peoples: the Global Origins
     of Constitutional Preambles', George Washington International Law Review
     (forthcoming, 2014).
2   Declaration of the Establishment of State of Israel, Israel Ministry of Foreign
     Affairs [www.mfa.gov.il/mfa/foreignpolicy/peace/guide/pages/declaration%20
     of%20establishment%20of%20state%20of%20israel.aspx accessed 10
     November 2014].
3   Elazar, D. J., *Constitutionalism: The Israeli and American Experiences*
     (University Press of America, 1990). pp. 61–63.
4   O'Toole, op. cit.

5   O'Dowd, T. J., 'Remembering the Constitution: The Easter Proclamation and Constitutionalism in Independent Ireland', Working Papers in British-Irish Studies, No. 104, 2011. Institute for British-Irish Studies, University College Dublin, p. 1

6   O'Dowd, op. cit., p. 6

7   Bulmer, W. E., *A Model Constitution for Scotland, Making Democracy Work in an Independent State* (Edinburgh: Luath Press), Article 1, section 1.

8   The Scottish Parliament, Michael Lloyd: The Mace [www.scottish.parliament. uk/visitandlearn/24496.aspx, accessed 29 July 2014].

9   The Commonwealth, Our Charter [thecommonwealth.org/our-charter, accessed 29 July 2014]

10   Hirschl, R., *Constitutional Theocracy* (Harvard University Press, 2010)

11   'Scottish Independence: Role of Religion Should be Recognised', BBC Website, 6 April 2014 [www.bbc.com/news/uk-scotland-scotland-politics- 26903855, accessed 6 June 2014]

12   'Secular Groups attack plan to make religion part of Scottish Constitution', *The Herald*, 7 April 2014. www.heraldscotland.com/politics/referendum-news/ secular-groups-attack-plan-to-make-religion-part-of-scottish-constitution. 23887937, accessed 6 June 2014]

13   International IDEA, Religion-State Relations? (Constitution Building Primers series) (Stockholm: International Institute for Democracy and Electoral Assistance, 2014

14   Williame, J-P., Religion, State and Society in Germany and France (A paper presented at the annual meeting of the Association for the Sociology of Religion, Atlanta, Georgia, 15 August 2003) [http://hirr.hartsem.edu/ sociology/willaime.html, accessed 5 May 2014]

15   Henderson, G. D., The Church of Scotland: A Short History (Edinburgh: The Church of Scotland Youth Committee, 1937). p.180.

16   Bonney, N., 'Scottish Independence, State Religion and the Monarchy', The Political Quarterly (83/2, 2012)

17   Freston, P. Protestant Political Parties in a Global Perspective (Aldershot: Ashgate Publishing, 2004), p. 1.

18   Constitutional Charter of France (1814) www.napoleon-series.org/research/ government/legislation/c–charter.html accessed 8 May 2015.

19   Constitutional Charter of France (1830) http://oll.libertyfund.org/pages/1830- french-charter-of-1830 accessed 8 May 2015.

20   Constitution of Poland, 1997. Preamble.

Chapter Seven

1   Oyugi, W.O., 'Bureaucracy and Democracy in Africa', in Oyugi, W.O., Odhiambo, E.S.A., Chege, M., and Gitonga, A.K., (eds) Democratic Theory and Practice in Africa, (London: James Currey Ltd, 1988) p. 106.

2   Sunstein, C., A second Bill of Rights: FDR's Unfinished Revolution and why we need it more than ever. (New York: Basic Book, 2006).

3   Constitution of Australia, s51(xxiiiA).

4   Basic Law of the Federal Republic of Germany, Arts. 73, 74 and 75.

5   Fulbright, J.W., *The Arrogance of Power* (Toronto: Random House Canada, 1966). p.224

6   Constitution of Kenya, Art. 41–43.

7   Constitution of Kenya, Art. 22(1).

8   Constitution of Kenya, Art. 22(2).

9   Constitution of Malta, Art. 21.

10   O'Dowd, op. cit. p.9

11   Wightman, A., 'A Land Value Tax for England: Fair, Efficient, Sustainable', Land Matters, 2013. [http://www.andywightman.com/? p=2351, accessed 20 July 2014]

12   Wearden, G., 'The 85 richest people are as wealthy as poorest half of the world', *The Guardian*, 20 January 2014.

13   Sheridan, T., Speech given at Methilhill Bowling Club, 2014 [https://www.youtube.com/watch?v=1PzGaDD7k04, accessed 28 July 2014].

Chapter Eight

1   Sandel, M. Democracy's Discontent: America in Search of a Public Philosophy (Harvard University Press: 1998).

2   Viroli, M. Republicanism (Hill & Wang, 2001).

3   Marquand, D., The New Reckoning: Capitalism, States and Citizens (Cambridge & Oxford: Polity Press, 1997); MacEwan, A., Neo-Liberalism or Democracy? Economic Strategy, Markets and Alternatives for the 21st Century (London: Zed Books, 1999).

4   Blond, P., *Red Tory: How Left and Right Have Broken Britain and How We Can Fix It* (London: Faber & Faber, 2010); Crick, B. & Lockyer, A. (eds.) *Active Citizenship: What Could it Achieve and How?* (Edinburgh: Edinburgh University Press, 2010); Critchley, P., *Aristotle and the Public Good*, (ebook, 1995) [www.academia.edu/705315/Aristotle_and_the_Public_Good, accessed 20 March 2014].

5   Constant, B., 'The Liberty of the Ancients Compared with that of the Moderns', in Fontana, B., (ed. & trans.) *Constant: Political Writings* (Cambridge: Cambridge University Press, 1988) p. 326

6   Milbank, J., 'Orthodox paradox: An interview with John Milbank' 2010 [blogs.ssrc.org/tif/2010/03/17/orthodox-paradox-an-interview-with-john-milbank/, accessed 9 September 2012].

7   Committee on Standards in Public Life, 'First Report of the Committee on Standards in Public Life' (1995) CM 2850. [www.gov.uk/government/publications/first-report-of-the-committee-on-standards-in-public-life accessed 1 June 2014]

8   Committee on Standards in Public Life, 'Standards Matter: A review of best practice in promoting good behaviour in public life' (Fourteenth Report of the Committee on Standards in Public Life, CM 8519 – January 2013).

9   Commission for Ethical Standards in Public Life in Scotland, Annual report 2011–12 (September 2012). p.2.

10   The Scottish Parliament, Code of Conduct for MSPs, Volume 1, 3.1.1. [www.scottish.parliament.uk/msps/16182.aspx, accessed 28 July 2014]

Chapter Nine

1   Elster, J., 'Constitution-Making in Eastern Europe: Rebuilding the Boat in the Open Sea', Public Administration (71/1-2, 1993). pp. 169–217.

2   Thomson, D., *Democracy in France: The Third and Fourth Republics* (2nd Edition) (Oxford: Oxford University Press, 1952).

3   Adams, J. C. and Barile, P., *The Government of Republican Italy* (3rd Edition) (Boston: Houghton Mifflin, 1972)

4   *Ibid.* (See also Viroli, M, *The Liberty of Servants: Berlusconi's Italy* (Shugaar, A., Trans.) (Princeton University Press, 2012).

5   'Tunisia approves new Constitution', The National (United Arab Emirates), 27 January 2014 [http://www.thenational.ae/world/tunisia-crisis/video-tunisia-approves-new-constitution, accessed 29 January 2014].

6   Darnolf, S., *Democratic Electioneering in Southern Africa: The Contrasting Cases of Botswana and Zimbabwe* (Goteborg, Sweden: Goteborg University Press, 1997). p. 219

7   Miller, L.E., ed., *Framing the state in times of transition: Case Studies in Constitution-Making* (Washington DC: United States Institute for Peace Press, 2010).

8   Elster, J., 'Forces and Mechanisms in the Constitution-Making Process', Duke University Law Journal (45, 1995). p. 364–394.

9   Smith, G., *Democratic Innovations: Designing Institutions for Citizen Participation* (Cambridge: Cambridge University Press, 2009)

10 Landau. D., 'The Importance of Constitution Making', Denver University Law Review (89, 2012). p. 611.

Appendix

1   On current population figures, this would produce the following distribution of seats, for a total of 120 seats: England, 65; Scotland, 20; Wales, 18; Northern Ireland, 17.

2   The alternative possibility would be to have two houses, one chosen on the basis of population, the other containing an equal number of members from each state, with a joint session or some sort of mediation committee to resolve conflicts between the two. Indeed, a bicameral arrangement of this sort would be more normal in federations. However, one could argue that such a bicameral structure would be over-engineered for the UK, given the relatively narrow range of competences envisaged for federal institutions in this Constitution.

Some other books published by **LUATH** PRESS

A Model Constitution for Scotland

W. Elliot Bulmer
ISBN: 978-1-908373-13-7 PBK £9.99

Scotland is a free, sovereign and independent commonwealth. Its form of government is a parliamentary democracy based upon the sovereignty of the people, social justice, solidarity and respect for human rights...

A Model Constitution for Scotland sets out a workable model for Scotland's future and includes detailed constitutional proposals together with informed discussion on the topic.

The independence debate has to break out of political elites and address the 'after independence' question. Elliot Bulmer's book is an important contribution to this, exploring how we make Scotland constitutionally literate, and how we shape our politics in a way which reflects who we are and what we aspire to be. Bulmer rightly argues that independence has to aspire to more than abolishing reserved powers, Holyrood becoming a mini-Westminster, and nothing else changing. A must read for independentistas, thoughtful unionists and democrats.

GERRY HASSAN, author and broadcaster

Bulmer deals with fundamental rights and freedoms in a broad-minded and incisive fashion.

NEWSNET SCOTLAND

A Modest Proposal

Edited by Angus Reid and Mary Davis
ISBN: 978-1-910021-05-7 PBK £9.99

There are few moments in history when the ruling class can be said to be on the back foot. It is only at such moments that parliaments concede any meaningful powers to people. This has been the case only at rare moments in the history of the UK, and this book takes the view that this is one of them. It shows you this history; it shows you how Scottish people have a unique chance to challenge the powers of the ruling elite and how they can change the political nature of the whole UK.

Inspired by the project growing across Scotland, which invites people across the nation to leave their mark of agreement and petition simultaneously against members of the parliament. The project demands an 'Agreement of the People', an act of people constituting a government, for Scotland's future

Small Nations in a Big World
Michael Keating and Malcolm Harvey
ISBN: 978-1-910021-20-0 PBK £9.99

Small northern European nations have been a major point of reference in the Scottish independence debate. For nationalists, they have been an 'arc of prosperity' while in the aftermath of the financial crash, unionists lampooned the 'arc of insolvency'. Both characterisations are equally misleading. Small nations can do well in the global marketplace, yet they face the world in very different ways. Some accept market logic and take the 'low road' of low wages, low taxes and light regulation, with a correspondingly low level of public services. Others take the 'high road' of social investment, which entails a larger public sector and higher taxes. Such a strategy requires innovative government, flexibility and social partnership.

Keating and Harvey compare the experience of the Nordic and Baltic states and Ireland, which have taken very different roads and ask what lessons can be learnt for Scotland. They conclude that an independent nation is possible but that hard choices would need to be taken.

Scotland could be made to work as an independent state but this implies not merely a change its external relations or formal status, but a rebuilding of its institutions internally. We know from the example of other small states that this requires bold decisions and hard choices.

Britain Rebooted: Scotland in a Federal Union
David Torrance
ISBN: 978 1 910021 11 8 PBK £7.99

Would federalism work in the UK?
Wouldn't England dominate a British federation?
How would powers be distributed between federal and Home Nation level?
What about the House of Lords?

In the run up to the historic referendum on Scottish independence there has been a plethora of tracts, articles and books arguing for and against, but there remains a gap in the literature: the case for Scotland becoming part of a 'rebooted' federal Union. It is an old, usually Liberal, dream, but one still worth fighting for.

It is often assumed that federalism is somehow 'alien' to the Scottish and British constitutional tradition but in this short book journalist David Torrance argues that not only has the UK already become a quasi-federal state but that formal federation is the best way of squaring the competing demands of Nationalists and Unionists.

He also uses Scotland's place within a federal UK to examine other potential reforms with a view to tackling ever-increasing inequality across the British Isles and create a more equal, successful and constitutionally coherent country.

Details of these and other books published by Luath Press can be found at:
www.luath.co.uk

Luath Press Limited

committed to publishing well written books worth reading

LUATH PRESS takes its name from Robert Burns, whose little collie Luath (*Gael.*, swift or nimble) tripped up Jean Armour at a wedding and gave him the chance to speak to the woman who was to be his wife and the abiding love of his life. Burns called one of 'The Twa Dogs' Luath after Cuchullin's hunting dog in Ossian's *Fingal*. Luath Press was established in 1981 in the heart of Burns country, and now resides a few steps up the road from Burns' first lodgings on Edinburgh's Royal Mile. Luath offers you distinctive writing with a hint of unexpected pleasures.

Most bookshops in the UK, the US, Canada, Australia, New Zealand and parts of Europe either carry our books in stock or can order them for you. To order direct from us, please send a £sterling cheque, postal order, international money order or your credit card details (number, address of cardholder and expiry date) to us at the address below. Please add post and packing as follows: UK – £1.00 per delivery address; overseas surface mail – £2.50 per delivery address; overseas airmail – £3.50 for the first book to each delivery address, plus £1.00 for each additional book by airmail to the same address. If your order is a gift, we will happily enclose your card or message at no extra charge.

Luath Press Limited
543/2 Castlehill
The Royal Mile
Edinburgh EH1 2ND
Scotland
Telephone: 0131 225 4326 (24 hours)
email: sales@luath.co.uk
Website: www.luath.co.uk

ELLIOT BULMER, after graduating with an MA in Arabic and Politics from the University of Edinburgh, was commissioned as a Logistics Officer in the Royal Navy and served in Iraq as part of a PSYOPS unit. After leaving the Navy, he completed a PhD in Politics at the University Glasgow while working as Research Director of the Constitutional Commission, a Scottish charitable organisation for constitutional education and research. He now works for the Constitution Building Programme of the International Institute for Democracy and Electoral Assistance in The Hague, Netherlands. He is the author of *A Model Constitution for Scotland: Making Democracy Work in an Independent* [?] (Edinburgh: Luath Press, 2011) and several articles on constitutional subjects in peer-reviewed academic journals, as well as being a frequent contributor to Scotland's constitutional debate in print and online.

[?] Press is an independently owned and managed book publishing company based in Scotland, and is not aligned to any political party or grouping. *Viewpoints* is an occasional series exploring issues of current and future relevance. All opinions is this book are the sole opinions of the author and do not represent the position of International IDEA, the Constitutional Commission or any other person or organisation.